WITHDRAWN

012729722

8|9|95

Teachers' stories

D0988195

Teachers' stories

Edited by David Thomas

LIVERPOOL
UNIVERSITY
LIBRARY

Open University Press
Buckingham • Philadelphia

Open University Press
Celtic Court
22 Ballmoor
Buckingham
MK18 1XW

and
1900 Frost Road, Suite 101
Bristol, PA 19007, USA

First Published 1995

Copyright © The Editor and Contributors

All rights reserved. Except for the quotation of short passages for the purpose of criticism and review, no part of this publication may be reproduced, stored in a retrieval system, or transmitted, in any form or by any means, electronic, mechanical, photocopying, recording or otherwise, without the prior written permission of the publisher or a licence from the Copyright Licensing Agency Limited. Details of such licences (for reprographic reproduction) may be obtained from the Copyright Licensing Agency Ltd of 90 Tottenham Court Road, London, W1P 9HE.

A catalogue record of this book is available from the British Library

ISBN   0 335 19255 6 (hb)   0 335 19254 8 (pb)

Library of Congress Cataloging-in-Publication Data
Teachers' stories / edited by David Thomas.
  p. cm.
  Includes bibliographical references and index.
  ISBN 0-335-19255-6. ISBN 0-335-19254-8 (pbk.)
  1. Education Biographical methods. 2. Teaching – Case studies.
  I. Thomas, D.J. (David John). 1932-
LB1029.B55143 1995
920'.0071 dc20   94-45444
                                                             CIP

Typeset by Colset Private Ltd, Singapore
Printed in Great Britain by St Edmundsbury Press Ltd
Bury St Edmunds, Suffolk

371
102
T40

Contents

Acknowledgements

The material for this book has been influenced by discussions with friends and colleagues, among whom I would like especially to thank David Hamilton, Waltraud Boxall and Eleanor Wright and also John Quicke for many stimulating and, occasionally, disturbing comments. A special thanks to the many students who explored aspects of their educational biographies with me over the years and who have allowed their 'private' text to move into the public domain. In building my collection of papers on teachers' stories, the effort of the staff of the Department of Education library, Liverpool University, must not pass without a grateful acknowledgement.

The majority of the chapters have been written specifically for this volume. However, as indicated in the Introduction, versions of some chapters have appeared in the *British Educational Research Journal* and a version of my chapter on 'Trustworthy or treasonable text' appeared in International Analyses of Teacher Education (edited by P. Gilroy and M. Smith and published in 1993 by Carfax, PO Box 25, Abingdon, Oxon).

Above all, I owe particular thanks to my dearest wife Maggie for her loving care during a long convalescence and for her indefatigable industry in seeing this volume through to publication.

List of contributors

Kath Aspinwall is a senior lecturer in the Centre for Education Management and Administration at Sheffield Hallam University. She teaches on Diploma and Masters' programmes on a variety of topics concerned with personal, professional, managerial and organizational learning. She is particularly interested in approaches such as biography work and action learning.

Waltraud Boxall, lecturer in education at Liverpool University since September 1984, is currently director of studies for the primary PGCE course. Her interest in multiracial education while a primary school teacher for many years has been extended to include international aspects of the primary curriculum, early literacy and media education. In addition, she is looking at the construction of cultural identity with particular reference to Irish studies in the primary school. She has responsibility for the teaching of English on the primary PGCE course. Her publications include contributions to multiracial education and teacher education.

Ardra Cole is a professor in the Department of Applied Psychology at the Ontario Institute for Studies in Education, Toronto, Canada. Her research, writing and teaching are in the areas of teacher education and development, and qualitative approaches to educational research, particularly autobiographical, narrative and life-history methods. Among her recent publications is a book, co-authored with J. Gary Knowles, *Through Preservice Teachers' Eyes: Exploring Field Experiences Through Narrative and*

Inquiry. She is currently conducting a life-history study of university teacher educators.

Florence Gersten was born in Liverpool in 1943. After graduating in English literature from St Anne's College, Oxford, she worked as an assistant stage manager in a variety of theatres before obtaining a Postgraduate Certificate in Drama, after a year's course at the University of Bristol. After two years' teaching in London schools, she returned to Liverpool in 1970, since when she has worked as an administrator in the Department of Education, University of Liverpool. She is actively involved in the conservation of buildings, choral singing and various kinds of theatrical activity.

Morwenna Griffiths is a lecturer in the School of Education at the University of Nottingham, where she lectures in philosophy of education, research methods and equal opportunities. She has previously worked in primary schools in England and in institutions of higher education in Isfahan, Iran and in Canterbury and Oxford, England and in Maine, USA. She is currently working on a book on feminism and the self. She is also collaborating with a local teacher on another book on social justice in the primary school.

Mary Jean Ronan Herzog is a lecturer in the Department of Administration, Curriculum and Instruction at Western Carolina University, where she teaches historical, social and philosophical foundations of American education to undergraduates and curriculum development and an advanced research seminar in curriculum to graduates. Her research interests are in qualitative educational research focusing on teacher stories, classroom ethnographies and students' perspectives on such issues as streaming and their personal histories of education. Other topics that she is involved in studying are school censorship and rural life and rural education.

J. Gary Knowles is a professor in the School of Education, University of Michigan, Ann Arbor. He teaches graduate courses in teacher education and development and qualitative research (particularly autobiographical narrative and life-history methods), and has written extensively in both of these areas. He also does research in the area of home education. Among his recent publications is a book on preservice teacher education co-authored with Ardra L. Cole. His current research activities include an auto-ethnographic study of teacher educators, as well as an autobiographical exploration of the place of artistic endeavour and aesthetic influences within qualitative research enterprises.

Doreen Littlewood is a qualified primary schoolteacher. In 1966, she moved into the teaching of children with special educational needs (SEN) and at present teaches in a special needs class. This is attached to a large mainstream primary school for which she is the SEN coordinator.

Anne Murray was, until recently, deputy head of a Liverpool primary school. She is married with three daughters.

Jennifer Nias has been 'composing her life' as a teacher for forty years. This composition has integrated elements as disparate as Headstart in California, a girls' secondary school in Nigeria and four different teaching institutions in England. At present she holds a part-time post as Rolle Professor of Education, University of Plymouth. Her chapter, based on longitudinal research into teachers' perspectives, arises from her conviction that the professional development of teachers can be fully understood, and facilitated, only when it is seen in the context of their other lives and concerns.

Elizabeth Thomas was a pupil at Queen Mary's High School, Walsall and is a graduate of Lancaster University. She has worked in various areas of residential and day care with teenagers and adults with both physical disabilities and learning difficulties. She is currently almost fully occupied in raising and educating three-year-old twins (Megan and Joshua), but still finds time to work with other children in a play-group and help an A-level psychology student with his studies.

David Thomas is an Honorary Senior Fellow in the Department of Education at the University of Liverpool and until his recent retirement, was senior lecturer in education in the Department of Education, University of Liverpool, and director of the Inservice and Professional Development Unit. His original interest was special education. His publications include *The Social Psychology of Childhood Disability* and *The Experience of Handicap*. He is a regular reviewer for the *British Journal of Special Education*. He taught on the MEd programme with options on biography in education and special needs curriculum and has been actively involved in developing a mentoring programme.

Peter J. Woods attended Loughborough Teachers' Training College and his first teaching post was in his native county of Norfolk, a county which continues to exert a strong influence on his life and writing. In 1981, he became headteacher of Brixworth Primary School, a position from which he took early retirement, in 1993 to concentrate on his other interests (archaeology, numismatics, ornithology, wildlife photography and writing). He is the author of a biography of the Yorkshire-born writer Leo Walmsley and a number of articles on Romano-British kilns and pottery. He has directed several major Iron Age and Roman excavations for Northamptonshire County Council. While at Brixworth he was instrumental in setting up the Rushavenn Project, which resulted in the publication of a full-length children's story. This won a prestigious literary award.

Introduction

David Thomas

In this volume, I attempt to introduce the reader to some examples of the range of responses which can emerge when education tutors facilitate the entry of the personal, the student's biographic experiences, into training. Some accounts may be grounded in specific intellectual, moral or literary theories or frameworks (e.g. feminism); others may use the framework of social transformation (Herzog).

As far as I am concerned, the scope of the book is introductory and its purpose is frankly evangelical to mark out and claim importance and significance for the personal in initial teacher training and in continuing professional development. I see a place for the following: the construction of an account of a particular intellectual and professional area/interest (e.g. a subject specialization); a more general education biography, and guidance in reflection on practice and experience; the generation of a journal of training experience, especially of school placement, teaching practice and/or mentoring. An examination of teaching methods and values through the above will provide an agenda in which the personal can claim a substantial part of the territory of initial training. The notion that the personal embraces the political is so well accepted as scarcely to require justification.

In Chapter 1, I introduce in a somewhat formal manner some of the issues associated with the use of, and interpretation, of, narratives. Among the issues is the importance, in a post-Skinnerian universe, of meaning and interpretation of human processes and behaviour and the rediscovery of the value of subjectivity. Another major dimension is the emergence of the recognition of stories as valued sources of information – indeed, storytelling as a 'primary act of mind'. In the shadow of Descartes and the triumphalism of the scientific method, we in our culture attempt to maintain a clear distinction between fiction and non-fiction and stories are more likely to be valued as belonging to the discourses of imagination than empiricism.

I note that storytelling can be captured in logs, diaries, research journals, vignettes, life-histories or autobiographies and through interview – recorded and transcribed. All these modes of expression can be seen as ways in which the person socially constructs him or herself.

As far as teaching is concerned, one of the clearest statements of the value of personal narrative is the following:

> In exploring an exceptional educational event in his school, a teacher had recourse to his life history. The event was the fullest expression in his teaching to date of his self, and to understand the event fully it was necessary to see how that self had come into being, developed, resisted attack, been mortified, survived, and at times prospered. His philosophy of teaching was rooted in these childhood experiences, which he saw as starkly divided between the alienating world of formal schooling and a natural world of real learning. Critical incidents and degradation ceremonies marked those occasions when the two came into conflict. The sense of marginality that resulted has stayed with him through life, though it has had its moments of exquisite pleasure as well as intense pain. In managing his marginality he has cultivated private places and a reference group of significant others who have supported and developed his preferred beliefs. But success in teaching is the main support.
>
> (Woods 1993: 447)

I have included illustrations of the varieties of narratives. Chapter 2 is a transcript of a student teacher's language biography as an instance of having teachers explore quite specific aspects of their own development – in this case, the aspect of language. The text is the full transcript of an audiotape which she produced at her home in response to my minimum prompts, 'Try to recall your language experience, perhaps in the following areas: reading, writing, mother tongue, foreign languages'. After reading the transcript, the student noted, with some disquiet, that the transcription had lost the dynamics of the spoken word, such as variations in speed, rhythms, stress and accents. However, the text did represent her views.

Florence Gersten, former teacher now administrator, created her education biography with minimum prompting. It, and the education biography of Anne Murray, are rich sources of lived experiences, through which more abstract issues may be illustrated and discussed. In Gersten's account, there is evidence of the linkage between home resources and opportunities and academic success. It also reminds us that happiness is not determined by academic success alone, but that acceptance and friendship are also important. Both Gersten's and Murray's education biographies, while rich in potential sources of ideas for sharing in a group, pose problems which Boxall touches upon – the extent to which material generated for one audience may be made available to another and under what circumstances. Both accounts, of course, raise issues about the reliability and trustworthiness of personal memories.

Boxall's chapter is a closely argued rationale for introducing journals/ diaries to primary PGCE students as they begin to grapple with the troubling, confusing and contradictory aspects of education, as practised in classrooms, compared with its description in textbooks and seminar rooms. Journals and diaries are resources with a number of uses. These include material for a grounded life-history: opportunities to record incidents which illustrate pedagogical processes and which can be evaluated at leisure. Journals provide space for students to share with tutors and others developing professional concerns which may be difficult to articulate in more formal academic assignments. Boxall's account also reveals something of the sensitivity the reader must bring to the task of interpretation and clarification. The value of journals to the experienced teacher is indicated in the introductory note to Doreen Littlewood's chapter.

Morwenna Griffiths tackles the theme of how action research can link the *personal* to the *political* and the *critical*. She suggests the pleasure of the personal can be connected to personal renewal and beyond to aspects of social reconstruction.

I wanted to include contributions from other cultures and also to illustrate the interactive nature of the dialogical process between teacher and researcher. The contribution from Ardra Cole and Gary Knowles indicates the value of distance from familiar surroundings in helping critical reflection, and the manner in which each reflection is assisted by having the reactions of an 'over-reader'.

I believe the teacher's story told by M.J. Ronan Herzog satisfies Griffiths' criteria for assessing the epistemological status of personal accounts in that, in constructing the account, the teacher Mrs Lauren integrates the process of personal renewal (value clarification) into a critique of her education system and how that system could be modified.

Chapters 10 and 11, by David Thomas and Peter J. Woods respectively, are based on work that appeared in the *British Educational Research Journal* (1993. Vol. 19, No. 5). The origin of these chapters was a stimulating paper by Professor P. Woods (1993), which included illustrative material for a grounded life-history of a teacher, Peter J. Woods. This evoked a reaction piece by Thomas, which was sent to Peter J. Woods. He, in turn, wrote a paper 'Keys to the past', in which he commented on both the original paper by Woods and Thomas's response.

Nias and Aspinwall have shown, in their contribution, how individual, subjective and solipsistic accounts can be woven into a research strategy using a stratified sample of primary school teachers and looking across their personal accounts for themes. This chapter is a powerful, condensed version of the research and reflection that has heavily influenced our understanding and concept of 'career' among women primary school teachers. The traditional view of career as a vertical ladder was enlarged and augmented by such notions as horizontal career patterns and parallel careers.

It should be clear that no story by a teacher can be regarded as typical or representative, but that, within each individual narrative, there will be episodes, experiences and emotions with which teachers can readily identify. It will be argued later that one of the signal virtues of the personal/biographic approach is that the narrative is grounded in an actual place-time and deals with highly concrete matters and specific affairs. Thus it is in contrast to the painless generalizations about children, teachers and teaching with which so much of the literature is 'embellished'. The encouragement of the entry of the personal into training and subsequent professional development, and the admission of the individual teacher's voice into educational monologue, is a powerful and necessary counterpoise to the discourse of teaching and training dominated for too long by those with claims to ownership of that discourse with its remote language of theoretical and propositional knowledge.

References

Thomas, D.J. (1993) 'Empirical Authors, Liminal Texts and Model Readers: a response to 'Managing marginality''. *British Educational Research Journal* 19(5), 467–74.

Woods, Peter J. (1993) 'Keys to the past – and to the future: the Empirical Author replies'. *British Educational Research Journal* 19(5), 475–88.

Woods, Professor P. (1993) 'Managing marginality: Teacher development through grounded life history'. *British Educational Research Journal* 19(5), 447–65.

1

Treasonable or trustworthy text: Reflections on teacher narrative studies

David Thomas

After the children started school, I put up the partitions in my mind. I would rush around in the morning braiding their hair, packing their lunches: then the second they were gone I would grow quiet and climb the stairs to my study. Sometimes a child would come home early and I would feel a little tug between the two parts of me: I'd be absent-minded and short-tempered. Then gradually I learned to make the transition more easily ... I no longer attempt to sneak off to my study to finish that one last page; I know that instantly, as if by magic, assorted little people will be pounding on my door requiring Band-Aid, tetanus shots, and a complete summation of the facts of life.

Anne Tyler, *Still Just Writing*

'That woman Estelle,' the note reads, 'is partly the reason why George Sharpe and I are separated today.' Dirty crepe-de-Chine wrapper, hotel bar, Wilmington, PR, 9.45 a.m. August Monday morning.

Since the note is in my note book, it presumably has some meaning for me. I study it for a long while ... Why did I write it down? In order to remember it, of course, but exactly what was it I wanted to remember? How much of it actually happened? ... the point of my keeping a notebook has never, nor is it now, to have a factual record of what I have been doing or thinking ... I have abandoned that kind of pointless entry; instead I tell what some would call lies.

Joan Didion, *On Keeping a Notebook*

Introduction

This is a general introduction to selected aspects of an approach to the study of teachers and teaching, which uses forms of narrative as a device for obtaining a perspective on life, work and career. It is directed towards teachers and, as well as considering some of the principals of this genre, it will also draw attention to some problems and controversial issues.

From machine to meaning

It is sometimes difficult to give a precise date to the beginnings of a change in intellectual climate, although in retrospect it is clear that a different era has emerged. An indication of a sea-change is often signalled by a *shift in dominant metaphors*. One such change can be described as the *rediscovery of meaning and interpretation* in human processes, both internal (mental) and external (interactions and communications). Among the characteristics of this climatic change was a challenge to the commanding position of the earlier quasi-axiomatic, behaviouristic approaches to social science research and to understanding. Among the 'taken-for-granted' positions was that knowledge growth was contingent upon perceiving human processes as a species of *information processing*: the prevailing image of the human brain was the computer and that mind was a special kind of software. Alongside this was also a mysterious (and essentially subjective) distrust of all forms of subjectivity. Truth was to be discovered in the objective and the observable and confirmed by public evidence of a repeatable, valid and reliable nature. A corollary of this was a perception that what people might *say* about themselves, their actions and motives and about other people, was not to be regarded as trustworthy evidence; at least, not in comparison with direct observation of behaviour or accurate measurement (Bruner 1992).

The swing away from the computer–computing image made possible the re-emergence into social science perceptions some long-banished concepts, such as *meaning* and *interpretation* in human affairs. This alternative perception took as *its* axiom that persons exist in cultural contexts. No psychology of the individual could rationally and realistically emerge without that psychology recognizing the person in his or her milieu. Consistent with this view was an appreciation that 'people in their context' are engaged in attempts at relating and communicating; that is, they are making efforts to understand and interpret their own behaviour and that of others in their community, context or milieu. These activities and strivings imply the possibilities of shared or negotiated meanings, and shared and negotiated interpretations of both behaviours and thoughts.

The assault on the behavioural ramparts was undertaken by a multilateral force: a mixed bag of philosophers, anthropologists, linguists and sociologists. These intellectual commandos looked critically, for example, at the metaphoric substrate of human communication (Lakoff and Johnson 1980) and cultural interpretation (Geertz 1973), explored human intentions (Searle 1983) and how the person was 'socially constructed' (Gergen and Davis 1985). An enduring contribution of this period was to alter the focus of attention from information and data to ideas, thoughts, perceptions and, in particular, meanings. It reclaimed the subjective as a legitimate zone of inquiry by challenging the hegemony of the objective: substituting more organic, more holistic, metaphors for mechanistic ones: contesting the notion that the principal goal for the study of persons was the prediction of their behaviour.

The importance of narrative

Crucial to this process was the affirmation of the importance of narrative. It began to be recognized that narrative was an ancient form of communication, reaching back to a pre-literate oral tradition. In all cultures, storytelling was a universal feature, and with its correlatives of 'storyteller' (narrator) and 'listener' (audience) could be celebrated as a 'primary act of mind' (Hardy 1986). Narrative had been reclaimed and given the status of a form of thought of equal validity to that used in logical thinking and in inductive argument (Bruner 1983). It has been credited with addressing something profound within the human psyche – the need to tell and hear stories – and as a part of the social cement which creates group cohesions. We seem to acquire the art and craft of storytelling alongside our language learning and become gifted with the capacity (or cursed with the imperative) to cast our experiences in narrative form. They are devices for communicating, interpreting and giving meaning to our experiences. So powerful is the impulse to tell stories, there is a sense in which 'we are told by our stories'.

Storytelling has its structure and strictures. Stories involve choice, selection and emphasis in the service of coherence; they require structural features such as plots, beginnings, middles and endings; they demand cause and effect, motivations and climaxes; and they require heroes, heroines and villains, romance, tragedies and comedies. While our culture has attempted to discriminate between narrative and non-narrative discourses (maintaining such distinctions as 'fiction' and non-fiction), it seems likely that inside most non-narrative discourses there is a story struggling to get out and within each narrative there 'stalks *the ghost of non-narrative discourse* [my emphasis]' (Rosen 1987; 12).

Education and research

In educational research, this *zeitgeist* expressed itself, in part, through the emergence of reactions to what were perceived as the restraints, limits and errors of traditional positivist positions and their concomitant, circumscribing research methods. Among these reactions can be identified the impetus for innovative forms of evaluation (Hamilton 1977), alternative styles of collaborative research *with* teachers (Stenhouse 1975; Carr and Kemmis 1983), a reappraisal of the value of the intensive case study (Simons 1980), and the dynamic, transformative presence of a feminist perspective on research which firmly linked the personal to the political (Burgess 1985). This led eventually to the present, overwhelming, puissance of the qualitative research paradigm in educational studies. Within these varied strands, it seems clear that one unifying aspect was the affirmation of the actors'/agents' right to speak for themselves: the advent of teacher as subject not object.

Entwined within the more global intellectual paradigm shift and its impact upon general educational studies, was a growing concern to find ways in which teachers' voices and stories could be heard and told. A landmark publication was Abbs' (1974) *Autobiography in Education*. This, together with Leonard Berk's (1980) lengthy paper signalled the arrival of a distinctive approach to the study of teachers and teaching. From these early beginnings, there has been a steady increase in the number of books, research reports and dissertations which have, through a variety of approaches, taken seriously the idea that much of value to the educational community can be learned by conversing with, and listening attentively to, what teachers have to say (it is worth noting the significance of words like 'conversation' and 'listening') about their classroom practices, their experiences of schools and of the formal and informal relationship within them, their insights into pupils as learners, and the corpus of professional understandings and craft knowledge that derives from experience. In addition, these research relationships have extended conversations with teachers to concerns beyond the classroom and school, both the personal and the private.

From this not so distant starting point, there has been an expansion of teacher-focused studies with a calculated intent to help teachers to tell their own stories and to find ways of getting these stories heard. Since the 1980s, there has been a near-global interest in teacher narratives. A signal feature of these narrative studies has been to provide a medium through which many so-called ordinary teachers, and not just a few *prima donnas*, have been able to make a personal and professional statement (Elbaz 1991).

Logs, diaries, journals, research journals, vignettes, critical incidents, life-histories and autobiographies

The media through which such teachers have been able to express themselves can take a variety of forms. These records may be in the form of logs, diaries, journals, research journals, vignettes, critical incidents, life-histories or autobiographies. Logs are factual records, usually containing brief, accurate statements and which provide an authoritative record, often in a well-structured format and in an impersonal style. Diaries are less structured, allowing for more personal decisions on content and style and where subjective aspects can find a place. Journals may combine the structured and objective aspects of a log with the freer format of the diary. An essential feature of the journal is the internal dialogue which the writer carries on with him or herself. Research journals focus upon a specific project and contain a record of events, remarks, data and notes. They provide an evidential store which can be used for interpretive and analytic purposes.

Vignettes have been used to provide snapshots of, say, classroom events, and can be compiled relatively easily and are used as the basis for self-reflection or for comment by others. Shulman and Colbert (1988: 81) define 'vignette' as 'a story about a particular event, experience or episode . . . a narrative . . . which describes what led up to an event and its consequences'. Critical incidents, like vignettes, concentrate upon episodes and especially those which identify specific pedagogic practices and which can be used to begin reflections upon the origins of these practices. Critical incidents also may refer to those events which provided or caused major shifts or changes in a life.

Life-histories are more ambitious undertakings. They have the potential for 'facilitating reflection upon the experience of society' (Quicke 1988: 92). They can help to make more clear to the individual, the way in which a personal life can be penetrated by the social and the political. Life-histories may be deliberately 'grounded' in a particular theoretical framework, such as social replication or radical feminism.

Autobiography, 'a work in which the hero, narrator and author have the same name', takes writing about the self into the region of literature. For Pascal (1960), autobiography involves the reconstruction of a life within the circumstances in which it was lived: its primary focus is the self, although clearly the self must address the external world, through which, in interaction with the individual, the personality comes to acquire its unique shape.

An important aspect of diaries and journals is the opportunity they provide for the writer to enter into a dialogical relationship with the self and with those who are permitted to share the text. As such, the text may help to *confirm* current practices and beliefs or *challenge* them. There is an obvious but significant distinction to be drawn between those accounts which are private, self-confessional and intended for solitary reflection, and those which are occasioned and designed to be shared. This latter will have implications for content, style and clarity of communication with the other reader. Here the writer will receive comments, analysis and contested perspectives which will themselves be a starting point for further, spiralling, professional engagement and critical reflection.

Experience suggests that those commencing journal writing may need support on such issues as focus, frequency of entries, quantity and style. Some teachers and researchers advocate a two-stage process in which an event or episode is recorded in an abbreviated form, near to the time of its occurrence, and then is reflected on, after an interval of, say, several days. A valuable guide to these practical issues can be found in Holly (1989).

Two types of teacher narrative research

Autonomous writings

As indicated above, there are two broad categories of teacher narratives. The first, less common type may be called *autonomous writings*, which are the spontaneous and unaided narratives of individual teachers. An example of this kind of writing is Carol Stumbo's (1989) account of her life, teacher-training and experiences as a teacher in a remote, rural county in Kentucky. She describes her pupils as named individuals, their family and cultural backgrounds, and sees their school experiences as being 'educated to fit into the majority culture and to devalue their own history'. Of her own initial expectation of these Appalachian children, she writes:

> I had come to ... teaching ... with a great deal of confidence, the kind of empty confidence that was based on no real understanding of the problem I would confront as a public school teacher. On my first day ... I asked all my students to do a piece of writing ... and I remember ... looking for the first time at what I had so casually asked them to write. Most of it I couldn't read, yet they had filled page after page. Here and there, I was able to understand the thoughts and feelings behind some of the writing and it was beautiful ...
>
> (Stumbo 1989: 90)

She goes on to describe and analyse how she began to get closer to her students through a project on oral history. The narrative shows how her reflections on the experience began to reshape not only her views about teaching one particular group of students, but also at a deeper, values level, her general ideas and ideals about teaching, her own education and her notion of community. One aspect of this change was a realization of the need to focus on the students in their community:

> I want to know more about the worlds my students bring into the classroom with them ... [If] teaching is to be a creative process ... I have to listen ... we can not sell students short because of [their] experiences and scars.
>
> (Stumbo 1989: 96)

Her narrative allows us to see the events which have led to reflective transformation. It also allows us to generate questions for ourselves.

Leslie Hills (1990), in *The Senga Syndrome*, writes of her time as a woman undergraduate in the early 1960s attending a Scottish university and of her career as a teacher, as an adviser and as a development officer with the Scottish Examination Board. This autonomous account is implicitly grounded in a dynamic view of feminism, moving from liberal gradualism to a more radical perspective. It takes as its central message the essentially cosmetic changes in the position of women:

> Along with many women of my generation I had a belief in gradual improvement and a hope for the future in which power relationships between the sexes could change. In education, as in many fields, our hopes have proved false. There has been superficial change.
>
> (Hills 1990: 165)

On her undergraduate days, she recalls both the inferior place of women and her own and other women's passivity to that experience: 'I barely said a word within the University for the next two years. All my lecturers were male. The professor of English refused to lecture to mixed classes' (p. 149). She recounts her entry into teaching ('for no good reason') and unexpectedly discovers in herself a gift for teaching difficult children:

> On my first day I was given a timetable and shown a room by the Head of English. I saw him once more in the next twelve months. I could not meet him informally because the staff rooms were segregated.
>
> (Hills 1990: 151)

As for teaching,

> There was no attempt to discuss the teaching I inflicted on my pupils. I was given to understand I was doing well and that the measure of this was I bothered no one with my problems.
>
> (Hills 1990: 152)

This record focuses upon the experience of one teacher-educator and goes beyond the particular and personal to address wider sociopolitical issues. Through it we see the growth of consciousness and we are thus able to make an assertion about the general status of women in the educational system: reminding us of Carl Rogers' 'What is most personal is most general'. The account offers us the possibility of comparing and contrasting our experiences with that of the narrator. Both Stumbo and Hills, through accounts which are situationally specific and anchored in experience, provide examples of teacher autonomous narratives directed at pedagogic, career, cultural and political issues. They are also examples of teachers finding their 'voice' through writing.

Collaborative accounts

The second broad category of teacher narratives may be termed *collaborative accounts*. These are teacher/student narratives which are created within a relationship with education tutors (pre-service and in-service) and/or researchers. Such activities are often formally labelled as collaborative in the sense that, as part of the process, the narrative is being continually transformed by the interaction of student or teacher with the tutor or researcher. One feature of the collaborative enterprise is that the partners give each other equal status. They attempt to offer each to the other, not only as professionals but also as persons. This collaborative process implies that the researcher does not possess the right to an absolutist interpretation of the narrative, but as a reader may offer to share with the writer reactions to the stories, but is not given judgemental powers. This duality of the professional and private may be seen in published accounts. Another aspect of this relationship is a relaxation or abolition of the right of one party to an absolutist or authoritative discourse. Teacher and researcher resign claims to a privileged interpretation of events. This does not mean an abdication of expertise and knowledge on the part of the researcher or the abandonment of craft skills and experience by the teacher. Neither, however, can assert that their positions and perspectives be given a special entitlement. Both attempt to bring to reflection and analysis distinctive approaches which are themselves the subject of discussion and debate in order to seek, if possible, a *rapprochement*. The theoretical perspectives of the researcher/educator are confronted by the specific realities of actual classroom and schools. The craft experiences of the teacher, expressed as 'private theories', may be challenged by alternative perspectives and theories provided by the researcher. Both may benefit from the heuristic dialogue.

An example of this interactive and collaborative style is Clandinin's (1989) work with 'one novice teacher'. Clandinin provides an account of Stewart, a kindergarten teacher, and how the narrative method used had, as its principle feature, 'the reconstruction of classroom meanings in terms of unities and rhythms in the lives of classroom practitioners'. The method involved biographical data, journal material, interview transcripts and field notes. The period of interaction was one year and Stewart kept a daily journal 'that recorded what seemed to him to be his most significant classroom experiences'. As well as frequent informal conversations, there were three semi-structured interviews in which the journal entries were discussed. Stewart was given a copy of the interview transcript of the previous meeting before the next one. Through this, Clandinin was able to have Stewart's reactions to her interpretations of his journal. At the end of the research, Clandinin explored the notion that Stewart has an image of teaching which is largely non-propositional in nature, has developed out of experience and with affective and moral dimensions. She sees Stewart shaping his experiences into a narrative form which extends to, and incorporates, aspects of the private life. For Clandinin (1989: 138), the distinction between professional and private worlds is almost arbitrary:

> A full accounting of the understanding a given teacher brings into and develops in the classroom requires an opportunity for inquiry into the whole of a teacher's life. The appropriate experience for reflection becomes all experience that led up to and contributed to the teaching experience.

Clandinin, like others, seeks to go beyond the specific and particular of the individual studied to make statements of a more general character. An important codification of this unity of life and work within a narrative convention is to be found in Connelly (1987). This process is described, elsewhere, as:

> [in] an understanding of the process [narrative inquiry] as one in which we are continually trying to give an account of the multiple levels . . . at which the inquiry proceeds. The central task is evident when it is grasped that people are both living their stories in an ongoing experiential text and telling their stories in words as they reflect upon life and explain themselves to others. For the researcher, this is a portion of the complexity of narrative, because a life is also a matter of growth towards some imagined future, and therefore, involves retelling stories and attempts at reliving stories. A person is, at once, engaged in living, telling, retelling and reliving stories.
> (Connelly and Clandinin 1990: 4)

The process attempts to grasp and convey something of the totality and wholeness of the teacher's life and work.

The diversity of research interests and approaches

A salient feature of research using narrative and biographic work is its diversity of foci and methods. The following is illustrative of this variety:

> Case-study approach involving a newly qualified teacher keeping a journal and a curriculum log, whose classroom teaching was observed by the researcher and was systematically interviewed (Bullough and Knowles 1991).
>
> One student teacher's autobiographical account based on narrative episodes and with reflections on these by the researcher (Berk 1980).
>
> One teacher's independent account and critique of his own practice (Bigelow 1990).
>
> One pre-service teacher who failed teaching practice gives an account of her experiences; shared with her tutors and on which they comment (Knowles and Hoefler 1989).
>
> Fictional-critical writing by teachers (Winter 1991).
>
> Life history interviews with retired women teachers (Weiler 1992).
>
> An examination of the interaction of teachers' life history with continuing professional development (Beattie 1992).
>
> The use of theatrical improvisation in reading teachers' narratives (Salvio 1991).
>
> Teachers of English write their autobiographies (Beach 1987).
>
> Deconstructing the image of teacher as 'mother' (Casey 1990).
>
> A study of teachers during their internship using field notes and interviews (Clandinin and Connelly 1990).
>
> Groups of teachers producing collaborative autobiographies (King 1991).
>
> Observational study of an exceptional teacher (Grant 1991).
>
> Focused study on women teachers' careers (Acker 1989).
>
> Large scale study of the professional and private careers of primary teachers (Nias 1989).

Given this range of interests, it is worth asking what is the rationale for getting teachers to tell and share their stories.

Rationale for stories

Why invite teachers to disclose stories of their life and work? Invitations to recount the personal will need to be justified, since modern society has found many ways to 'legitimize' intrusion into private and family lives. The helping professions, 'doctors, teachers, psychologists, child guidance experts and juvenile court officers', all claim rights of access to personal territory (Goodson 1991). Oral historians, biographers and ethnographers assert rights of access to the personal landscape for epistemic reasons. It is no longer possible for the educational-researcher-ethnographer (the 'hero-ethnographer') to justify probing into teachers' lives on the basis of the rarity or novelty of such stories; it requires some additional moral prop beyond inquisitiveness.

There will be many possible answers to the question set out above. Trying to address some of the issues, I offer the following as a possible justification. It is asserted that under certain conditions, biographic work by teachers, either autonomously or collaboratively with researchers, helps with their professional development. From that point, it might be possible to claim that gains in teacher professional development has positive advantages for pupils and, where the work becomes professionally and politically trans-forming, to believe it has the potential for helping more systemic changes.

Knowingness

From personal experience of working within this genre (Thomas 1991), I have come to accept it *can* make *some* teachers more *knowing*. Writing and sharing experiences of teaching and learning is influential in changing self-understanding and developing critical reflective skills. However, it should be noted this way of working does not suit everyone. The term 'knowing' carries with it some personal meanings for me, and these include a 'sense of an expanded and deepened awareness of the roots of professional prac-tice: beliefs, behaviour and values'. These roots or foundations reveal the armature between propositional and non-propositional professional know-ledge. These are connected to both formal training and in-service experi-ences, as well to those formative experiences and relationships of a personal character which lie outside the narrowly defined professional life.

Within this view are assumptions about the ways in which the individual's past affects present attitudes and behaviour. There is strong evidence that what teachers 'know' about teaching derives from the links between personal life-history and professional career. In this way, 'experience' and 'self' become key constructs and the biographic work must entail an examination of these.

The self in teaching

In teaching, it is difficult for the teacher to separate, convincingly and reliably, his or her self from the professional persona. It seems to me to be in the nature of teaching, that the mask of the role player is likely to slip: the enactment of the role is threatened by the intrusion of the self. Teachers are under such an intensity of scrutiny from an audience of psychologically acute observers that the professional persona become permeable to their gaze. Some teachers will attempt to inhabit their professional persona to the uttermost, whereas others agree with Paulo Freire on the value of 'being human in the classroom', while for most teaching involves a continuing shifting from persona to person and back again.

Biographic work almost inevitably obliges the writer to reflect, and in that sense the teacher-writer is addressing the self as well as a readership. We can think of the present self communicating through writing with earlier versions of the self: consulting on editorial matters such as selection, censorship and discourse conventions. It hardly seems possible to engage in any substantial biographic work without the writer coming up against the universal questions of personal identity and the meaning and purpose of existence.

Jensen (1984) suggests that narrative work, 'honest journals or memoirs', can be undertaken and read as attempts at 'intra-communication'. He notes, as others have, the difficult problem of memory (its accuracy and fidelity) and the advent, recognition and interpretation of habitual patterns of thought, behaviour and relationships in narratives, like rocks after an ebbing tide. Through personal reflection upon these recurring patterns, it becomes possible to engage in intra-communication, which can be transformative.

This argument is taken up by Aufenanger (1985) in his work with teachers on their narratives. Like Jensen, he finds recurring patterns in the stories and often these are to do with problems and difficulties in teaching, but 'which have their origins outside the classroom'. He takes as an issue the classical Kantian dilemma of how to reconcile submission to legal authority with the idea of personal freedom. Within the classroom, this dilemma takes the form of teachers' judgements and beliefs about the balance to be struck between children's autonomy and teachers' control. Aufenanger states that in seeking for the right balance, having in mind the pupils' stage of development and age, teachers can make mistakes – either allowing too much freedom or exercising too much control.

Biographic work with teachers produced evidence that the handling of such dilemmas was not only a matter of technical judgement, but arose from tensions within the self derived from 'unresolved' conflicts over matters such as freedom and discipline. Classroom dilemmas highlight aspects of the personal biography which are unresolved or unsettled, which compound the difficulties of professional judgement. For Aufenanger, teachers' behaviour can reveal 'patterns of reaction' or 'every-day life theories', which the teacher may use automatically as recipe solutions. He sees the pragmatics of teaching as containing an important element of un-thinking, for it is '. . . typical for the profession of educator to act spontaneously without rational legitimation in the same moment' (Aufenanger 1985: 4).

A vital part of professional development is the exploration of these 'everyday life theories'. His method is via the *spoken* autobiography (more spontaneous, and less governed by literary conventions) and the asking of questions in interviews. Transcripts of interviews are provided by the researcher for further mutual reflection. The task for the interpreter, suggests Aufenanger, is to inquire about the meaning of the experiences set down in the text. Working together, it becomes possible to explore and sometimes deal with the unsettled aspects of a life and this process he calls 'self-education'.

Personal-practical knowledge

Consider a body of knowledge, which, when effectively transmitted and acquired, would equip one to be a teacher. Presumably, such a corpus would contain both broad philosophical foundations as well as a hierarchy of practices and skills (Calderhead 1990). This body of propositional knowledge creates an 'imperial relationship' between those who claim to have it and those who do not: as between education tutors and their students (Gilroy 1990). No doubt, beginning teachers often come to their training in the expectation of this transmission model of autocratic knowledge and go away disheartened if the imperial bounty does not seem to have much purchase upon their experience of teaching (practice). For PGCE students, their dominant experience of knowledge, its transmission and successful regurgitation, has been of the domineering kind. However, students and teachers have another kind of knowledge which is a potent alternative resource when propositional knowledge proves impotent in the face of the specific reality of an actual classroom. This alternative knowledge derives from experience and may not be formally expressed, but is the basis for much of the behaviour and values which inform the practice of teaching. This is not to say that the two discourses – propositional and experiential – do not, to an extent, overlap and interact.

Teacher narratives are vehicles for bringing out aspects of their accumulated experiential knowledge. Among the distinctive features of this knowledge is its anchoring in the concrete and the specific. Teacher knowledge comes from within 'a particular school, school system and society' (Elbaz 1991: 13); it is 'high-context knowledge', compared with researchers' 'low-context knowledge' or 'de-contextualized discourse'. Grumet

(1987) suggests that one dimension of this personal-practical knowledge resides in its discourse form. That is, we 'tell' our experiential knowledge in story form:

> Personal knowledge . . . is constituted by the stories about experience we usually keep to ourselves, and practical knowledge, by the stories that are never, or rarely related, but provide, nevertheless, the structure for the improvisations that we call coping, problem-solving, action.
>
> (Grumet 1987: 322)

Therefore, we might say that invitations to teachers to relate the rarely related is, simultaneously, to give us a window on their world and to solicit them to disclose that which has been guarded and privileged. While teacher narratives are a valued source of ideas and insights, their extraction imposes an ethical constraint. However, there are significant epistemological questions relating to how we should consider teachers' accounts of their practice and whether that knowledge can exist outside of the discourse conventions and relationships which produced it. Is it a 'textually produced phenomenon' without an entity independent of the practices which produced it?

Career

One of the areas of research which has most effectively used the narrative form, is that of teachers' careers. The work of Acker (1989), Ball and Goodson (1985), Nias (1989) and Nias and Aspinwall (1992) illustrates the value of the biographic approach; the latter noting the willingness of teachers to talk in the presence of a 'neutral but friendly outsider'. This is not the occasion to review in detail the findings of these researches, however, the work has revealed the necessity of having an expanded notion of what the term 'career' can mean, especially as far as women teachers are concerned. Nias (1989) noted that some of her primary schoolteachers, for whatever reason (e.g. child-care or other family responsibilities), had been denied a vertical professional career pattern but had been able to create and maintain an alternative career, what Nias called a 'horizontal career':

> Some women, usually with children . . . made a virtue out of necessity. Disadvantaged, in terms of the single line vertical structure of teaching, by the multiple roles they carried, by the prejudice which existed against their promotion to senior posts in schools and by the mobility sometimes enforced upon them by their husbands' jobs, they had redefined the concept of career to mean progressive opportunities for personal learning and extension.
>
> (Nias and Aspinwall 1992: 8)

This lateral career may involve self-chosen moves into a variety of short-term posts on the margins of mainstream teaching, or the choice of a personally satisfying role within a school within which one can grow professionally and personally. Another group constructed what are called 'parallel' careers, where teaching co-exists alongside another interest or occupation, such as painting or creative writing.

These studies identified themes recurring within individual lives as well as themes shared by many. In the act of telling their stories, it appears that teachers are, in a sense, creating the meaning and shape of their lives through the act of narration. This shape and meaning is, in part, an understanding of the present through a reflection on the past. However, as Nias and Aspinwall remind us, the act of storytelling may result in different stories being told at different times, leading to different conclusions.

Voice

> The ordinary teacher is the silent subject who has not always been given a position as subject in our discourse.
>
> (Elbaz 1991: 8)

The idea of finding ways to enable us to hear the voice of teachers has been a central value of a great deal of narrative work (Grumet 1987; Henry 1990). It has taken the form of trying to understand the frames of reference, or perspective, teachers use in describing their role, and more deliberately in relation to notions of empowerment. If we deconstruct the word 'voice', we find it implies a contrast with silence; having something to say and a language in which to say it; that the voice belongs to a person and that there is a listener prepared to hear what can be said (Puckett 1989). In assisting teachers' voices, a number of different approaches have been tried, including autonomous narratives, collaborative ones, fictional accounts and theatrical presentations. Teachers' voices imply a surrender by academic researchers of their unchallenged autocratic discourse on teaching and opens up the possibility of rejecting a common criticism of teachers; that is, their understanding of their art and craft is concealed from themselves – their knowledge is only 'tacit' (Diamond 1992). It may be suggested that the act of writing itself is a critical adjunct in clarifying experience. The activity is a process which helps to create a personal voice. The possession of a voice is a source of potential empowerment.

The treasonable text

In this way, we can come to see teacher narratives as 'treasonable texts' (Robinson 1983), for they offer the possibility of an alternative set of stories about teaching and the education system. They are redressive, with disclosures from the classroom and staffroom as counterweights to those deriving from positions of power and policy-making. The extent to which this process can be threatened by hegemonic definitions of the person should not be underestimated; a problem Bahktin saw as attempting to speak in a language 'over-populated with the intentions of others' (quoted by Weiler 1992).

Problems

So far, the advantages of the narrative approach have been stressed. However, there are a number of concerns needing consideration. Among those beyond the scope of this account are 'post-modernists' conception of the self' (Griffiths 1991) and 'the nature of experience' (Winter 1989). Among those which will be considered are 'intrusion and collaboration', 'analysis and interpretation', 'questions relating to knowing' and 'reflection and action'.

Intrusion and collaboration

Measor and Sikes (1992: 210) have set out the agenda of ethical concerns relating to life-histories, defined as: '. . . one respectable way of indulging our wish to have evidence from the lives of others that we are not alone in our difficulties, pains, pleasures and needs'. They consider the value of the relationship between researcher and biographer being placed within an 'honest project' and founded upon Kantian notions of 'respect for persons' and his categorical imperative to 'treat other people as ends in themselves and never as means to an end' (Warburton 1992). To these are added self-determination and confidentiality. Since narrative studies, including life-histories, are likely to involve a close relationship between researcher and participant, a clear and agreed understanding of the nature of the work and the relationship needs to be negotiated and established from the outset. Measor and Sikes (1992: 214) draw upon their experiences in one project to share their ethical dilemmas:

> We have emphasized . . . the quality of the research relationship, but we need to acknowledge . . . the relationship was, after all, one primarily developed for the purposes of collecting data. None of the researchers maintained any of the relationships after the period of data collection was over. We, as researchers, were primarily in those relationships for research purposes, not for more general purposes of friendships. That was made clear to the respondents.

The discourse conventions that narrative and biographic research are embedded in are those most closely allied to intimacy and friendship, yet by the requirement to make data and conclusions public, those conventions of friendship are violated in favour of the role of informant. If the conventions of friendship are maintained, then the researcher's own role becomes ambiguous. Other ethical issues are also considered, such as the problem of how honest the researcher has to be with the respondent about the real intention of the research ('being a bit shifty') and how much of the teacher's time the project will actually take. Concepts like 'negotiation' and 'ownership' are central, yet problematic for this kind of research.

Other researchers, such as Munro (1991), have seen in teacher narrative studies a chance to develop relationships with respondents which strive for genuine collaborative equality. Munro's account is of the dilemma of attempting to produce an objective report from an intimate, participatory experience. A key problem is that of the presence or removal of the researcher's own biography from interaction with the respondent. Among the choices are whether the researcher's life and experiences are rendered either invisible ('disembodied ethnography') or made manifest ('self-indulgent ethnograph'). A third approach is to have a clear separation of the voices of the researcher and the respondent.

This latter point touches upon an issue which arises out of collaborative work. In practice, it is self-evident that academics have more chance of getting material into learned journals than do teachers with autonomous accounts. Those familiar with the requirements of journals are likely to want to shape their reports and articles into the discourse forms which communicate comfortably with editors and readers. This implies that at the publication end of the collaborative relationship, the power equation is not balanced. Willinsky's (1989) deconstruction of the notion of 'collaboration' begins by insisting the relationship between teacher and researcher is an enduringly problematic one. 'Collaboration' is seen as a metaphor for an ideal ethical relationship but not readily attainable in the real world, since the researcher-interpreter (in addition to power/status differential) is anxious to see and indeed to impose, patterns, images and meaning on the narratives. Moreover, when both parties are seeking to achieve an interpretive consensus as to the understandings to be derived from the narrative, that search for consensus may dampen down the individual voice:

... collaboration entails a suppression, or at least a masking of that very individuality ... the research project works hard to recover in teacher and researcher ... Individuality may be ploughed under in labouring for a collaboration of voices and the production of shared meanings.

(Willinsky 1989: 255)

This emphasizes the relevance of how the relationship is conceptualized as well as how it is actually handled.

The relationship issue is especially difficult in the case of education students and their tutors. Here problems are acute about making the private public, in the context where disclosure may be related to assessment, where a critique of course content, delivery or personalities, in 'private' journals, may be read by those whose pedagogic or interpersonal skills are being challenged. Similarly, there are questions which arise over *enforced* journal writing demanded in the name of giving students transformative, empowering experiences and greater autonomy. For tutors, there are dilemmas over dealing with the therapeutic problems which journal writing can reveal while, perhaps, wishing to focus on those concerns which are normally more central for teaching and learning. Training versus self-education perhaps?

Analysis and interpretation

Among the areas where development is required is in the analysis and interpretation of teacher texts. Tochon (1992) has argued that the present state of analysis is limited to 'rough thematic analysis' and to the discovery of the metaphoric foundations of teacher stories. He advocates the use of more sophisticated textual tools, such as markers, signal use, framing categories and story grammars. Fielding and Lee (1991) have compiled a guide to the use – and dangers of – computer programs in the coding and classification of data from interview transcripts. There is a growing feeling among researchers that the cruder forms of thematic analysis, exhausted categories and progressive focusing, require the support of more demanding forms of textual analysis. As well as the technical aspects of analysis, the interpretation of texts seems to be moving towards striving for a better balance between the solipsistic and the sociological.

For Weiler (1992), a part of that striving involves developing a critical stance towards the perspectives on self and life offered by teachers in their narratives and considering them in relation to a hegemonic definition of both teaching and gender. She sees one of the problems as how to interpret memories shaped by experiences which themselves are products of particular social and historical circumstances. That is, one task for the interpreter is to position the narrative within Foucault's (1973) 'archaeology of memory' and how individual memory and experience has a constructed character, for, as Graham (1989) expressed it, the key question is not 'Who am I?' *but* 'Where do I belong?'. In this sense, the teacher text has the potential to be doubly treacherous. Another area for growth is that of attempting to provide a clearer image of the role of the interpreter's own autobiography in the dynamic of the interpretation offered. If there are no innocent texts, there are no privileged interpretations; although as readers we can benefit by the guidance of a thoughtful leader to take us through the narrative maze. Barone (1992) notes the need to have both an intimate view of the text while giving it a cool assessment.

Epistemology

An important issue is what counts as knowledge in this genre? Memory is potentially unreliable; events may be described which are unverifiable and interpretations offered which are manifold. Lyons (1990) sees this issue as involving teachers' general knowledge, their specialist subject knowledge, their knowledge of pedagogy, their knowledge about pupils as learners, their 'knowledge in action', their personal knowledge and their understanding of knowledge structures. Extracting these varieties of 'knowing', providing an epistemic map through narratives and journals, is seen as challenging, especially as Lyons' own work suggests individual teachers' epistemic cartography is under irregular review: the knowledge map is dynamic. Graham (1989) is of the view that autobiography with its 'original sin of coherence and rationalization' presents difficulties in pinning down teacher knowledge. For this reason, Tripp (1994) recommends the use of 'critical incidents' rather than autobiography or life-history, since the incidents tend to identify specific teaching practice and it then becomes possible to work from the particular event to current classroom practices and from there towards 'aspects of its genesis'. He alerts us, however, to the '... real danger of the approach ... that ... critical incidents and journal accounts of our espoused theories, have great and compelling explanatory power, the conservative force of which should not be underestimated' (Tripp 1994: 13).

As interpreters of teacher texts, we seldom have the opportunity to validate the accounts provided. We have no way of ascertaining the story's link with actual events, but does it matter? If we regard all narratives as belonging to fiction rather than 'data' or 'objective evidence', then we can begin to apply to teacher texts the canons of literary criticism. The controversial suggestion regarding the adoption of literary criteria for truth and trustworthiness is an intriguing one and is reminiscent of Foucault's claim to have written only fiction (Barone 1992). Its significance is related to finding some way of assisting the process of reflection on narratives as a basis for action.

Reflection and action

It is a regular feature of teacher narrative research to claim for it the capacity to evoke reflection. Reflective teaching involves a concern for the aims, consequences and effectiveness of teaching. It requires an openness of spirit and an enquiring mind. It is a spiral of action, monitoring and evaluation, and attempts to integrate in its judgements both self-reflection and the insights from other relevant disciplines (Pollard 1988). These are qualities needed, as perhaps never before, in teaching. However, I believe such processes may appear spontaneously as a result of journal keeping or life-histories but are more likely to emerge in collaborative enterprises. In the absence of support for reflective journal writers, the benefits from the activity may be dissipated. Among the benefits could be to help the individual to understand his or her experiences within the nexus of social, economic and political structures.

Narrative work is difficult and demanding (Atkinson 1991). Both writers and readers require ways of responding to text and interpretation in ways which will lead to perceptions of reliable (but not permanent) bases for actions. Like Mishler (1990), teachers and tutors will want to move from considered reflection to beliefs that the foundation for their mutual professional development is trustworthy. That is, to move from writing to reflection to accepting the possibility of a personal professional response which has as its focus the classroom and then widens out beyond the school to a consideration of the moral purposes of education – the imagined future.

References

Abbs, P. (1974) *Autobiography in Education: An Introduction to the Subjective Discipline of Autobiography and its Central Place in the Education of Teachers.* London: Heinemann.

Acker, S. (Ed.) (1989) *Teachers, Gender and Careers.* Lewes: Falmer Press.

Atkinson, P. (1991) 'Supervising the text'. *Qualitative Studies in Education* 4(2), 161–74.

Aufenanger, S. (1985) 'Patterns of interpretation and the autobiographical method: Some remarks for educators'. Paper presented at the Annual Meeting of the American Educational Research Association, Chicago IL, March/April.

Ball, S.J. and Goodson, I.F. (Eds) (1985) *Teachers' Lives and Careers.* Lewes: Falmer Press.

Barone, T.E. (1992) 'On the demise of subjectivity in educational inquiry'. *Curriculum Inquiry* 22(1), 25–38.

Beach, R. (1987) 'Differences in autobiographical narratives of English teachers, college freshmen and seventh graders'. *College Composition and Communication* 38(1), 56–69.

Beattie, M. (1992) 'Creating classrooms and school communities for learning: Places where lives meet lives'. Paper presented at the University of Liverpool, Department of Education Conference 'Teachers' Stories of Life and Work', April, Chester.

Berk, L. (1980) 'Education in lives: Biographic narrative in the study of educational outcomes'. *Journal of Curriculum Theorising* 2(2), p. 88.

Bigelow, W. (1990) 'Inside the classroom: Social vision and critical pedagogy'. *Teachers College Record* 91(3), 437–48.

Bruner, J. (1986) *Actual Minds: Possible Worlds*. Cambridge, MA: Harvard University Press.

Bruner, J. (1992) *Acts of Meaning*. Cambridge, MA: Harvard University Press.

Bullough, R.V. and Knowles, J.G. (1991) 'Teaching and nurturing: Changing conceptions of self as teacher in a case study of becoming a teacher'. *Qualitative Studies in Education* 4(2), 121–40.

Burgess, R. (Ed.) (1985) *Issues in Educational Research: Qualitative Methods*. Lewes: Falmer Press. Calderhead, J. (1990) 'Conceptualising and evaluating teachers' professional learning'. *European Journal of Teacher Education* 13(3), 153–60.

Carr, W. and Kemmis, S. (1983) *Becoming Critical: Knowing Through Action Research*. Geelong, Victoria: Deakin University Press.

Casey, K. (1990) 'Teacher as mother: Curriculum theorising in the life histories of contemporary women teachers'. *Cambridge Journal of Education* 20(3), 301–19.

Clandinin, D.J. (1989) 'Developing rhythm in teaching: The narrative study of a beginning teacher's personal practical knowledge of classrooms'. *Curriculum Inquiry* 19(2), 121–41.

Clandinin, D.J. and Connelly, F.M. (1990) 'Narrative, experience and the study of curriculum'. *Cambridge Journal of Education* 20(3), 241–53.

Connelly, F.M. (1987) 'On narrative method, biography and narrative unities in the study of teaching'. *Journal of Educational Thought* 21(3), 130–39.

Connelly, F.M. and Clandinin, D.J. (1990) 'Stories of experience and narrative inquiry'. *Educational Researcher* 19(5), 2–14.

Diamond, C.T.P. (1992) 'Accounting for our accounts: Autobiographic approaches to teacher voice and vision'. *Curriculum Inquiry* 22(1), 67–81.

Didion, J. (1974) On Keeping a Notebook, in J. Didion *Slouching Towards Bethlehem*. Harmondsworth: Penguin.

Elbaz, F. (1991) 'Research on teachers' knowledge: The evolution of a discourse'. *Journal of Curriculum Studies* 23(1), 1–19.

Fielding, N. and Lee, R. (Eds) (1991) *Using Computers in Qualitative Research*. London: Sage.

Foucault, M. (1973) *The Order of Things: an archaeology of the human sciences*. New York: Vintage Books.

Geertz, C. (1973) *The Interpretation of Cultures*. New York: Basic Books.

Gergen, K.J. and Davis, K.E. (1985) *The Social Construction of the Person*. New York: Springer-Verlag.

Gilroy, P. (1990) Professional knowlege and the beginning teacher, in Carr, W. (Ed.), *Quality in Teaching: Arguments for a Reflective Profession*, pp. 101–14. Lewes: Falmer Press.

Goodson, I. (1991) 'Studying teachers' lives: Problems and possibilities'. Paper presented at the Annual Meeting of the American Educational Research Association, Chicago IL, April.

Graham, R.J. (1989) 'Autobiography and education'. *Journal of Educational Thought* 23(2), 92–105.

Grant, G.E. (1991) 'Ways of constructing classroom meaning: Two stories about knowing and seeing'. *Journal of Curriculum Studies* 23(5), 397–408.

Griffiths, M. (1991) 'Change and the self'. Paper presented at the British Educational Research Association Conference, Nottingham, August.

Grumet, M.R. (1987) 'The politics of personal knowledge'. *Curriculum Inquiry* 17(3), 319–29.

Hamilton, D. (1977) *Beyond the Numbers Game: A Reader in Educational Evaluation*. Basingstoke: Macmillan.

Hardy, B. (1986) Towards a poetics of fiction, in *Novel: A Forum*. Providence, RI: Brown University.

Henry, M. (1990) 'Voices of academic women on feminine gender scripts'. *British Journal of Sociology of Education* 11(2), 121–35.

Hills, L. (1990) The Senga syndrome: Reflections on twenty one years in Scottish education, in Paterson, F. and Fewell, J. (Eds), *Girls in Their Prime: Scottish Education Revisited*, pp. 148–66. Edinburgh: Scottish Academic Press.

Holly, M.L. (1989) 'Reflective writing and the spirit of enquiry'. *Cambridge Journal of Education* 19(1), 71–80.

Jensen, M.D. (1984) 'Memoirs and journals as maps of intrapersonal communication'. *Communication Education* 33(3), 237–42.

King, J.R. (1991) 'Collaborative life history narratives: Heroes in reading teachers' tales'. *Qualitative Studies in Education* 4(1), 45–60.

Knowles, J.G. and Hoefler, V.B. (1989) 'The student teacher who wouldn't go away: Learning from failure'. *Journal of Experimental Education* 12(2), 14–21.

Lakoff, G. and Johnson, M. (1980) *Metaphors We Live By*. Chicago, IL: Chicago University Press.

Lyons, N. (1990) 'Dilemmas of knowing: Ethical and epistemological dimensions of teachers' work and development'. *Harvard Educational Review* 60(2), 159–81.

Measor, L. and Sikes, P. (1992) Visiting lives: Ethics and methodology in life history, in Goodson, I. (Ed.), *Studying Teachers' Lives*, pp. 209–33. London: Routledge.

Mishler, E.G. (1990) 'Validation of inquiry-guided research: The role of exemplars in narrative studies'. *Harvard Educational Review* 60(4), 415–42.

Munro, P. (1991) 'Multiple "I'S": Dilemmas of life history research'. Paper presented at the Annual Meeting of the American Educational Research Association, Chicago IL, April.

Nias, J. (1989) *Primary Teachers Talking: A Study of Teaching as Work*. London: Routledge.

Nias, J. and Aspinwall, K. (1992) 'Composing a life: Women's stories of their careers'. Paper presented at the University of Liverpool, Department of Education Conference 'Teachers' Stories of Life and Work', April, Chester.

Pascal, R. (1960) *Design and Truth in Autobiography*. London: Routledge and Kegan Paul.

Pollard, A. (1988) Reflective teaching: The sociological contribution, in Woods, P. and Pollard, A. (Eds), *Sociology and Teaching*, pp. 54–73. London: Croom Helm.

Puckett, T.F. (1989) 'Towards womanspeak: Explication and critique of Spender, Lacan, Irigaray and Kristeva's perspective on women speaking'. Paper presented at the Annual Meeting of the International Communication Association, San Francisco, CA, May.

Quicke, J. (1988) Using structured life histories to teach the sociology and social psychology of education, in P. Woods and A. Pollard (Eds) *Sociology and Teaching*. London: Croom Helm.

Robinson, L.S. (1983) 'Treason our text: Feminist challenges to the literary canon'. ERIC Document No. ED245959, Wellesley: Centre for Research on Women, Wellesley College.

Rosen, H. (1987) *Stories and Meanings*. NATE Papers in Education. Sheffield: NATE.

Salvio, P.M. (1991) 'On the use of theatrical improvisation in reading teachers' autobiographical narratives'. Paper presented at the Annual Meeting of the American Educational Research Association, Chicago IL, April.

Searle, J.R. (1983) *Intentionality: An Essay in the Philosophy of Mind*. New York: Cambridge University Press.

Shulman, J.H. and Colbert, J.A. (Eds) (1988) *The Intern Teacher Casebook*. San Francisco, CA: Far West Laboratory.

Simons, H. (1980) *Towards a Science of the Singular*. CARE Occasional Publication No. 10. Norwich: University of East Anglia.

Stenhouse, L. (1975) *An Introduction to Curriculum Research and Development*. London: Heinemann.

Stumbo, C. (1989) 'Teachers and teaching'. *Harvard Educational Review* 59(1), 87–97.

Thomas, D. (1991) 'Teachers as unexplored persons, pre-service teachers' narratives, diaries and field notes'. Paper presented at the British Educational Research Association Annual Conference, Nottingham, August.

Tochon, F. (1992) 'Presence beyond narrative: Semiotic tools for deconstructing the personal story'. Paper presented at the Annual Meeting of the American Educational Research Association, San Francisco, CA, April.

Tripp, D. (1994) 'Teachers' lives, critical incidents and professional practice'. *Qualitative Studies in Education* 7(1), 65–76.

Tyler, A. (1992) Still Just Writing, in J. Sternburg (Ed.) *The Writer on her Work*. London: Virago Press.

Warburton, N. (1992) *Philosophy: The Basics*. London: Routledge.

Weiler, K. (1992) 'Remembering and representing life choices: A critical perspective on teachers' oral history narratives'. *Qualitative Studies in Education* 5(1), 39–50.

Willinsky, J. (1989) 'Getting personal and practical with personal practical knowledge'. *Curriculum Inquiry* 19(3), 247–64.

Winter, R. (1989) *Learning from Experience*. Lewes: Falmer Press.

Winter, R. (1991) Fictional-critical writing: An approach to case study research by practitioners and in-service and pre-service work with teachers, in Nias, J. and Groundwater-Smith, S. (Eds), *The Enquiring Teacher*, pp. 231–48. Lewes: Falmer Press.

2

My language experience

Elizabeth Thomas

Editor's note

There is some debate over the rival merits of written narratives as opposed
to oral accounts. It is claimed by some that oral accounts or interviews leave
less room for second thoughts, authorial adjustments and amendments; that
is, they provide *more* authentic accounts. In this chapter the account is
derived from an interview in which the respondent spoke without interruption for nearly 45 minutes, giving this account of her 'language development'. The text here is a complete transcription of the recording. In order
to highlight some of the qualitative differences between oral and written
accounts no attempt has been made to alter the spoken words into the more
formal register of written English: it is here, like Cromwell's portrait
instructions.

Foreign language learning

I've decided to begin with foreign language learning as this is something that
I feel quite strongly about. The Junior School that I went to taught French
to everybody from the second year upward so I first began to learn French
when I was only eight years old, and I really enjoyed it. I thought it was great.
We had this system that used records and pamphlets and everyone in the
class had a pamphlet which had cartoon strips with sentences underneath;

the sentences were playing on the records with a gap in between for you to repeat what was said. They must have been stories that appealed to children because I enjoyed them and I learned a lot of French. We weren't ever taught any formal grammar but I think we absorbed it in the way that you absorb the grammar of your own first language. We also learned songs in French, carols and things like that, and when it was parents' open days we would occasionally put on a short play in French.

Then, at eleven, I started grammar school with a lot of people who hadn't learned any French before and we were back to square one, but being taught in a very formal way. We had a great deal of homework, two or three times a week, and it would be exercises. There would be sentences with spaces into which had to be fitted 'du' or 'de la' or 'des' or something like that, and it was really boring. I was good. I think I was probably the best in the class at French but I just found it so boring that I didn't really do any work. We used to have lists of vocabulary to learn. Rather than just absorbing it through translating things that interested you would be expected to go home and learn a list of words, which I never bothered with. Instead of having percentages in exams we were graded. 1–5 was a pass, 6 and 7 were fail; I used to get grade 1's. I think I had a talent for French even though I didn't do much work but gradually through the school my marks got worse and worse because I just got more and more bored and put in less and less effort. So by the time I got to 'O' level I only got a grade 3; then I went on to do French at 'A' level because it was an 'easy' option and I only got an E.

I think if I'd put in more effort I could have got a much better mark but, again, I found it really boring. All along I felt that the emphasis was wrong. The importance of learning a language is to communicate with other people. It's about making yourself understood and understanding other people. It's not about writing things down and getting your agreements right on the ends of your words and things like that which is what the focus seemed to be in French 'O' and 'A' level.

My school did organize trips for people who were doing French at 'A' level. There was an exchange visit with a school in Paris but, unfortunately, the year I was in the sixth form we didn't go. The school said that our February half-term was at a different time to the French holiday so therefore we wouldn't be able to go. This was such a shame because I'd have loved to have gone to France but I didn't go abroad at all until I was twenty-three. When I eventually did get abroad I felt quite inhibited about speaking the language. I think I'd had it drilled into me at school that what I'd written in French was *not* acceptable unless it was grammatically absolutely perfect and spelt perfectly. This makes you inhibited about speaking to people because you think that they are not going to understand you. It takes quite a lot of travelling abroad before you begin to realize that people do understand you and that all you need is to link a few words together and people can understand what you're getting at. I also think that there's an awful lot that's missed out. Teachers could make French really interesting at school. We could have learned things about French culture and history. It would have been nice to learn something about food and about the people and the music and geography and all those kinds of things. As it was, at 'A' level you spend your time translating French to English and English to French, doing compositions and a bit of French literature which was also pretty boring because it was writers like Balzac and we would have to go round the class translating it word for word. That was really tedious.

I also learned German at school and I feel similarly about that, although I hadn't learned German from such an early age. Being bored wasn't such a problem because it was something new. But German was taught in exactly the same way as I think all languages were in my school. I think it's a shame and I also think it's one of the reasons that kids in this country are not very good at foreign languages. They've had it bored out of them.

Learning to read

I can just about remember learning to read. I started school in the term in which I was five and I think I was ready to learn to read and write but my parents hadn't done anything about it at home. They were worried that anything they did might interfere with the method they used at school. So when I came to school I think I was ready and I picked it up really quickly. I learned using 'Janet and John' and I can remember finding that boring. I'm not sure whether we used a phonic system or 'look and say'; I think 'look and say'. When my Mum used to read with me at home she used phonics and I can remember finding that difficult. I could understand how to sound out the letters c-a-t but I could never really put them together. If I put that word together I would get cu-a-tu. I got lots of extra sounds in that weren't supposed to be there. So I found that a bit difficult. But I did enjoy reading.

I can remember at the age of six being given *Pinocchio* and really enjoying that, and then, slightly older, liking *Alice in Wonderland*. That was my favourite book for years and I read it many times. I think I must have been good at reading in the infants' school because, when one of the teachers left and wrote a letter to everybody at school, I was the one chosen to read it out in assembly. So I must have been a reasonably good reader. Also I remember the school gave a sort of prize. If a group of children had been reading to the headmistress she would let us all have a book to take home and keep. I used to be the one allowed to choose first which book I would like because I'd read well.

I carried on being interested in reading right through junior school. When I was nine, ten and eleven, when asked what I wanted for birthday or Christmas presents, it was always books. I had loads and loads of books and it was what I spent most of my pocket money on. I spent a lot of time reading and I got an awful lot out of it. Quite a lot of the books my parents bought me were difficult. They would buy me things like *What Katy Did*, *Good Wives* and classics like that, and I'd struggle with them and then give them up because I found them too difficult. But funnily enough it never bothered me. I actually liked having books as presents whether I could read them or not, and I've still got those books now. So I was quite happy with them even if they were too difficult, just to have them on the shelf.

When I bought books for myself I used to buy an awful lot of Enid Blyton books. I must have read my way through most of the series of the mystery stories and quite a lot of 'Famous Five' and 'Secret Seven'. I had a large collection of paperbacks. Rose, my sister, and I used to make libraries out of our books. We made cards for all the books and organized them on our book shelves and had a sort of booking-out system to borrow them.

When I was slightly younger, about seven or eight, my mum used to choose books for me from the library. I can remember she used to go to town shopping on a Saturday, and Rose and I would be at home. She would come in with her big bags of shopping, late Saturday morning and we would rush to the bags. Partly we were looking to see if there was anything interesting to eat like biscuits, but partly we were looking for library books. We used to be really excited at what she'd brought back. My mum was, apparently, a keen reader when she was young and was teased by her parents for always having her nose buried in a book. I think she thought it was a valuable activity which hadn't particularly been encouraged in her so this is one of the reasons she encouraged it in me. Because, although I did really like reading, when I expressed an interest in other things, like learning a musical instrument, or having ballet lessons that wasn't encouraged; but my interest in reading was always very strongly encouraged.

I stop reading

At the age of eleven I started a grammar school and I stopped reading. Just like that. It's almost like it happened overnight. At one time, looking back on it, I thought it must have been the quality of what I was reading. I explained it by the fact that I was reading Enid Blyton books because if I'd been reading better quality books, (maybe Roald Dahl or C.S. Lewis), I'd have carried on, *but I don't think it was that*. I think it was something to do with the amount of homework that I had. We were given three or four lots of homework a night and by the time I'd finished that I didn't want to be in the house. I wanted to be out on my bike or outside playing with the other kids in the street. So I stopped reading. I read virtually nothing until the summer I finished my degree. Friends of mine read and I used to go to the library with them when I was about thirteen or fourteen. A lot of them were into historical novels and they went through a phase of reading James Bond stories as well. Well, I never read any of them. I never found them interesting. When I was older, sixteen, seventeen, eighteen, if there was anything that I was particularly interested in I would read it to find out what all the fuss was about. I can remember reading *Clockwork Orange* because there was a film of it and everyone was talking about it. In the same way I read *Brave New World* and *1984* but generally I didn't read. I probably read no more than half a dozen books between being eleven and being twenty-two and finishing university. This was strange because I actually studied English at university; not as a main subject but in the first year you did three subjects of equal weight and one of mine was English. I studied English at 'A' level as well. I was quite good at it. I enjoyed it and was able to write essays about the poetry we were studying, or whatever, but I never did any reading, in my spare time, purely from interest.

To some extent I lost, and still haven't regained, the ability just to read a book purely for enjoyment. I quite often take on books that I think are going to be worth reading even though I don't particularly like them, and then I'll try to persevere with them even if I'm not enjoying them. It's as though the enthusiasm that I had when I was a child, where I would read things because I enjoyed them and if I enjoyed them I would read them again and again and if I didn't like them I would just put them back down and not come back to them, is gone. Now if I start a book I feel as though I have to finish it. If I'm not enjoying it, it will really slow me down and I'll plod on with it for weeks and weeks to try to get it finished, and sometimes I just don't but it stops me reading anything else. I think a great deal of that is to do with the fact that I lost this enjoyment of reading books when I was eleven. To me reading books has been something I've associated with studying; studying 'A' level and doing English at university.

When I finished university I was unemployed for most of the summer which was the really hot summer of 1978 and I can remember doing a lot of reading then. Suddenly I didn't have any course books to read; you finish your degree and you are left with this feeling of emptiness because for three years there has always been, at the back of your mind, this guilt that there's something that you ought to be doing: and suddenly that was gone and I discovered an enjoyment of reading again, and I went back and read an awful lot of things that I hadn't read when I was a child, like Alan Garner books and children's books of quality.

One of the things I enjoyed most about the teachers training course that

I did at B— was the literature course. The tutor that ran the course gave us the space and the time to look into kids' books ourselves. There were boxes and boxes of them and we would just choose one and read it, and maybe jot down a few notes to trigger our memory about what we thought about it. It was really nice to have the space to do that and they had some wonderful books there. I really enjoyed it. There's a really good bookshop a few miles outside Huddersfield, a children's bookshop, that I went to a couple of times when I was on teaching practice and bought some books. Well, I could get the books from the library but they were just so nice to have. There were some lovely children's books around and I did enjoy them. I still like children's books a bit more than adult books, quite-often. A lot of the newer ones now have such lovely illustrations and quite often they are very funny.

It's odd: one memory that came back to me was when I had a babysitting job when I was in the sixth-form. One of the kids that I was babysitting for had a book that was one that I'd read when I was learning to read. I must have been about five or six and I could remember all the stories in it but not in any detailed way, in the way that you remember a film if you've seen it a couple of years before. You sort of vaguely remember the incidents but not all the details or you remember what's going to happen just a couple of seconds before it does. And I knew that I had learned to read using this book. That was very strange.

Reading as part of cultural luggage

I think I still see reading as something valuable even though I don't do it very much myself. I feel guilty that I don't read a great deal. It's not so much that I wish I was reading more books now but that I wish that I had read an awful lot of books that I haven't read but that it seems everybody else has; the Brontes and writers like that. There's an assumption that everyone has read these books and other classics; books by Graham Greene and Ernest Hemingway and people like that who I just don't know anything about but most people seem to have as part of the general knowledge they have in their heads. But I do still value reading. I mean, when I go out to buy friends' children birthday presents and Christmas presents at least half the time I will buy them books. It's partly because they're the easiest things to post but partly because I think they are valuable and something they'll have for years whereas some plastic toy or cuddly toy will probably be damaged or thrown away in twelve months.

I've still got a lot of books I had when I was a child. My mum saved them for me in her loft and I've now got a lot of them in my home and I'm saving them hoping that I will be able to read them to my own children.

I've also got a lot of books that I bought when I was on teaching practice saved for the twins that I'm expecting. I had a good clear out after I finished the course at B—— and gave a lot of things away but I kept the books because I thought they were worth having.

At B—— the idea of learning to read with real books was very much encouraged. The books we were encouraged to read were by Frank Smith, Jill Bennett and Liz Waterland. I thought it was a really good idea, the method that was suggested: kids learning to read with proper books rather than with reading schemes. The schools where I did my teaching practices, both of them, used reading schemes and I felt sorry for the kids, having to use them. They were really boring. Both the schools I was in on teaching practice used 'Link-up' which is supposed to be good for a town environment. It talks about the language that's around them and there are street signs, notices on buses, people reading newspapers and magazines and that sort of thing. It's a great idea in theory but in practice the actual books themselves are boring. There wasn't a story in them. The second school only used 'Link-up' in the first four stages and after that the kids went onto real books which were colour coded according to the level of difficulty. That was a lot better. There were a lot of fairy stories as well as modern children's books. I used to quite enjoy listening to children read when they were reading proper books but I used to find it hard to concentrate when they were reading the 'Link-up'.

I remember one girl in my class on my second teaching practice. She'd have been seven. She suddenly got into reading in a big way. She was reading proper children's paper-back novels. She was way ahead of the rest of the class, even the good readers. Whenever she'd got a spare minute she'd be reading one of these books. She reminded me a bit of what I was like, when I was a bit older. I thought it was great; a really valuable thing for her to be doing. So I think I probably encouraged her: if she wanted to do that rather than playing in the Wendy house or the sand she could read her book instead. I thought it was a good idea.

Writing: quality and mechanics

I've got a few memories about learning to write too so I might as well include them here. I always found writing difficult. I think it was because I was never taught to hold a pen properly. I still don't hold a pen properly even now. When I have to do a lot of writing, particularly during exam times, my fingers get really sore. My smallest finger drags across the paper and it wears away the skin and gets really shiny and hurts. When I was young I think I held a pen with virtually all my fingers on it and as I've got older and my fingers have got bigger they won't all fit on, but I still hold the pen in the same way rather than the way most people hold it. I think this is why I find writing quite a strain. I find it very, very hard to write neatly though I think I probably learned to write reasonably easily. I don't remember much about the process in infant school. I can remember that we were taught to write the alphabet and that I already knew it. The teacher wrote it out on the board and we had to copy it. She wrote half one day and the other half on another day. On one of the days I was off school, poorly, and I only had half the alphabet in my book. I can remember the teacher questioning me about this. Why did I have only half of the alphabet? But I did know it already.

I can remember, in the second year juniors, it being written on my report, and my Mum being told when she went to see the teacher at the end of the term, that the quality of what I was writing was good but I just wasn't writing enough. And I can remember taking it to heart and deliberately trying to speed up. The following year my Mum was told that, yes, I was now writing more, but my work was very untidy. And it carried on being untidy. I used to get comments written on my work until I was fourteen or fifteen about how untidy it was. And it was, terribly untidy. In the junior school we used to write with old-fashioned pens with open nibs and an inkwell. They are hard to write with anyway, those really scratchy pens, and I used to find it a real strain trying to write neatly with those. But I felt as though they either wanted me to write a lot and they'd have to settle for it not being tidy or I could write neatly and there wouldn't be so much of it.

When I was in the top class in the junior school there was a boy, David, who came into our class from a different school and he'd been taught a different sort of writing. We did 'Marion Richardson' which was very plain and round, and he'd been taught, I don't know what it was called, a different style with loads and loads of loops. All the up-strokes had loops on. H's and t's and l's and letters like that had loops on and all the down-strokes on y's had loops on. I thought it was lovely. I think a lot of the kids in our class liked this writing and a lot of us gradually introduced fancier bits like loops on the y's and things like that into our writing and we were told off about it. We were told that it was alright for him to do it but we shouldn't be doing it. But it was a novelty and we found it more interesting with all these loops.

I now find I can write neatly if I make an effort. If I don't my writing just goes off terribly. I've always enjoyed the content of the writing rather than the actual mechanics of it. I used to enjoy writing stories, particularly at secondary school. I enjoyed essay writing in English. I wasn't so keen on writing for other subjects but to write the imaginative work was good. In the junior school we had a book that was called 'Imagine Read and Write'. I really enjoyed that. There would be a passage that you would read and then it would give you some suggestions as to things you could write yourself, maybe on a similar theme. I enjoyed that and my mum bought me a similar book which was called *Imagine and Write* and I did a lot of those exercises at home as well because I enjoyed them so much.

On my second teaching practice I didn't really see the kids being taught to write. They just did some writing. Some of them were very good and some of them very poor but I didn't see any formal teaching of writing. In the school where I did my first teaching practice the children were slightly younger. They were five and six and were all in the process of being taught to write. The school had taken part in some sort of project which involved teaching the kids cursive writing. So these children were being taught to write 'joined-up' before they had written in script, which I thought was crazy. They were using the 'Link-up' reading scheme and I felt that the lettering that they were writing should be as close as possible to the lettering that they were reading, but it seemed to be a separate thing. They did a lot of exercises. To start with they would be doing things like tracing patterns; maybe zig-zag lines and things like that. There would be a dotted line and they would have to go over it and then they would move on from that to tracing letter shapes, like rows of e's all joined together. From that they moved on to actually doing real words. They would write a whole page full of the same word like bed, bed, bed, bed, bed. It seemed a waste of time to me. I'm sure you do need to have some formal teaching of hand-writing but the more it can be related to what writing is about, which is, you know, about jotting something down so that you've got a permanent record of it, or a way of expressing yourself so that somebody can read something at a later date that you've said. The more writing is related to that, I thought, the more sense it would make to the kids. The most ridiculous thing about the way those children were taught to write was the fact that the letters were open. For example, the letter 'b' would be a down-stroke and then a curve but it wouldn't come back round into the down-stroke. It would be open. So for most readers they were quite difficult letters to recognize. I mean most b's are closed. A lot of the letters were like that. F's had really long curly tails that curled backward. I don't know how the kids coped with it because a lot of them, when they were actually actually starting to write were writing using the letters that were in their 'Link-up' books and their 'Link-up' work books, but alongside that they were being taught to write in this different way. I'm sure it must have been confusing for them.

In the school where I did my second teaching practice there were a few children there, particularly the girls, who were really getting into writing in 'a big way'. They'd be set something to do by me or by the teacher and the other kids in the class would write maybe half a side, if you were lucky, – some just a couple of lines. But these particular children would really get into the idea of writing a story. Once one or two had started it a few of the others picked up the idea. I don't think they were exactly trying to compete with one another but when they'd seen someone else write a *really* long story and teacher would make it into a book by stapling the sides together, they wanted to have a go and write their own. Some of them were writing stories that were ten pages long. They wanted to do that rather than much of their other work. They seemed to get a great deal out of it. Yet again, I saw this as valuable. I thought that if they were quite happy to spend their spare time writing, I was quite happy for them to be doing that rather than a lot of the other things that were going on in the classroom. In the infant school a lot of the children's time is spent playing with Lego, in the home corner, playing with sand and water and stuff like that. I think it's important for kids to have these experiences as well but if they're really getting into reading and writing at a particular time I felt that it was good to encourage them. I felt sorry for the ones that found reading and writing difficult. There was one particular child in the class, Andrew, who had a lot of trouble with it. I didn't know how he was going to manage when he went on to junior school because he really couldn't do either properly. Of course there isn't the space or the time in the classroom when you've got thirty odd children to give the individual attention that a child needs. I felt that I'd done well at school because I'd learned to read when I was young and, as a result, I was seen as being bright. I was put in the top class in the infants'. I went into the A-stream in junior school and then to grammar school and ended up at university. I think learning to read and write early had a lot to do with this. I felt that those kids who were leaving infant school without having learned to read and write were never going to catch up. I felt quite sorry for them really.

A personal voice

I want to say something about learning to talk though I find this the hardest area. I can't actually remember anything about learning to talk. All I can remember is being older, junior school age and older than that, and being corrected by my parents for my speech. They would tell me off for dropping my h's or the way I pronounced certain words. It was one of the minor things that I used to get nagged about like standing with my shoulders straight and things like that.

When I was a child I wasn't aware that I had an accent because I was speaking the same as everyone around me. I just thought I spoke BBC, Queen's English and I remember going on holiday when I was eight or so and other children there saying how we talked strangely and I couldn't understand what they were on about. It wasn't until I was about fifteen or sixteen that I think I realized that I did have a Midland accent. I started going away to other areas and people used to tease me about my accent and I hated that. The Midland accent is one of the most unpopular accents. I think it makes people sound really thick and I didn't like having it at all. I still don't like it. I think I've lost quite a lot of it now and I feel glad about that. I think it's been replaced by a Northern accent and I've got a mixture of Northern and Midland but I think it sounds better than just a Midland accent. I had problems when I was about seventeen or eighteen meeting new people and they would ask me my name. I would say Liz and because of the long 'e' sound that you get in a Midland accent people wouldn't understand and would think I was saying 'Lees' and then think I was called Lisa or Liza or something. I would repeat my name several times and I couldn't get this 'e' sound in the middle any shorter. It's really hard when you tell someone your name and they can't understand what you're saying. That was one of the most difficult things about having a different accent. When I went to university I was spending most of my time with people with other accents and I found that I gradually did start to notice that I'd got an accent myself. I started to hear it in my own voice and I didn't like it. For a while I went through a phase of not liking the sound of my own voice. That was quite difficult.

The grammar school that I went to fancied itself as a bit of a private school. It had a preparatory school although there was only one child in our year who had actually been to it. But I think it thought it was a cut above the ordinary school and we were given elocution lessons once a week for the first three years in school. I quite enjoyed those because they were easy. We used to learn poetry and we had to stand up in class and say it. But we had to do some silly things as well. There were exercises that we used to have to repeat, the whole class together. Things like, 'No-one in the class has a pass mark', and I remember the teacher said I had an expressive face and voice but she was always on about my long 'a' sounds because I used to refuse to say 'cl-ah-ss' rather than 'cl-a-ss'. My mum says 'b-ah-th' and things like that and it jars because I don't think it goes with the rest of the accent. I could never understand this emphasis. They didn't pick us up on anything else to do with the accent, just this long 'ah' sound. The Midlands accent like a Northern accent has a short 'a' in words like class and bath and to put an 'ah' in the middle just isn't right. I think it sounds really strange.

I'd like to say something about studying linguistics at university. I think I've always been interested in language and I still am. I think if I was to go on to do some kind of post-graduate qualification, a Master's degree or Ph.D. I'd quite like to do something to do with language or communication studies. I studied linguistics at Lancaster as one of three subjects in my first year which were of equal weight. English and psychology were the other two. I then went on to study it as a minor subject. I found it very interesting and I also found that I was better at it than psychology. I think probably that if I'd carried on with it I might have been able to get a first but I found that psychology was more relevant and I thought that I'd probably be able to use it more in my future life than I would linguistics. Also the focus on transformational grammar irritated me. I don't know whether it's still like that but at the time I was at university they thought Noam Chomsky was the bee's knees and everything revolved around transformational grammar. I thought they had got the emphasis wrong. I thought then, and I still do, that the main thing about language is communication. It's about meanings. It's about making other people understand what you want to say and understanding what other people are trying to say. There was very little in this course about meanings. We did a bit about semantics but it was very rarely touched on. The centre of the course seemed to be transformational grammar and the linguists at Lancaster seemed to think that the *essential* part of language was grammar. As far as I can see grammar is an incidental thing. I mean it's something that you have to make language easier, so you can understand one another. I mean, 'man bites dog' is different from 'dog bites man' and the reason you need grammar is so that you can communicate those differences. But it is incidental really. It's not the essence of what language is about because language is about communication.

Doing linguistics as a minor subject you do two units as part of your degree and one of those was supposed to be transformational grammar, and one other course. I read somewhere in the prospectus that, with special permission from the head of department, you could do something else if it was relevant to your career. So I actually went along to see him and said that I wanted to be a teacher and that I didn't particularly want to do transformational grammar. I thought that other courses would be more useful for the kind of career that I wanted. I actually did two courses, one called 'Language in education' and one called 'Sociolinguistics'. Both of these courses were really good and I enjoyed them both. I got firsts in both those units which had a lot to do with the fact that I enjoyed what I was doing. In 'Language in education' we looked at Bernstein and his restrictive and open codes and we looked at the fact that a lot of Afro-Caribbean kids were failing in our schools and the way that their language is regarded. In 'Sociolinguistics' we looked at the different uses of language.

In both courses we had to do some study of our own. In 'Sociolinguistics' I and a friend, Sue, did a study of some of the careers advisers at Lancaster. We recorded them on tape and then we analysed the uses of their language when they were interviewing students and we worked out our own system of analysis for the kinds of uses that the language was being put to. The study that I did for 'Language in education' was even more interesting. I went into school and did a survey of children's reading. I went into two different schools in the West Midlands. One was an open-plan, integrated day, very middle-class kind of school in a big housing estate with detached houses, and the other one was in a much poorer area with a very, very high immigrant population and a lot of old terraced houses. I worked with six and seven-year-olds and I gave them a simple questionnaire about what sort of books they'd been reading recently and what books they enjoyed reading and why. Then I looked at the kind of books that were being named and compared the two schools. I went out and got a lot of the books and read them. I really enjoyed doing that. I wrote quite a detailed survey. I worked on it through the holiday and I seem to remember getting quite a good mark for it. I wrote an awful lot and I enjoyed reading the children's books. As always, I do enjoy reading children's books.

Spelling

Another area that springs to mind is the issue of spelling. I think I've got a bit of a thing about spelling. My mum is a very, very good speller. If you're not sure how to spell a word, if you ask her, she always knows. You never need to look up a word in a dictionary. I think this is years of doing secretarial work, and I think I've picked up a lot of her attitudes. I think bad spelling is appalling. I don't mind it too much just in private letters to friends and things like that but I think that if you go into a public building and there are notices on the wall that are spelt wrongly, I think it looks terrible. I remember going into the post office, and they had this sign in neon lights. Those little lights that flash on and off so that it looks as though the words are moving from right to left across a kind of screen – and this little screen was saying something about Parliament and they had missed the 'a' out of Parliament – parl-i-ment – it wasn't in there. This was an official thing up in these lights. I was really shocked, I can remember telling my husband about it and he can never understand what all the fuss is about. I don't know why I've got such a thing about spelling.

I've found that in the jobs that I've had, working as a Residential Social Worker, I've come across quite a few people who can't spell very well; sometimes I've had team leaders who know they can't spell very well and they've asked me to go through things that they've written and correct them. I suppose in some ways I can see that spelling isn't all that important but I do think it has an effect on people. I think that if you're applying for a job or something like that and your spelling is not very good I think you might be judged to be not particularly bright. I don't know whether that happens. I think its really important to try to get it right. I hate to spell words wrongly myself although I probably do without realizing it.

Lastly I'll say something about what I think I might be doing in the future.

I've already said that I would be interested in doing a further qualification in communication studies or something like that. I've also considered a career in the teaching of the deaf although I think it's very unlikely now that I'm going to go into teaching. At the moment I'm looking around wondering what else I could do. As I'm expecting twins I think I'm going to be at home most of the time for the next few years. But I'll be looking at what courses I could do part-time. One of the things that appeals to me is the part-time courses that are offered in Huddersfield Technical College in Urdu and Punjabi. I think I'd like to go to college to study something like that. I think that might open up various jobs working with people but, if not, I think it would still be interesting. I like learning foreign languages.

Language development

I'm looking forward also to helping my babies to learn to talk and read. I've often read that twins tend to be behind in their language development by something like six months when they start school. I think this is partly because the parents have less time to spend with them because there are two of them and partly because they tend to rely on one another for contact as much as their parents so they don't need to learn to talk with the same urgency. I want to see if I can do something to counteract that. I've already discussed with Huw that we should spend time individually with each of them, that I should have one and he the other and that we should deliberately spend time talking to them and playing with them to try to stimulate their language. I don't see this retardation in twins' language as being inevitable so I would be interested to see whether it *is* possible for them to develop as fast as a single baby. I'm also looking forward to reading them books and to them learning to read. The book shop that I mentioned before – I'm looking forward to being able to take them there to buy books because it's a smashing bookshop. And, like I say, I've already got a lot of books that were left over from my teaching practice. Also I've got a lot of books from when I was a child, *Pinocchio* and *Heidi* and books like that which I will put in their bedroom.

Well that's about it for now. I'm going to get this tape finished and get it into the post to you. Let me know if there are any other things that you think I could have talked about. I'm finding it quite hard to think of the sort of things that you'd want me to talk about and I don't really feel that what I've said is actually a great deal of use. So if you can think of anything else, just let me know.

3

The pupil experience: A view from both sides

Florence Gersten

Background

I was born in January 1943, the third and youngest child of an orthodox
Jewish family. My brother was at that time aged twelve, my sister almost
six. My parents had moved to Liverpool immediately after their marriage,
in 1929, and had settled in Anfield, a relatively poor area. Ten years later,
my father obtained the post of cantor and head of Hebrew studies at a
newly opened synagogue and my family moved to a house nearby.

My first five-and-a-half years were spent almost exclusively in the company of my family. There were no other children in our street, and I was
extremely shy and resistant to attempts made to introduce me to the
children of family friends. Our house was fairly large with a large back
garden. I spent hours outside, examining plants and insects, constructing
nests in which birds obstinately refused to live, and playing with and inven-
ting imaginary friends, some of whom were cats, others human, but with
not-quite-human properties. Much of my father's work took place in the
evenings and at weekends and he was often free during the daytime. In the
summers before I started school, I used to spend whole days with my father
on his allotments, just down the road from our house. At other times, I
liked watching him making furniture in the carless garage which served as
workshop and lumber room.

My home provided many resources for informal learning. There were
shelves of books in almost every room, including a huge range of fiction

and books about politics, philosophy, religion, history and language. There were books in Hebrew, German, French, Greek and Latin. All the members of our family loved music, which we heard frequently on the radio and on 78 gramophone records. My sister began to have piano tuition when I was still very young and she developed into a competent pianist. My family held animated conversations among themselves and with friends, on all kinds of topics. Much of this must have impinged on me, although it was rare for me to talk to anyone outside my family.

Many writers have pointed out that social class and home environment predetermine, to a great extent, the individual's educational and life pattern. Katherine Clarricoates (1980: 27) writes: 'Research has shown that social class can handicap children from early in their lives, for it is influential in such areas as streaming, helpful parents, and teachers' expectations'. Obviously, social class can also have a very positive early influence. Dale and Griffith (1965: 14) note that: 'For a long time teachers have been aware of the influence of the home on individual pupils, but the influence's strength and pervasiveness were not fully appreciated'. Elsewhere, they point out the importance of parents' educational background in influencing the progress of their children's education. I would say that, by the time I commenced formal schooling, I was very strongly predestined to educational success but very inadequately prepared for socialization.

Infant school

By 1948, the post-war 'bulge' was creating problems for primary schools and a school place was not available for me until September of that year, by which time I was nearer six than five years old. My family had attempted to teach me to read and write at home but I was strongly resistant to this, as I was to prove to be to all attempts at formal teaching in my home.

My junior mixed and infant school was within easy walking distance of my home, but it served quite a mixed area, including some relatively disadvantaged neighbourhoods. My comparatively gregarious brother and sister had been happy and successful at the school. My brother, who had begun his schooling in Anfield and could remember some rough fellow-pupils, had found Mosspits a haven. It was not to prove so for me.

My memories of my first two years at school are very hazy. There was a very short period during which we played with blocks and other constructive toys; then the process of learning to read and write, to add and 'take away', and to recite our tables began. I can remember nothing about these processes, but my sister has told me that when my family asked me to read aloud, at home, I said I could not read. Eventually, my worried mother spoke to my class teacher, who said that my reading was progressing very well. I was transferred from class to class very quickly, so I must have been making good progress in general but I do not think I was told this. I was just informed that I was to move to another room, another set of children.

The infant school was quite a gentle institution and I do not think there was much about it to make me unhappy except, perhaps, a growing pressure to succeed. The physical conditions were adequate, if unappealing. The infants were based in a single-storey brick building with a flat roof, upon which it was intended to place a second storey. During my early days there, it was what John Stroud (1960: 69) described as 'one of those Junior Department/Senior Department places, all dark green paint and brown glazed tiles'. There was a large hall in which infant school assemblies and concerts were held. Playtime and games lessons were held in a large paved area, which was strictly out of bounds to the juniors. There was no barrier, however, between the playground and the 'field' where the juniors played, which was a large area of sparse grass and bare earth. Every so often the infants' playground would be invaded by some of the 'big' boys from the juniors, who chased the smaller children, pinched them and pulled their hair. On one occasion, a junior boy found the ragged remains of a large black bird on the roof of an old air-raid shelter and ran round swinging it by its wing. On a number of occasions, I was waylaid on my route home by a group of three large boys, who surrounded me and would not let me pass until I managed to break through. On the first of these occasions, I was in trouble with my mother for being home late and found it very difficult to make her believe my excuses: one never, of course, 'told on' these offenders to the teachers. Flora Thompson (1939: 175) recalls the strong code of honour about such matters during her own late nineteenth-century schooldays. We all knew a version of the rhyme which she quotes:

Tell-tale-tit
Your tongue shall be slit!
And every little puppy-dog
Shall have a little bit!

The junior school came to loom ahead as a place of some terror.

I was not on unfriendly terms with most of my classmates, but I did not make friends. I was regarded as an oddity for a number of reasons. First, I could not join in games lessons properly. I suffered from what I later realized to be very poor coordination and was unable, for example, to learn to skip with a rope. Second, my interest in plants and insects was regarded as very peculiar, especially for a girl. Official 'nature study' included such pursuits as growing mustard and cress on blotting paper and inducing broad beans to sprout, but did not really encourage one to pick up earthworms, caterpillars and spiders, as was my habit. Third, since school dinners were not 'kosher', and therefore banned to the child of an orthodox Jewish family, I always went home for lunch, as I was to continue to do until I left school. This meant that I was excluded from a period of the school day when informal activities took place and friendship groups were formed. On the other hand, it meant that, every day, I had lunch with both my parents and my sister. I was not to realize for many years how unusual this was.

As far as my formal education was concerned, I was quickly revealed as being strong on the verbal side but weak at arithmetic. There seem to have been curious gaps in my learning. A visiting uncle was disconcerted to find that I could not, at the age of about seven, recite the alphabet. At around the same time, my brother discovered that I could not tell the time. In both cases, I protested that I did not want to learn these things: I could not see the point of them. For once, however, my resistance to being taught at home was overcome. I was somewhat in awe of both my uncle and my brother and I learned to recite the alphabet and to tell the time.

By this time, I had become an obsessional reader and this proved to be another isolating factor, since I tended to spend playtime sitting on the ground with a book. This, among other things, made me a target for teasing.

Success in the 'important' subjects was rewarded by special seats in the classroom and by what Holt (1964: 165) describes as 'petty and contemptible rewards – gold stars, or papers marked 100 and tacked to the wall'. I occasionally won this kind of approval. My arithmetic remained poor and my writing neat but very slow. I was very slow and clumsy at any activity requiring dexterity of hands or feet. My reading, however, was acknowledged to be very good, and my stories and poems were regarded as well above average. This probably won me a little esteem from class-mates, since competitiveness was already becoming important.

At some point late in my infant school years, we were given what was referred to as a 'spelling test', but which was in fact a kind of vocabulary test. Each child in my class was called separately to see a teacher who handed out a long list of words, starting with common, simple ones and ending with difficult and unusual ones. Each child was asked to read these aloud and was sent away as soon as a mistake was made. I listened – rather smugly, I am afraid – as one of my classmates told a friend that she had been stopped at 'anticue'. My own stumbling block proved to be 'sepulchre', an utterly unfamiliar word to a child unfamiliar with the New Testament. My mother, on hearing my story, told me the pronunciation and meaning of the word and told me that I had nothing to worry about. I suspect that this test had some bearing on the way in which we were treated on our entry, soon afterwards, to the junior school.

Junior school

Entry into junior school coincided with some important changes in my life.
A girl of my own age came to live in my street and became my 'best friend'.
Our activities were quite diverse, including trying to make pottery, creating
an insect zoo in our back garden and building a 'plane in her parents'
garage. We also played something we called 'The Game', which involved
the acting out of some fairly lurid fantasies and in which I invented most
of the plots and acted most of the roles. However, our friendship brought
me some mundane but useful pieces of instruction. My friend taught me,
at the age of seven, to climb ladders and strike matches. Her mother taught
me how to tie a bow.

At about this time I began to have piano lessons and I also began to attend
the Hebrew and religious instruction classes which the Jewish community
held in some of the junior classrooms on Tuesday and Thursday nights and
on Sunday mornings. During one year I was in the class which was taught
by my father, which I found a humiliating and disturbing experience. My
normally gentle and patient father seemed to be endlessly finding fault with
me. This probably gave me my first glimpse of the fact that a teacher has
to perform a role. Typically, I was very resistant to learning Hebrew and
resented having to attend these classes, while I looked forward to the piano
lessons.

There were important changes in life at school, too. We were now
streamed and, although we were not informed of the fact, it gradually
became apparent.

The post-war bulge was by this time burgeoning. When the long-awaited
upper storey was built on the roof of the infants school, it was immediately
filled by infants and their teachers. The junior school remained in the single-
storey wooden shed which had been erected as a supposedly temporary
measure, but which is still in use today. Our classes of fifty pupils were
crammed into rooms not nearly large enough. A new decorative scheme,
introduced in accordance with the latest ideas, changed the dark green and
cream paintwork to pastel shades of pink and blue, but this did not do much
to hide the inadequacies of the premises.

Our county junior school was an eleven-plus factory. The headmistress
was, to us and no doubt to many parents and teachers, a terrifying woman,
very tall and erect, with iron grey curls and very bright blue eyes. She was
apt to appear suddenly in classroom doorways, searching the room for
inattention and worse sins. Her favourite expressions were: 'I have *blue* eyes
and blue eyes are the *sharpest* eyes', and 'Work hard, play hard!' In fact,
play was not much encouraged. The headmistress' successful aim was that
her school should have the highest proportion of eleven-plus passes in
Liverpool. Almost everything was sacrificed to this end. There were token

periods of 'art', 'music', 'crafts' and 'scripture'. We even had occasional history lessons in which we were told rather randomly about Ancient Romans and Britons, Roundheads and Cavaliers. There were also, of course, periods of games. But most of the timetable was devoted, unequivocally, to subjects which were going to be needed for the eleven-plus examination. Razzell (1968: 27–9) describes this kind of regimented and unimaginative junior school schedule, in a school where he worked during the mid-1940s.

Various kinds of segregation became apparent. Different games were played by boys and girls, and boys began to do woodwork while girls were taught to sew. I think this was my first conscious experience of the different expectations for boys and girls. Stanworth (1981: 14) refers to 'the myriad of subtle ways in which the educational process brings to life and sustains sexual divisions – the process of, quite literally, teaching girls to be women and boys to be men'.

Another way in which this distinction was impressed upon me was the attitude of the teachers to my growing aggression. I had always been a target for teasing and this became worse during my junior years. I reacted instantly and very badly to jokes about my gradually increasing size, my interest in books and insects and, less explicably, my name (Florence). These latter ranged from shouts of 'Nightingale!' and 'Where's your lamp?' to the shortening of my name in ways I found unacceptable. My reactions were usually out of all proportion to the offence and I quite often attacked the jokers physically. When this was reported to, or observed by, teachers, I was lectured about my temper and for being 'unladylike', while fights between boys went more or less unremarked. When I read *Jane Eyre* (Bronte 1847) and *David Copperfield* (Dickens 1991a) at about this time, I felt a great empathy with the scholarly Helen Burns, punished for her unfeminine untidiness, and for David Copperfield, punished and humiliated for his unchildlike violence.

There was a substantial number of Jewish pupils at Mosspits. The Jewish children in the Junior School only attended assembly on Fridays. On other days, we were sent into one of the classrooms and issued with school bibles, which we were free to read, or not read, at our leisure, under the eye of a teacher. The Old Testament was fairly familiar to me, so I began to dip into the second half of the book. References to the 'crucifixion' puzzled me and I asked a schoolmate, with whom I sometimes walked home, what this unfamiliar word meant. Her explanation horrified me and I exclaimed that surely no-one could have done such a thing to another human being. My companion said, 'Yes they did. You did it'. She explained, in response to my indignant disclaimer, that she meant that the Jews had done it. It was left to my mother to try and sort this out for me. This incident was, I believe, my introduction to anti-semitism.

There were a few Chinese pupils but the Jewish children formed the only distinct ethnic group of any size. Customs which made us deviate from the norm were frowned upon. For example, our absences for the religious festivals, and our leaving school early on Fridays, when the short winter days brought early sunsets on the eve of the Sabbath, were looked on with disfavour. Probably as a result of this, I came to resent these customs.

There was a general feeling, by the pupils, that the Jewish and Chinese children were 'picked on', but I do not know if the following incident had anything to do with this. During one Friday assembly, when I was sitting on the floor with the rest of my class, listening attentively to the head-mistress' notices, she suddenly said, 'Florence Gersten, go out', and I had to stand up and leave the hall in front of the whole junior school. The pro-cedure when this happened was for the offending pupil to stand outside the headmistress' room until summoned. I waited with increasing terror, but she did not come. A teacher found me there in tears and I explained that I had no idea what I had done wrong. She advised me to go back to my classroom. I never found out what, if anything, I was supposed to have done, but the sense of unfairness stayed with me until I left the school. Children have strong feelings about being treated unfairly. Barry Hines (1968: 81) gives a good description of such an incident in *A Kestrel for a Knave*, when a boy sent on an errand to his headmaster is automatically caned because he is outside the door with the boys sent for punishment, an incident which seems to amuse the teacher to whom it is told but rankles with the boy who recounts it.

A complete change came in my second year in junior school. The burgeoning 'bulge' could no longer be contained in the school's premises and two-thirds of the year were farmed out to other buildings. We were completely re-divided. A mixed class remained on the original site, a girls' class, including me, was sent to a neighbouring church hall, and a boys' class was sent to a nearby school.

This was my happiest year at the school. Pupils who stayed for school dinner went back to the main school site and we joined the rest of the school for Friday assembly; otherwise the whole week was spent at the church hall. We were taught by one of the older female teachers, an experienced and wise person, who probably brought out the best in me and in many of my class-mates. I found the absence of the 'threatening' male pupils a great advantage and began to make friendships, some of which were to last me beyond my school years. My self-confidence certainly increased and I felt myself respected for some of my abilities, particularly my ability to write creatively.

During these years, between the ages of seven and eleven, I did more serious reading than I was ever to do again. Most of this was done at home. I read my way through most of the voluminous fiction in the house, including Dickens' entire opus, and also dipped into plays, books on history and natural history and anything else which caught my attention. I was also a keen member of the local library.

Obviously, I cannot have understood everything I read. Holt (1964: 164) writes that:

> The bright child is willing to go ahead on the basis of incomplete understanding. He will take the risks, sail uncharted seas, explore when the landscape is dim, the landmarks few, the light poor.

I suppose I was a 'bright' child, but I was also greatly helped by being able to discuss what I read with members of my family, especially with my sister. When she attempted to pass on to me some of what she was learning at grammar school I was, predictably, very resistant. When I was aged about ten, however, we found that we were reading some of the same things and this undoubtedly created a bond between us.

Returning to the original school site for the final two years of my junior schooling was not pleasant. We were re-divided into three mixed classes, each still with fifty pupils. We had now been definitively streamed and this quickly became very obvious. I was in the 'top' class, all of whose members were expected to pass the eleven-plus. Class 2 was more mixed. About two-thirds of its members were expected to pass the eleven-plus and the whole class was constantly warned to work hard 'or else'. Class 3 was the year's 'rubbish dump'. It was made quite clear that none of its members were expected to pass and that they would go to the local secondary modern school, after which their expectations in life would be very low indeed. The kinds of work they were expected to do – window-cleaning, selling fruit from barrows, serving in shops, refuse-collecting – were quite explicitly held in front of us as examples of what not to be. Our schoolmates in class 3 were pointed out to us as lazy, badly behaved and bound to fail. Predictably, the behaviour of many of these unfortunate children followed suit: they did not work, they were badly behaved and they were often punished, sometimes in front of the rest of us. We had by now more or less ceased to know our former classmates in the third stream and were certainly not expected to mix with them. Hargreaves (1967: 73) writes of 'the depth of the mutual fear and distrust' between different social groups in the same school. Bernstein *et al.* (1966: 163) write: 'One might wonder whether the stratified, ritualized school does not evoke *shame* as a major controlling sentiment in the pupils'.

Absolutely no concern was shown for the welfare of our class 3 schoolmates. They were, needless to say, generally from backgrounds which differed considerably from ours. Illich (1970: 6) writes:

> It should be obvious that even with schools of equal quality a poor child can seldom catch up with a rich one. Even if they attend equal

schools and begin at the same age, poor children lack most of the educational opportunities which are casually available to the middle-class child. These advantages range from conversation and books in the home to vacation travel and a different sense of oneself, and apply, for the child who enjoys them, both in and out of school.

In this country, the distinction has as much to do with social class as with finance. Efforts to counteract this situation seem always to have been unavailing. Elsie Pettigrew (1989: 30), writing of the end of her schooling in 1924, recalls:

> By this time I was doing well at school. I was getting good marks for essays, poetry and acting skills. I found that I was in the scholarship class, which at that time was an exam for a free place in a grammar school. I can't remember what my marks were, but I don't think it really mattered as you were judged on your social position also, and the winner of the place was the daughter of the local dentist who really was in a position to pay for his daughter's education.

It is to be feared that the move into comprehensive education has made very little difference to this situation.

My parents were actually very worried that I might not pass the eleven-plus. Although I was good at 'English', my arithmetic was still poor and I was still a very slow writer. I realized later that it was most unlikely that I would have failed, but it became a matter of serious anxiety to my parents. They explained that they felt it would be a serious disadvantage to me not to go to grammar school and that, in their circumstances, they could not pay to keep me out of the secondary modern school. This reinforced my impression that the secondary school, which was actually quite a good one, was a dump for substandard children. I felt very much under pressure, both at home and at school. I became terrified at the prospect of 'eleven-plus day' and deeply frightened of the possibility that I might disgrace myself in the eyes of the school, disappoint my parents and end up in the educational 'dump'.

The day, when it came, was not as terrifying as I had expected, but the day upon which the results came out was very frightening indeed. The entire junior school was summoned into the school hall. Our headmistress mounted the platform and began to read out the names of those who had passed, each of whom, as his or her name was announced, went up on to the platform to the accompaniment of general applause. We had no prior warning of the results and the names were not read out in alphabetical order. My last conscious memory of my junior school headmistress is of her reading out my name, almost at the end of the list, as if she grudged having to include me, by which time I was feeling sick with fright.

A clearer and more poignant memory, however, is of the rows of eleven-plus failures who were left sitting on the hall floor, stamped as failures in front of the whole junior school. I think that, at the time, I was simply relieved not to be one of them, but it did not take long before, looking back on this episode, I saw how cruelly these children had been treated.

I left my county primary school in July 1954, determined that I would never set foot there again.

Grammar school

The high school for girls I attended had only 400 pupils and the advantage of pleasant buildings and grounds. The central building was a large, late eighteenth-century house and the later buildings dated mainly from the early years of this century. The grounds had belonged to the house and included large, well-kept lawns, extensive flower beds, trees, a shrubbery, tennis courts, and so on. There were only thirty girls in each form, which seemed an incredibly small number after the overcrowding at my junior school.

When I entered the school, my sister was starting her final year there. We saw little of each other, sixth-formers being regarded with considerable awe in a rigidly hierarchical school. However, I knew quite a lot about the school before I became a pupil there and my sister's presence gave me a feeling of belonging.

I had looked forward enormously to being a pupil at the school. I think I saw it as a larger and longer-lasting version of the girls-only year I had spent at the church hall during my junior years and, in many ways, the atmosphere was comparable. During my first two years at high school, I was occasionally a target for teasing by one or two aggressive classmates and slightly older girls. However, I learned to defend myself better than I had at primary school and the teasing came to a natural end. In most respects, the high school seemed a haven of peace and security.

The school had a very strong ethos, which was strengthened by many of the 'consensual rituals' described by Bernstein *et al.* (1966: 160):

> In general the consensual rituals consist of assemblies and ceremonies of various kinds together with the consensual lineaments of dress, the imagery of signs, totems, scrolls and plaques for the revivifying of special historical contexts and other symbolic features. An important component of the consensual rituals is the ritual of punishment and reward.

We wore a fairly distinctive uniform, which gave me a kind of pride by identifying me, in the eyes of the outside world, with the school. At the start of each school year, each form elected a form captain and deputy form captain who wore special badges, as did the head girl, deputy head girl and prefects, at the top end of the pupil hierarchy. At the daily assembly it was reported if anyone had behaved particularly badly, for example by persistent lateness. It was also announced if anyone had done anything particularly meritorious. At the special assembly, held on the final afternoon of each term, the best academic results were announced in the form of reports with an overall 'A' grade, and the results of the ongoing 'house' competitions were reported. The annual prize-giving or 'speech day' conferred particular honour on pupils who had distinguished themselves academically, but all GCE certificates were also handed out on this occasion. The annual summer garden party provided a less formal opportunity for pupils' relatives and friends to see samples of artwork and needlework, displays of dancing, and so on.

On the walls of the school hall, polished wooden boards displayed in gilded lettering the names of pupils who had gained state and city scholarships or Oxbridge entrance. I think that it was, quite early on, my secret hope that my name might one day be added to these.

There were three levels of loyalty in the school: to the school itself, to one's 'house' and to one's form. The school was divided into four 'houses', each named after a prominent Liverpool family of former times. Bernstein *et al.* (1966: 161) write of 'house rituals':

> These are rituals which delineate fictional communities within the school, and each community has its own set of consensual and differentiating rituals together with their inductive subsets. The whole is supported by the lineaments of dress, the imagery of signs, totems, the associations and sentiments invoked by scrolls, plaques, chants, etc.

Each pupil at the high school wore a metal badge denoting her house. These badges bore the coats of arms of the families which had given the houses their names. There was a continuous competition between the houses and the result, as mentioned before, was announced at the end of each term. Outstanding work, in particular 'A' reports, won points for your house. Inter-house sports matches were another method of gaining points. There were four small 'house gardens', each consisting of a bed of earth within the walled enclosure which once must have been a kitchen garden. At some point, I voluntarily took over responsibility for the garden belonging to my house and I begged or purloined plants and cuttings from my father. My work won the house garden competition for my house many terms running, which gave me satisfaction and a small amount of prestige. But we could lose points for our houses too: detentions lost points, as did exceptionally bad work.

I quickly became tremendously absorbed in the school. It was almost the whole of my social life and events there assumed the status of high drama. A few episodes stand out.

Outings from the school were very rare, but we were taken each year to a special schools concert at the Philharmonic Hall. Good behaviour on these occasions was very strongly enjoined and the eating of sweets was strictly forbidden. When I was in my third year at the school, a number of pupils, including some of my form-mates, were observed to be eating sweets during a concert. One of these was our form captain, Margaret, a conscientious and hard-working pupil. In consequence of this crime, she was stripped of her badge in front of the whole school. We were then requested to elect another captain. Many of us, having discussed the situation, nominated Margaret again and refused to consider anyone else until a compromise solution was agreed. This exciting occasion assumed, for me, the properties of a major political event.

We were normally a well-behaved form, but good behaviour was the norm in an almost exclusively middle-class school. Michael Fielding (1987: 56) refers to 'the partiality of privilege which, for example, cherishes the clarion call for the return to grammar schools on the tacit assumption that one's own children will not find their way into the local secondary modern school'. Having survived the eleven-plus ordeal, we had not found our way to the local secondary school. Our school, although maintained by the local education authority, had something about it of the feel of privilege.

There were, of course, some less well-behaved pupils in the school. There were even some 'naughty' forms. A division became apparent, quite early, between the high-achievers, who worked hard, behaved well and looked demure, and some of our schoolmates who did the minimum of work and sometimes behaved badly. Some of these daring girls even dyed their hair and wore make-up, although this was strictly forbidden by our rather puritanical headmistress. The two groups felt a certain degree of scorn for each other, based precisely upon those characteristics which differentiated them. Hargreaves (1967) as mentioned above, writes of the fear and distrust between social groups in the same school and notes that the brighter boys ignore the lower streams. Things were perhaps not as polarized as that in our high school, but there was an element of this situation and friendship groups tended not to cross this divide. Hargreaves also notes, however, that games tend to unite pupils from different groups and this was observable at our school.

The school was academically sound but perhaps not particularly inspiring in its teaching. It was quite clear that it was meant for girls who, like myself, had a value for learning. Little encouragement was given to pupils who had intelligence but lacked the support and help at home which many of us took for granted. Dale and Griffith (1965) point out the problems caused for many children by the lack of facilities such as a warm and private room where they can do their homework. Parental encouragement and the presence of books are, of course, also of great importance.

The emphasis at our high school was very much on subjects which could be taken for GCE, which included art but not music. On the timetable, music consisted of a single period each week. This was, during my first three years at the school, exclusively devoted to group singing, mainly from the *National Song Book*. Then, the rather elderly music master retired and was replaced by someone much younger and more energetic. She formed a school choir, which I promptly joined, and organized other extra-curricular musical activities such as concerts and record recitals. She received no encouragement from our headmistress, who was not very interested in music, and was not well supported by the pupils. She remained at the school for only two years, but I think it was her influence which suggested to me, later, that I should revive the school Music Society, defunct for several years. I ran this during my last two years at school and received quite a lot of support from schoolmates. The greater importance given to visual art as part of the school curriculum was, I believe, owing to the strong character of the art teacher, who had worked at the school for many years. The quality of work produced by her pupils was very high and there was a steady stream of entrants to art colleges. I can only remember, during my seven years at the school, one pupil who took up music professionally. Goodman (1962) points out the extent to which music, among other activities which might be classed as 'non-academic', has been undervalued by adults as a part of education.

The attitude to academic subjects was very serious, but the chief aim of our teaching was to help us pass examinations. This was treated in a much gentler way than at my junior school, but nevertheless probably produced something of the barrenness and crushing of individuality described by Goodman (1962). We were not precisely *Gradground*: 'Upon the principle that two and two are four and nothing over' (Dickens 1992: ch. 2), but there was just a little of this feeling in our education. I found that I was so concerned with mastering facts, getting homework done and passing examinations, that much of my creativity was stifled. I no longer read or wrote nearly as much, at home, as I had done while at primary school.

A full range of sciences was taught at high school, but we had to make curriculum choices at a very early stage and only the determined scientists ever took physics or progressed beyond basic chemistry. Stanworth (1983: 11) points out what a small proportion of girls take sciences and mathematics beyond a very low level. However, the point at which curriculum choices were enforced, when I gave up all science except biology in order to take an additional modern language, gave me the chance to drop the girls' subjects which I hated, cookery and needlework, in neither of which I had succeeded in mastering even the most basic skills.

I was never a good 'all-rounder'. I was very good at English, good at modern languages and quite good at history. On the other hand, I was poor at mathematics and geography, bad at art and atrocious at PE and needlework. In some way, nevertheless, my academic prestige in the school was fairly high. I was expected to 'do well' eventually, and did. The two highlights of my time at high school came at the end of the fourth year and half-way through the final one.

At the end of my fourth year, I won a prize for a poem in the school magazine, to which I was a regular contributor. I also received an 'A' report, for the first and only time, and I won the main part in the school play, Marlowe's *Dr Faustus*, which was to be performed at the end of the following term. I experienced a quite unfamiliar gush of self-confidence.

From the fifth year onwards, we were steered in the direction of suitable careers or courses. The most academically able were urged towards university, although given little advice regarding appropriate courses or universities. The second level of pupils were guided in the direction of teacher training or nursing and the rest were, via the very minimal careers advice which we received, nudged in the direction of secretarial work, librarianship, and so on. Stanworth (1983) notes the way in which girls are channelled towards careers considered 'suitable' for their sex.

During the first two terms of my second year in the sixth-form, I sat the entrance examinations for Cambridge and for two Oxford colleges. I was accepted by St Anne's College, Oxford, in the spring term of 1961. This was something of an achievement in the school's eyes, since Oxbridge entrants normally stayed at school for an additional year. Rather to my surprise, I found myself congratulated by large numbers of pupils of all ages, who seemed genuinely excited on my behalf. I left school feeling more successful than at any other time in my life.

Universities

I had two rather different experiences at two different universities. My euphoria at winning entrance to Oxford turned rather quickly to terror at leaving home for the first time and doubts regarding whether or not my academic ability would be adequate in such exalted surroundings. To some extent my fears were justified. Although I made some friends, mainly within my own college, my extreme shyness prevented me from having much social life. I felt unable to take advantage of the vast range of opportunities offered by Oxford, and much of the time I felt very isolated.

The collegiate set-up seemed, in some ways, very strange. To ex-boarding school pupils, which many of my fellow-students were, having to be in at a relatively early hour and being locked in probably seemed quite normal. To me, even coming from a very sheltered home, this seemed far from normal. The combination of relative restriction and relative independence was quite disconcerting.

I found my studies quite a problem, too. Goodman (1971) notes that school tends not to encourage independent thought and I found it very difficult to study independently. Despite the enclosed atmosphere of the college and the individual attention bestowed by the tutorial system, the level of support for students was not high. The pressure on students, on the other hand, was very great indeed. Students who wanted to achieve good results but who did not want to spend their entire time studying were often placed under great strain. Depression was common and breakdown far from uncommon.

I dealt with my problems in various ways. Oxford is probably an outstanding example of the dislocation, noted by Goodman, between universities and their neighbours. At times, my sense of unreality became so strong that I would go and sit in Woolworth's cafeteria or the little fish and chip cafe quite near my college, just to remind myself that there was still a world outside the university. Finding difficulty in creating a social life, I became very much involved in the university's theatrical activities, first acting, then stage management. This made acquaintances for me and was absorbing and, sometimes, exciting.

The rigours of essay writing and examinations were too great to allow many students to neglect their studies totally, and a burst of frenetic work before and during the period of my degree examinations secured me quite a good degree. However, I left Oxford feeling very dissatisfied with myself and with the feeling that I wanted no more to do with academic institutions. I had decided that I wanted to work 'in the theatre', starting with stage management. This was discouraged, as far as possible, by the university careers adviser. Oxford had two quite separate advisers for male and female students, and no doubt they gave quite separate kinds of advice. To quote Stanworth (1983: 17–18): '. . . what little evidence there is available suggests that teachers and careers advisers may wittingly or unwittingly steer girls and boys towards traditionally feminine or masculine goals'. My proposal to take up a career in the theatre was greeted as unrealistic. It was suggested that theatrical activities would make a nice hobby and that I should consider teaching or social work as careers.

During the following year, I found myself three stage management jobs and one non-theatre one while I tried to persuade Liverpool Education Authority to give me a grant for a one-year course in stage management. I was allowed the grant but too late to give me a place on the desired course. Instead, during the academic year 1965–66, I was a student at the

University of Bristol's Department of Drama, on the one-year course leading to a Postgraduate Certificate in Drama.

This course, and indeed the whole department, was at that time an uneasy mixture of literary study and training in stagecraft. I enjoyed the practical side of the course, without finding it of any use in the furtherance of a theatrical career. Advice from the academic staff was not particularly helpful, but on the other hand there were much closer relations between lecturers and students than I had ever encountered at Oxford, and I had many stimulating and thought-provoking discussions with members of both groups. Bristol reminded me in many ways of Liverpool and I always felt, and have continued to feel, at home there.

However, on finishing my course at Bristol I was unable to obtain work in the theatre, and ended up by taking an administrative post at the General Medical Council which I held, with some unhappiness, for two years.

Teaching

In the autumn of 1968, I resigned from my administrative post and became a supply teacher. During two academic years, I taught in three London schools and had every assumption I had ever made about education totally and irreversibly disrupted.

During 1968–69, I taught for four days a week at a girls' secondary modern school in Walworth, London. This school really was what we had been led to believe our local Liverpool secondary school was: the dump for unwanted female pupils in its neighbourhood. It was quite a small school on a split site. Both buildings dated from the nineteenth century and were in a poor state of repair, but the lower school, where I worked, was very much the poorer of the two.

Almost every girl in the school had educational problems. These were of differing degrees of seriousness and of vastly differing kinds. Approximately ninety per cent of the pupils were immigrants, many only recently arrived in Britain. They included a high proportion of Pakistanis and Turkish Cypriots, many of whom knew almost no English. There was also a large number of Jamaicans, several of whom had never been to school before coming to this country. Many of the girls came from extremely unhappy home backgrounds and suffered from severe emotional disturbance. Finally, there was a small number of English pupils who, on the whole, seemed to have very little intelligence. Dipak Nandy (1971) notes the failure, from the 1950s onwards, to identify the several problems of immigrant children in British schools and to deal with them in specific ways.

I, an untrained teacher, found myself expected to do remedial work with a group of twelve of these children; half of a first-year class reckoned to be of the lowest ability. What did I have to help me with my approach to this work? My middle-class background, selective and privileged education and total lack of contact, since childhood, with working class children?

On realizing that I was expected to teach arithmetic, I reacted with dismay and explained to the head of the lower school that I was practically innumerate. 'Two and two?' was her reaction. I was disbelieving, but she was, of course, quite right about some of my pupils. It took me some time to gain any idea of their abilities, about which I had been given very little prior information.

The first time I met my group I was rather puzzled by behaviour which included their folding themselves up and disappearing under their desks. This was a favourite joke and seemed to happen according to some invisible signal.

I decided to test their reading ability and asked each girl to read from the very simple book which had been given to me. The results were poor but each girl did read, until it came to twelve-year-old Marcia's turn, when there was silence. When I tried to persuade her to read she told me that she could not. My reaction was to tell her not to be silly, whereupon she repeated that she could not read and behaved in a way which seemed to me to be sullen. I passed on to the next girl and suddenly realized that Marcia was wandering around the room, moving objects about and looking, as I thought, ill-tempered. It gradually dawned on me that her reaction was one of unhappiness. At the end of the lesson, I asked her privately if she really was unable to read and, on being assured that it was true, I felt a terrible sense of shame.

Hargreaves (1967: 83) writes of the problems which many teachers experience when confronted by pupils from a radically different background: 'Their attitudes and values are naturally those of settled middle-class adults, whose lives are rooted in the town and its environs, but in a contrasting social setting to that of the pupils'. Hurt (1979: 113), writing of a very much earlier period, noted teachers' lack of comprehension regarding the conditions in which their pupils lived.

I did make efforts to compensate for my lack of comprehension, by reading the children's record cards and by talking to the children themselves. Many of the specific problems were disturbing enough. A great many of the girls were living in very overcrowded and unpleasant conditions. A large number were children of broken marriages and the emotional disturbance caused by this was compounded by the particular circumstances. Many of the Jamaican children had been left, as infants, with a grandmother or aunt when their parents came to England. They had lived very happily in Jamaica, often with little or no schooling, until suddenly sent for by a parent who had often, by that time, made a second marriage. Within days of arrival in London, these children, having had to accept life with families to which they felt they only partly belonged, were compelled to sit at desks, in a ramshackle and gloomy building, and to accept efforts to give them information which they certainly did not want and perhaps did not need. Razzell (1968: 36) writes:

> To liken a class containing young children to a prison is a harsh analogy but, as Caldwell Cook, a writer of the First World War period, observed, 'We have abolished the stocks for our felons, but we keep our young children incarcerated in desks for long hours every day'.

For many of the children at the school in Walworth, and at the two schools where I worked subsequently, school really was like a prison. I listened with some dismay to the descriptions some of the Jamaican girls gave of their homeland, which sounded like a paradise: sun, sea, breadfruit which could be picked from the trees. I tried, without much success, to imagine what it must have been like to be suddenly plucked from such a home and transplanted into a dirty, ugly, impoverished London district.

For some of the Moslem children there were other problems. Many of them came from fairly repressive homes and were, I think, confused by the lack of discipline in the school and the freedom enjoyed by their English and West Indian schoolmates. Their parents expected them to work at school and to learn useful skills, but they would soon have marriages arranged for them and would be bringing up their own children before they were out of their teens.

I became totally bewildered about what I was supposed to be doing for these children. I thought, at least, that it would be worthwhile trying to help them to read, write and do simple arithmetic, but I had no training to enable me do this. When I asked a younger colleague, recently emerged from a college of education, how I could learn to teach reading, she replied: 'Teach reading! Do you think they taught us how to teach reading? We learned how to use equipment that this school will never be able to afford, but teaching reading . . .'.

I had rather less of a problem teaching arithmetic. Having found this very difficult myself, I could empathize with pupils who were experiencing problems. I began quite soon to use small squares of cardboard to represent digits and this suddenly seemed a familiar technique. I realized that I had simply gone back to the 'counters' which had been used to help us learn arithmetic, twenty years earlier. Actually, some of the Cypriot and Pakistani pupils were already quite good at arithmetic. Their main problem had been mastering the English language, thus enabling them to understand instructions. Numbers themselves are, after all, a kind of lingua franca.

I continued to have difficulties with the teaching of English. Marcia was the only one of my regular pupils who could neither read nor write, so I tried to persuade other pupils to practise their English by reading, writing and, far too rarely, by talking. Barnes (1969) writes much about the importance of talking as a part of education. I am afraid that, much of the time, I felt that encouraging my pupils to talk would distract them from the serious business of reading, writing and doing arithmetic. Some of my pupils would have felt this too. But I was to realize, after I had left the school, the opportunities I had missed of using my pupils' own experience to help them learn.

I even acted repressively with regard to the dialect of some of my pupils. Bush *et al.* (1985: 96–7) write of the attitudes to West Indian before the growth of concern about multicultural education:

> Hazel Carby's analysis of these early attitudes makes horrific reading. She quotes references to West Indian dialect as an 'inadequate language', its speakers having only a 'partial mastery of English' and this 'deficiency' being a 'major part in this culturally induced backwardness of Afro-Caribbean children'.

I was so concerned with the apparent importance of teaching my pupils 'correct' English, that I ignored the claims of their own brand of the language, which might have made a fruitful basis for learning.

Most of the children had, I am afraid, a low value for themselves. At the age of eleven, they had been given a few tests, the results of which decided the schools to which they were sent, even though the eleven-plus officially no longer existed. All the pupils at the school knew that they had been allocated the lowest status girls' school in the area. I would sometimes receive doleful accounts of the local comprehensive school, with its modern premises and superior equipment, attended by the siblings of some of my pupils.

There was not really much effort to educate the girls at the school. The highest possible attainment at the school was CSE. Pupils who wanted to take GCE had to transfer to other schools. Some were well capable of it. One pupil, Shamshad – a charming, intelligent and imaginative Pakistani who had been condemned to the school because of her lack of knowledge of English at the age of eleven – hoped to become a nursery nurse. I have always wondered if she was helped to realize this ambition. Most of the girls, however, were expected to achieve virtually nothing. Sheila Cunnison (1987: 2) writes of the female pupils in a co-educational secondary school:

> The girls were mainly working class, the teachers, by standards of education, residence and income, were middle class. And middle class women, even teachers, can be expected to be fairly complacent about working class girls going into dead-end unskilled jobs.

Anthony Green (1977) remarks on the generally low expectation of the capabilities of working-class pupils in a primary school.

Despite all this, there were sporadic experiences which gave me a small amount of satisfaction. One was an occasion when I talked to my pupils about the reasons for learning arithmetic and had them talking quite enthusiastically about the problems of reckoning up one's bill at the supermarket. On another occasion, when illness had reduced the group to four, I took them around the school on a 'writing hunt', to see how and where writing was used. We wrote a list of examples we found and my pupils seemed quite interested to find words on the underside of furniture, on doors, walls and equipment.

Marcia, whose total inability to read and write had taught me an early lesson, always worried me. She was an extremely nice girl, a pleasure to have in the group and possessed of a good intelligence. However, she seemed to make no progress with her reading and writing. I noticed that, while trying to write, she would transfer her pen from one hand to the other indiscriminately, using whichever hand was the less tired. She could not write with either hand, however, and I concluded that she must have some kind of organic problem. Her attempts to copy letters resulted in misshapen and usually unrecognizable marks. I bought a copy of the Ladybird book on handwriting and traced some of the patterns on to paper. I then asked Marcia to trace these patterns on to fresh sheets of paper, hoping that the continuous motion of the pen in her hand would in some way help her. She did this reluctantly, feeling it to be a childish exercise. Shortly before I left the school, I suggested that my group should try writing letters. Marcia told me that she would like to write to her grandmother in Jamaica, but did not see how she could do it. I asked her questions about what she had been doing, family news, and so on, and from her answers constructed a simple letter which I printed in large letters on the blackboard. Marcia copied this very carefully on to paper. A few days later she told me that her letter was now on the way to Jamaica. I can still see her joy and excitement, as great as Joe Gargery's on seeing his name written down by Pip (Dickens 1991b: ch. 7).

My next school, another comprehensive, was a very different proposition from the first. It had 2000 pupils contained in buildings on a single site, which had once included both a grammar and secondary school. Discipline at my first school had been poor, but the bad behaviour had been the result of natural ebullience and unnatural restriction, with little in it of real aggression or malice. My second school included pupils with a wide range of abilities. It also included some very powerful, aggressive and embittered pupils. Violence against teachers was not uncommon; completely uncontrolled behaviour was very common indeed. This was something of a shock to me, probably analogous to Edward Blishen's dismay on first entering Stonehill Street Secondary School: 'shocked, stung and frightened' by the sheer noise, rudeness, bad language, fighting and, worst of all, contempt for the teacher's intentions (Blishen 1966: 13).

There were a number of pupils with educational problems similar to those of the pupils at my first school, but the school had the resources to deal with those. My contact was with the 'ordinary' pupils. I was deployed much more as an ordinary supply teacher than I had been before and I met a wide spectrum of pupils, in terms of age and ability. Used to thinking of pupils as 'children', I found that many of them were not. Postman (1983: 120) refers to 'the disappearance of childhood ... after its long sojourn in Western civilization', but perhaps childhood never really existed for certain sectors of society.

The school's teeming population included pupils whose mothers were prostitutes, pupils with both parents in prison, and some whose fathers beat them up. For many of them the school offered no haven and no sanctions which could compare with those of home. They were obliged by law to continue attendance there until the age of fifteen, by which time many of them looked and behaved like adults and were already involved in life-styles resembling those of their parents.

Blishen and Goodman express doubts about the supposed virtues of extending the school-leaving age and, at both schools, I came to doubt its usefulness. But then I came to doubt so many things about 'education'. Having believed without question, all my life, that education was a 'good thing', having had some kind of unarticulated idea of what 'education' was, and what it was for, I suddenly found that I could make no assumptions about it any more. I did not doubt the usefulness of teaching mathematics or the virtue of studying literature, creative writing, sciences, languages, the arts, etc., for those who wanted to learn about these subjects and could assimilate and make use of them, but this was plainly not what was happening for many pupils. Young people were being kept in prison until the age of fifteen and I did not know why they were there. The more intrepid among the pupils sometimes walked out of lessons and disappeared, and I did not blame them.

When I tried to express my confusion to other members of staff, I was accused by one of the younger teachers of wanting to drag my pupils into the middle-classes. While I could see that this might be true and might be undesirable, I wondered if I had the right *not* to try to help our pupils out of the station to which they were accustomed. Green (1977: 269) refers to the 'reproduction of social stratification as a material formation in the classroom, of which the teacher was constrained to be a part'. I became aware of the constraint but did not know in what direction it should be broken or how this could be achieved.

No conclusion

The 1969–70 academic year saw my last experience inside a school classroom. My brief experience of teaching has, however, always haunted me. Over the years I have talked to many people about their own experiences as pupils and as teachers, and I have formed the impression that the desire to change the system has not, despite many efforts, really succeeded in changing it. Holt (1965: 171) writes: 'Schools should be a place where children learn what they most want to know, instead of what we think they ought to know'. This is undoubtedly true, but how are children to know what they most want to know? Is it possible to create circumstances in which children's real needs and desires can emerge uninfluenced by factors beyond the control of homes, schools and the children themselves?

Goodman (1971: 116) believes '. . . that every child must be educated to the fullest extent, brought up to be useful to society and to fulfil his own best powers'. I suppose no-one would disagree with this as an ideal goal, but how to reach it and what exactly it means are quite another matter.

References

Barnes, D. (1969) *Language, the Learner and the School.* Harmondsworth: Penguin.

Bernstein, B., Elvin, H.L. and Peters, R.S. (1966) 'Rituals in education'. *Philosophical Transactions of the Royal Society of London.* **251.**

Blishen, E. (1966) *Roaring Boys.* London: Panther.

Bronte, C. (1847) *Jane Eyre.*

Bush, L., Coulby, D. and Jones, C. (1985) *Urban Schooling: Theory and Practice.* New York: Holt, Rinehart and Winston.

Clarricoates, K. (1980) 'The importance of being Ernest . . . Emma . . . Tom . . . Jane'. The perception and categorization of gender, conformity and gender derivation in primary schools, in R. Deem (Ed.), *Schooling for Women's Work.* London: Routledge and Kegan Paul.

Cunnison, S. (1987) 'Let's take these thoughts with us into the day': macho culture in the school, in A. Booth and D. Coulby (Eds), *Producing and Reducing Disaffection: Curricula for All.* Milton Keynes: Open University Press.

Dale, R.R. and Griffith, S. (1965) *Down Stream: Failure in the Grammar School.* London: Routledge and Kegan Paul.

Dickens, C. (1991a) *David Copperfield.* London: Mandarin.

Dickens, C. (1991b) *Great Expectations.* London: Mandarin.

Dickens, C. (1992) *Hard Times.* London: Dent (Everyman Library).

Fielding, M. (1987) Liberte, Egalite, Fraternite, ou la Mort: towards a new paradigm for the comprehensive school, in C. Chitty (Ed) *Redefining the Comprehensive Experience.* Bedford Way Paper No. 32. London: Institute of Education.

Goodman, P. (1971) *Compulsory Miseducation*. Harmondsworth: Penguin.

Green, A. (1977) Structural features of the classroom, in P. Woods and M. Hammersley (Eds), *School Experience: Explorations in the Sociology of Education*. London: Croom Helm.

Hargreaves, D.H. (1967) *Social Relations in a Secondary School*. London: Routledge and Kegan Paul.

Hines, B. (1968) A Kestrel for a Knave. Harmondsworth: Penguin.

Holt, J. (1964) *How Children Fail*. London: Pitman Press.

Hurt, J.S. (1979) *Elementary Schooling and the Working Classes, 1860–1918*. London: Routledge and Kegan Paul.

Illich, I.D. (1970) *Deschooling Society*. London: Calder and Boyars.

Nandy, D. (1971) Foreword in J. McNeal and M. Rogers (Eds), *The Multi-racial School: A Professional Perspective*. Harmondsworth: Penguin.

Pettigrew, E. (1989) *Growing Up in Liverpool from 1912 Onwards*. Liverpool: Toulouse Press.

Postman, N. (1983) *The Disappearance of Childhood*. London: W.H. Allen (Comet Books).

Razzell, A. (1968) *Juniors: a Postscript to Plowden*. Harmondsworth: Penguin.

Stanworth, M. (1983) *Gender and Schooling: A Study of Sexual Divisions in the Classroom*. London: Hutchinson.

Stroud, J. (1960) *The Shorn Lamb*. Harmondsworth: Penguin.

Thompson, F. (1939) *Lark Rise to Candleford*. Oxford: Oxford University Press.

4

An education biography and commentary

Anne Murray

1. I was born in Liverpool. My father drove an articulated lorry and my mother took care of their home and six children. For five years I was their only child.

2. I was my maternal and paternal grandparents' first grandchild and the first niece of many doting aunts and uncles. Attention was heaped on me and I thrived on it. I was an obviously bright child, quick at developing the various childhood skills: I walked and talked in coherent sentences very early. Before my fourth birthday, I could read, write, recite endless rhymes and stories and had noticeably good coordination. One of my aunts was a teacher and was clearly very impressed with me. She asked my parents to allow her to take me away to attend her school because she felt that the local primary school would not open up the same opportunities for me as her own school could. My parents would not hear of it but their expectations of me were mounting with pride. I, too, had fairly high expectations in the light of several overheard conversations from my perch at the top of the stairs.

3. My first day at school left me thunderstruck and almost speechless. Having waved my mother a nearly tearful and somewhat apprehensive goodbye, I was ushered into a room full of distressed children being wrenched from their parents with loud assurances that all the children would be fine once the mothers had gone. However, they were not and one or two received a hearty slapping around the legs in an attempt to

quieten their protestations. I stood, rigid, my head echoing with the sound of my own heart pumping and watched the sea of faces seeming to float about, with a mixture of emotions too varied for my bemused mind to comprehend. The teacher approached me, smiling, and ushered me to a table. On it were thin scraps of paper and a large box of grubby crayons in the centre. The children already at the table were sitting scribbling, but I just sat and watched the teacher. She had a shrill voice and spoke to groups and individuals alike, as if she were addressing the whole class. This kept me vigilant because I was not at all sure when the smiles would turn to anger and who the somebody would be who got slapped. At some point, we were given tepid milk to drink and there were more shrill cries about the shame of some children wasting it. I am sure I drank mine.

4. When my mother came to meet me, she was full of questions that seemed impossible to answer. It was clear that she expected me to have had a good time and have done lots of interesting things. I seem to remember lots of trips home from school of a similar ilk. I was obviously supposed to do something to which the teacher would respond positively and on which I could give a report on the way home. I could not explain that what we were supposed to do was not always clear: we were given hard lumps of grubby plasticine to 'make things' with; small pieces of thin paper and stubby crayons to 'draw something' with; we went to the toilets in a 'nice straight line' and 'peed to order'. Nobody asked you what you could do: we seemed to be in the business of learning how to be there.

5. I was beginning to *experience for the first time* a strange inability to speak when spoken to. When the teacher asked me a question, I found it difficult to get my mouth to respond. The reply was always in my head but, before I could effectively communicate, someone else always seemed to answer for me. I was therefore never chosen to do any of the numerous small tasks which she doled out to her emerging chosen few. The rule seemed to be to please her in order to get some attention. You could dash to carry her bag and be allowed to walk to the staff room with her or tidy the classroom and sometimes get a sweet.

6. A month after I started school, my baby sister arrived, amid joy – and whispered worries. She had been deprived of oxygen at birth and, within the first twenty-four hours, began having the tell-tale convulsions, warning that all was not well. All indeed was not well and many years of worry and growing concern followed for my parents. It was never quite understood what was wrong: we belonged to that age when people still spoke in hushed voices about those whose brains did not function in conventional ways. She was eventually described as being slow and probably educationally subnormal. In contrast to me, she developed skills

only gradually and often performed much less proficiently. My parents
were told she would have to attend a special school. They visited those
suggested and, having decided they would not be of benefit to her, insisted
that she be allowed to attend a 'normal school'. Normal school, however,
belonged to a system that barely catered for the 'normal' pupil, in that
it provided statutory education in a statutory way for pupils with
non-statutory needs.

7. My sister might have been housed at the back of each classroom with
the rest of the slow or disruptive pupils, in relative oblivion, had it not
been for her over-sensitive nature. She could not bear herself, or other
children, to 'get into trouble'; under such circumstances, she would sob
pitifully. Sometimes I could hear her, from my classroom upstairs, as she
was ushered along one of the downstairs corridors and a wave of
embarrassment, mixed with anxiety, washed over me. Both her teachers
and my parents tried to teach her in the only way they knew how. As
patience gave way to frustration, there were many more tears.

8. I was in school for a full five years before my sister joined me and,
while some moments are fixed sharply in my head, much of the experience
is a hazy memory of vague feelings. I had developed into a daydreamer
and my responses to questions from teachers remained painfully slow. In
school I was slow and dreamy, and outside school I was bright and alert.
At home I could read and in school I couldn't. The teacher would hold up
a flash-card and I would know the word but I couldn't get it out. I knew
that I knew the answer and I wanted the teacher to know that I knew the
answer. But, while I struggled, other children would shoot up their hands
and answer before I could. At the end of such a session, I would find
myself directed to go with a group which, I was acutely aware, was
considered by the teacher, and other children, as the 'slow group'. We
were given dull lumps of plasticine to occupy our fingers, while the others
were given brand new exercise books and sharp pencils. I so much
resented being in this group and desperately wanted to be associated, in
every way, with the top group and to get the teacher's approval.

9. One or two children in the slow group were good at sport and were
much in demand at playtime. Inside my head I knew I could show them
all that I was at least as physically competent as them. In practice, after
one or two abortive attempts, I became an unwanted liability to my peers.
I was not unpopular with them, just not popular. I was not disliked by the
teachers, just overlooked. On the odd occasion when I did seem to be able
to do some task or other, I would begin with a flourish and then be
frozen with fear at the last moment. It seemed that, within the confines of
school, my expectations of myself were at a point below zero.

10. I can recall once, when I was about six, doing a good piece of work in my writing book amid the many red-biro scarred pages of previous efforts. The teacher was very pleased. She gave me a brand new exercise book and said that if I could do more good work the next day, with beautiful writing, I would be allowed to sit with the top group. She called a girl from the top group to show me her work. I gazed at the beautifully written pages, interspersed with colourful illustrations. The book was covered in wall paper with a neat white label on the front. The girl was neatly dressed, with two matching ribbons in her hair, and she and the teacher beamed at each other. It was a much longed for opportunity to show that I was not the slow and stupid person I had been labelled.

I went to my uncle's house that night and he showed me how to draw a face, using numbers. With my new book in mind, I asked him to show me how to draw a beautiful lady, which he did to my satisfaction. I didn't need showing twice. I reproduced it perfectly. He remarked to my aunt how quick I was at picking things up and she came to look at my efforts. She expressed no surprise, saying that I had always been quick but admonished him for teaching me 'grown-up things like that'. He retorted that there was no harm in it. No warning bells sounded in my head I just thought that the more grown-up the drawing was, the more impressed the teacher would be and I would join the top group.

The following day I wrote my story very carefully. I had sneaked in an extra-sharp pencil from home and a small scrap of paper to try words out on. I was oblivious to everything around me as I worked away. When I had finished I surveyed my efforts with pride, with just a slightly nervous feeling lurking inside me. However, I pressed on and drew my lady. I reproduced my uncle's sketch but replaced the straight skirt he had drawn with a flamboyant ball gown with splendid trimmings. I sharpened the fat crayons with my nails in order to colour the finery, and thought about the coloured pencils you were allowed to use in the top group. When at last I had finished, I took my efforts to the teacher with my heart thumping: I just knew it was good. She took one look at the drawing and said she did not want to see me or the book again. She did not look at rude pictures and I had better rip the page out before 'Sister' (the headmistress) saw it. I was dumbfounded and sick. Other children came scurrying round to look and she roundly admonished them too. I discovered, through the taunts in the classroom and the playground, that my uncle had taught me to draw a large bosomed figure, which was not allowed. I knew that anything I did now would be wrong. I went back to daydreaming and being as quiet as possible.

11. At least, up to this point, my unhappiness had gone largely unnoticed at home. There was little or no contact between school and home, and, in

any case, home was now busy with another baby, my first brother. In the junior school, I was conscious of greater divisions among the pupils. There were now more books to be written in; there were spelling tests and multiplication tables to be learned and tests on Friday. I watched the top group as they closed their eyes or stared into space and silently mouthed the tables and spellings. I copied them but when it came to saying them out loud I looked long and hard, to no avail, for the answers. One day, I was walking behind two children from the top group, on my way home from school. They were reciting their three-times table. I caught the rhythm and wanted to join in but I just did not seem to know the words. They turned and saw me and asked me if I knew mine yet. I said 'no'. They invited me to join them and I was greatly honoured. We reached the vicinity of their houses and I continued my journey ecstatically repeating them to myself. Friday came and we all had to recite the table in unison. I chorused with the best of them, wanting to catch the teacher's eye and show her that I could do them too. The teacher darted questions around the room. When she asked me a question it was bathed with a quip: 'And let's see if the bottom group has learned anything'. The answer froze on my lips. A voice inside my head was almost hysterical, urging me to answer, but nothing came before she said, 'Can somebody tell her?'

12. I gradually became aware of the vicious circle I was in. The teachers did their best to teach. They tried to explain things to the whole class. Once most of the children seemed to understand, work was set to practise and test. Those who failed were usually the ones who were expected to, and there developed a chasm between those who could and those who couldn't. I knew I was on the wrong side of the chasm but, as yet, my parents did not know. The end-of-year tests were a rude awakening for them. I came near to the bottom of the class. My mother went to see the teacher and demanded to know what had gone wrong. The teacher was sorry for her because she was disillusioned in thinking that she had a bright child. She was told that I behaved very well, tried very hard and that, if I was at fault in any way, it was only that I appeared to daydream quite a lot. Basically, I was *a slow learner*. This was a bitter blow for my mother: first to have one child with problems and then to have the brightness of the other wiped away in one short interview.

13. When my parents talked it over they decided to help me more at home. This was disastrous in every way. I had, by this time, suffered the loss of the doting adults who had surrounded my earlier years. They were married with children of their own. I had gone from being the centre of their world to not even being on the periphery in many cases. By now I knew I was an absolute disaster at school and then came the rift with my parents, and especially my father. My father tried to help me and ended

up angry and frustrated. Worse than that, amid the recriminations of both of them, I became convinced of my total failure as a child to deliver any of the goods I was sure parents had the right to expect. I prayed that God would do something. Perhaps I would wake up one morning or bang my head in some accident and be released from this stupidity.

14. The next blow came when I failed the 'eleven-plus'. My parents, family and friends were convinced I would walk through it. Sometimes I believed this too. I felt clever outside school and, besides which, I had said a great many prayers. At home I was reliable: I could shop for several neighbours, dealing with various amounts of money. In the local 'fruit and veg' shop I helped to weigh the foodstuffs and knew how much per pound the various goods were. Despite my difficulties in school, I retained a lot of information in my head from books and the radio and my conversations were lively and informative. I was perceived, by all round me at home, to be a bright and able child. The shockwaves were tangible when news of my failure was released. My two worlds could not have reacted more differently. At home they reacted with utter disbelief: *school* was busy congratulating the successful. There was no doubt who would pass and, of course, they had done so. Most of the rest of the pupils were happy with their lot; they had never expected to pass anyway. Only one of my friends passed unexpectedly and her attitude to me changed almost overnight. She would not be able to come round as often now as she had homework to do. At moments like this I pretended to be preoccupied, not to listen. I busied my mind with other thoughts.

15. However bad the secondary modern seemed at first encounter, it brought with it a bag of mixed blessings: I was not bottom of the heap any more; I made a few good friends; I developed a crush on the maths teacher and my maths improved considerably. The art teacher saw that I was one of the better behaved girls who tried hard. She liked me and began to encourage me and I became very good at art.

16. I so admired the rough element in the school: they were frightened of no-one. They formed their own groups, turned their backs on any attempts at academic success and stood up to any teacher at the slightest provocation. As a group they were physically adept and had the utmost respect of the PE teacher. Given the choice, if I couldn't belong to the clever set, I would have given much to belong to this group, but I lacked the courage. I once had to run the gauntlet of some of the older members of this group, as they draped themselves across the foot of the main staircase. As I passed through their midst, they began to taunt me and made remarks about me being a '----ing sucker-up' to the maths teacher. While my heart thumped violently, they could have beaten me to a pulp and I would not have changed one jot.

17. The fact that 'I' was no longer at the bottom of the academic heap any more might have raised questions about the standards in the school, but it did a lot for my ego. I was delighted to make new friends who did not belong to the bottom group. My parents, unfortunately, did not approve of my new friends, which caused more problems at home. One of the friends I made was a year older than me and a fellow admirer of the young maths teacher. I adored this teacher, from not too far away, because she travelled on the same bus as me. I frequently carried her bag to school and nearly 'broke my neck' opening doors for her. I so wanted to impress upon her that I was not stupid. Perhaps because of my willingness to please her she took time to explain things to me and I began to get more things right. However, I did not feel at all in control of this new found success: my head was like a dark store cupboard of information. When I wanted to retrieve a piece of information, sometimes it would still be there but at other times there would be no trace. The fact of this made me constantly anxious. The reason for it puzzled me.

18. Within eighteen months of my starting secondary school, I was entered as a candidate for the 'thirteen-plus' and, much to my astonishment, I passed. I can remember being so thrilled that I had at last achieved something that would make my parents proud of me. But there remained in my mind the underlying question of how I had managed it. Added to this there was some confusion that I could not make sense of at the time. The school had another scholarship on offer and I was given extra tuition from the art teacher in preparation for it. It was to the Liverpool Junior College of Art. My parents did not appear to be too thrilled about this, but the school seemed to indicate that it was my only chance. Given that I had only just scraped through the first scholarship, I was not eligible for a place at the better known grammar schools.

19. I duly went to the art college but, because of a not very straightforward tonsillectomy, I started a month later than the rest of my peers. The first piece of homework I was given was to draw a map of the world for the history master. Because of my late start I did not realize that maps could be traced, and after several abortive efforts I coloured in my best version and it came back with '2/10: Terrible!' written on it. This typified most of my experience at this school. I had found myself at the bottom of another heap.

20. While in hospital having my tonsils removed, I had met a nun who lived in a convent not too far from my home. She befriended me and asked me to come and see her after I had recovered. I did so and was soon enlisted, with a group of other girls, to assist these nuns in the care of the elderly. I was awe-struck to discover that most of these girls were

thinking of becoming nuns. They seemed quite ordinary to me. My
imagination was fired. I read copious books on the subject and began
copying pictures of the saints in my art classes which endeared me to
no-one at the school. For some reason, I was not particularly attracted to
join these nuns. By chance I met another nun from an order based in the
South of England. She was very impressed with me and invited me to
come and have a holiday at her convent. This I did and, while there,
decided that I would like to become a nun. The sisters were all delighted
but said that I should finish school first. After all, I was a scholarship girl.
The horror of this hit me immediately. If they discovered what a failure I
was, maybe they would not be so keen to have me join them. The answer
to this dilemma was not long coming. In my readings I had discovered the
value put on 'God's calling'. It meant leaving everything, scholarships
included! I had read about how Therese de Lisieuz had been allowed to
join the Carmelites at fifteen. I was nearly fourteen.

21. I survived another year at school, during which time I worked hard on
my parents and the nuns. I told them I couldn't wait much longer: I needed
to follow God's call. I left school and worked for a short time, after which
I was accepted into the convent. From the moment I mentioned I wanted
to be a nun, the adulation from friends and extended family began.
Suddenly I was the brightest, most attractive girl ever – and I was giving it
all up for God! My parents were no part of this admiration society but,
sadly, by now, that was 'par for the course' and too painful to deal with.
So I buried it and drank deep from this new source of nourishment.

22. The nuns saw me as a girl from a good home who was scholarship
material and, although the next six years were to hold much pain and
sadness, under their expectation I partially emerged from my chrysalis. I
did a number of correspondence courses and obtained a few 'O' levels. The
grades were not very good but the excuses were many. We devoted six
hours a day to prayer and the students were not totally released from their
other duties. Added to this my body, in collusion with my mind, was
given to psychosomatic illnesses that caused me to be laid up at
appropriate moments. In some respects, this saved my sanity.

23. After five years in the convent I was allowed to go to a college of
further education to do some 'A' levels. I still prayed fervently that God
would allow me to be clever, for it still seemed a matter of chance
whether I was able to learn and show evidence of this or not. I wondered
how long it would be before others would discover this too. There was a
dreadful sense of guilt that somewhere along the line it was my fault that I
could not learn properly, but I so much enjoyed the high expectations
everyone had of me.

24. During my period at this education establishment I fell very much in love with my English tutor. It was not at all reciprocated, but he did have an uncanny recognition of my plight. As I proffered ill-formed essays, riddled with spelling errors, he gave me nothing but encouragement. He listened and seemed to value my ideas. He introduced me to many of the great authors and poets. Reading became like a drug I could never get enough of, but which was immensely satisfying even in the meagre doses my busy life usually allowed.

25. It is interesting to reflect that, while I was able to recall great chunks of literature and appreciate the most sensitively expressed allusions, the business of recall under exam conditions was still a haphazard one. I still feared a return to failure.

26. By the end of my year in college I had decided to leave the convent. I left with an abiding sense of failure in yet another area of my life. The nuns had really believed in me, but I was unable to fulfil their expectations. Within a month or two I obtained a place at a large teacher training college where I trained to teach infants. Throughout my time at this college I was carried through by sheer hard work and an innate ability to teach. I received several distinctions for various areas of teaching and for any course work that I did but still, under examination conditions, I floundered. I thought I had come to terms with the fact that I was a practical person, not terribly academically inclined, but the eve of the final exams found me on my knees pleading for miracles.

27. The day I discovered I had passed my exams I wept tears of joy and, in my head, I heard myself saying over and over again, 'You're not a failed anything any more: you are a teacher'. For a long time afterwards I glowed when people asked me what I did. 'I am a teacher', I would reply, as if it indicated a certain type of human being – a fully paid-up member of the 'OK Society'. At last I had a piece of paper to show that I was not stupid. It did not fool me but, as long as it satisfied everyone else, I was content.

Commentary on my education biography

The purpose of this commentary is to explore aspects of pupils' experience of the education system and to consider what lessons might be drawn which would be of value to myself and others involved in education, especially teachers. In pursuit of this, I have written an account of my own experiences as a pupil from my first day at school until the day I qualified as a teacher: an education biography. The main theme that emerges from this biography is that at no time were my experiences taken into account by the teachers into whose hands I was entrusted. That is to say, I was not treated as a consumer who could and should have been consulted about the services on offer and how they were being delivered. In the light of this experience and of my reading, I have chosen to consider two issues: the experience of pupils as 'consumers' within the education system, and the effect of the lack of consultation on the learning experiences of these pupils. I propose to explore these issues by examining five aspects of the experience of the pupil:

- the quality of the relationship between pupil and teacher;
- the expectations the teacher has of the pupil;
- the expectations the pupil has of him or herself;
- the way in which the pupil interacts with other pupils and pupil groups;
- the match or mismatch of pedagogy with pupils' learning processes and styles.

What is the quality of the relationship between the teacher and pupil?

The quality of the relationship between the pupil and teacher is not easy to assess or quantify, not least because it has to do with feelings and emotional responses. My first encounter with my reception class teacher was in many ways sadly disastrous. She was not specifically unkind to me, but her treatment of my fellow pupils left a chasm of distrust between us that was never crossed (Biography, para. 3). Relationships with other teachers thereafter began with a similar mistrust and fear, and always there was a degree of confusion between their agenda and mine. My experience was that my needs and feelings were not on their agenda at all (Biography, para. 4).

Dennis Thiessen (1989) interviewed two students who had experience of being labelled as having learning disabilities. One of the students, Trevor, clearly expresses his need for a good working relationship with his teacher when he speaks of the need to 'do little favours for the teacher, in order that, when you ask them for help after class they will give you five minutes' (p. 96). This experience of bartering in order to get on the agenda shows a degree of initiative and maturity which the student, in this case, was never credited with. In his heroic effort to be accepted as normal, Trevor put in what he describes as 'a hundred and ten per cent effort' (ibid., p. 91). He reiterates the importance he attaches to teacher–pupil relationships: 'If there are good student–teacher relationships they will want to get along, to understand each other' (ibid., p. 96). This is not so much a statement of fact but rather an expression of hope that, given the one, the other will follow.

When relationships between teacher and pupil have completely soured, pupils frequently react by forming their own groups with their own agenda which is diametrically opposed to the agenda of the school or class teacher. Paul Willis (1983) refers to these groups as a 'counter-culture' who have given up trying to develop a working relationship with their teachers and set and adhere to their own rules and codes of conduct. Willis, in a discussion with such a group about their relationship with their teachers, was told by a pupil called Joey,

> It's sort of a challenge, coming to school thinking, 'How can I outwit the teachers today?' like. The teachers are the establishment, they've done things to you, you don't like what they've done. How can you get back?
>
> (Willis 1983: 113)

It is easy to dismiss Joey and his group as delinquents who form the disruptive element in a school, but by doing this we ignore the implications for our society, and admit that our education system is not for the benefit of all pupils but suited to and aimed at a much smaller portion of the pupil population. This highlights the conflict between the overt and covert aims of education and the reality of the experience of our pupils. Clearly, without consultation, the experience of the pupil will never influence the agenda of the education system. Joey's aggression would appear to stem from his discovery that his needs were not on that agenda.

During my primary school years, I vacillated between conscious efforts to establish good relationships with my teachers and rapid withdrawals when this failed (Biography, paras 9, 10 and 11). In school, I experienced a quite desperate need to be accepted as a worthwhile person, to be liked and to receive approval. I wanted to be given an opportunity to show what I could do and to get help for what I could not do. Consultation was not on the agenda, however, and although I did develop some of the bartering strategies used by Trevor, they did not effect any consistent or significant changes. The reason why these strategies sometimes worked and at other times failed left me confused (Biography, para. 10). My experience was of a clever mind somehow trapped in an inflexible system that labelled me without ever knowing anything about me (Biography, paras 8, 10 and 27).

Margaret Meek (1988), author and Reader in Education at the University of London, was a successful pupil who describes herself as: 'Industriously pleasing my teacher [and enjoying] the approval which linked pleasure with virtue' (p. 5). It would appear that most pupils at least start by trying to develop a good relationship with their teachers. Teachers, too, for the most part, are anxious to enter into a good working partnership with the pupils in their care, but the system denies them *both* access to the time, place and opportunity for consultation and effectively restricts them from making any significant changes.

The expectations teachers have of their pupils

The relationship between teacher and pupil is considerably influenced by the expectations the teacher has of a pupil. I was aware, through experience, from quite an early stage in my primary school of the correlation that existed between teacher–pupil relationships, teachers' expectations and pupil performances. Within each classroom pupils were streamed into groups and the expectation the teacher had of these groups varied, as did the materials with which the pupils in the groups were expected to work. The performance was almost predictable – even to a five-year-old (Biography, paras 3, 4 and 8). A pupil's current and past performances are often the basis on which teachers form their expectations. Pupils from deprived areas, poor social backgrounds, girls, shy, hesitant pupils, etc., even in this enlightened age of 'equal opportunities', also provoke a degree of expectation from teachers. Pupils tend to respond in accordance with the expectations teachers have of them. This then produces an upward or downward spiral of performance related to expectation that is self-perpetuating and hard to intercept or change. Even when pupils break loose and expose their ability, and even if a teacher is perceptive enough to be aware of it, the moment is often lost within the mechanisms of school life. Ted Hughes (1988: 5), teacher and poet, made some poignant remarks about this:

> We actually have no idea what any child's real abilities are . . . I have felt it myself – the teacher's pang of despair when he glimpses a pupil's real potential, and knows there is no way of catching hold of it and developing it . . . it is beyond what any ordinary educational methods are designed to deal with, and even, in a way, beyond what our society can accept.

A significant number of adults when questioned about the subjects they perceive themselves not to have performed well in at school, will link their acceptance of this, as fact, to a teacher informing them directly or indirectly of their expectations of failure. This expectation of probable failure, because of innate inability, may be implanted as early as eight years of age and remain with some people for the rest of their lives. These expectations are not based on true ability because, like myself, many of these pupils become academically successful in adult life. Rather, they are based on the results of assessable performances linked to fixed criteria (Schostak and Logan 1984: 75).

At the end of his eighth grade at school, Trevor was told by his teachers, 'You won't be able to make it through and get an education' (Thiessen 1989: 96–7). He reflects:

... they recommended I go to a vocational school. A vocational school was not for me. My mind was made up. I knew I needed an education to get a half decent job in this world. I knew if I got into a normal high school, if I got the chance, I could do it. I wanted to prove my elementary school wrong ... a vocational school would have been a wrong thing for me. I wanted to prove I could handle a normal class. I just needed a little help here and there. My 110 per cent was to prove that I was capable of handling normal teachers and classrooms from grades nine to thirteen.

(Thiessen 1989: 97–8)

For Trevor, the drive to be treated as normal and the occasional success he achieved in this gave him the incentive to battle against the low expectations of his teachers.

Most pupils, however, do tend to conform to the expectations of their teachers for better or worse. Even Joey, who had opted out of the role of conventional pupil, was still conforming to expectations. He was in fact conforming to the low expectations of a school that gave him 'Nothing hardly relating to school work ...' (Willis 1983: 101) by doing as little as possible and trying to '... go through the term without writing anything. 'Cos since we've come back I ain't done nothing' (Willis notes that at this point he is at midpoint in the school term) (ibid., p. 102).

Pupils' expectations of themselves

I did not begin to succeed in any real sense until somebody began to have consistently higher expectations of me than I had experienced throughout my life (Biography, paras 22 and 24). The effect of this was a gradual and somewhat spasmodic change in my belief and expectations of myself. Up until that point, I had experienced a conflict which, while it was similar to Trevor's in that I knew that I was more capable than I was being labelled, was more complex because subconsciously I reflected on the *results* of anything I did and was convinced by the evidence that the labels were about right (Biography, paras 8, 10 and 27).

Pupils' expectations of themselves are based on the feedback they receive from parents, teachers and peers. Those expectations are likely to become self-fulfilling prophecies that govern their school life to good or ill effect. Negative expectations formed early in a pupil's school life are frequently reflected in feelings of inadequacy, lack of confidence and low self-esteem as an adult. In my experience of teaching adults, I have found that even in the face of evidence to the contrary, they will say they are 'thick' or 'no good' at something because of their experience of failure as pupils in school.

Jennifer Rogers (1977: 34), commenting on the feelings of some of her adult students, said:

> There is often a deep sense of inadequacy in my students, even though many of them are successful professional men and women. They associate written work with tests, marks and examinations and therefore with potential failure.

As an adult student myself, I have had to come to terms with the ghosts of past failures haunting me with self-doubt and fear of innate inadequacies (Biography, para. 26).

It is incredible to reflect how pupils exist side by side in the same classroom with the same teacher, receiving the different hidden messages that separate, divide and label them so effectively that it can alter their perception of themselves (Meighan 1986: 114). Sheila Tobias (1988) comments on the effects of self-expectations on the mathematical performance of boys and girls. She suggests that girls expect not to be good at mathematics and therefore interpret failure as an almost inevitable consequence and success as chance or good fortune: boys expect to be good and interpret failure as ill fortune and success as just reward.

It is hard to redirect downward spiralling self-expectations. Ted Hughes recounts an experience he had with a class of 'backward boys'. He had had little success teaching them multiplication tables. He persuaded them to try an experiment which merely involved calling out the first answer that came into their heads. He explained that this would allow their brains to work without interference. He obviously convinced them to some extent, because it worked: for the last ten minutes of the lesson he asked them questions and they shouted out the correct answers. He reports:

> By the end of the lesson the boys were wildly excited – and bemused. Neither they nor I knew what to make of it. Our problem solved itself, however. By the next lesson, the miracle was over. Their idea of their own limitations had moved in the night, and sealed off the escape route I had opened, and was now on guard. I was never able to open it again.
>
> (Hughes 1988: 5–6)

This is a sad yet familiar tale to me. It seemed throughout my school life there were many such experiences of teachers opening up an 'escape route' for me, and time and time again I would rise only to fall deeper into the pit of inadequacy from which I felt doomed never to escape (Biography, para. 10). I reflect on those experiences now as making the journey out of the pit longer and more fearful, because they served to entrench me in my expectation that I would inevitably fail. Yet I never once wanted to resist them nor do I now regret them, because without such experiences I might never have glimpsed the possibilities that were to come.

The way pupils interact with each other and the effects of pupil groups

Pupils' expectations of themselves are influenced by a number of factors, an important one of which is the expectation of their peers. Pupils' perceptions of each other are closely aligned to the evidence that is presented to them by such sources as the teachers' attitudes, results of tests and various assignments, and covert or overt grouping of pupils within the different subjects. The influence of one's peers is an intensely powerful one from which one receives informal labels that are not easily discarded.

Any group of five-year-olds will be able to identify who is 'good at what' in their class and who are in the top and bottom groups (despite the groups being labelled by colours, animals or solar systems!). This often leads to an unwritten pecking order which the pupils seem quite accepting of. It does not preclude fierce competition between individuals within these groups, but rather a general acceptance that the 'blue group' is always on a higher set of reading books than the others and the 'Milky Ways' are always the last to tidy their table and be ready. This, too, can lead to self-fulfilling prophecies. The 'blue group' is likely to generate a good deal of competition among its members that keeps them in the first division. The 'Milky Ways' might well develop a camaraderie that gets a perverse pleasure from keeping the rest of the class waiting. Pupils need to find soul mates in large or small groups; they need to develop a status and an identification which helps them to cope. Joey clearly feels the value of his group: 'You know you have to come to school today, if you're feeling bad, your mate'll soon cheer you up like, ... [mates] They're about the best thing actually' (Willis 1983: 104).

In the case of the counter-culture groups there is an element of solidarity. It is them against the 'ear-'oles' and the teachers who they see as trying to make them '... subject to their every whim ...' (Willis 1983: 113). Belonging to a group gives them status. To some extent, they are able to make their stamp on what is, to them, a somewhat oppressive and limiting regime by passively resisting attempts to make them work (ibid., p. 102). The so-called 'ear-'oles' are rewarded by their own success and consequent approval from their teachers and such rewards keep them relatively happy with their image and status.

As a primary school teacher, I took an interest in the progress of a class through their primary years into their mid secondary school. I observed the effect of the school's grouping of these pupils on the pupils' grouping of themselves. There was always least difference and movement in the groups at the extremes. Those whose experiences had led them to believe they were top were often friends both in and out of school, with evident approval of both teachers and parents. Those whose experiences had led them to believe that they were low achievers were often divided into two groups: one in which they seemed happy with their lot, their teachers' and parents' expectations of them being limited and their association with like-minded peers providing them with an acceptable image and status; the other group, whose parents seemed not at all interested in them and who were labelled as 'trouble-makers' by both teachers and pupils, were more disruptive and angry. In between these two groups were a large number of pupils. They, too, formed themselves into groups but gravitated at frequent intervals either to the top or bottom groups. These pupils seemed least in charge of their own destiny. Sometimes, through a chance experience of success, they would suddenly find themselves in with the top groups. Some would manage to maintain their position socially, whereas others would eventually find themselves lost, looking for another group to belong to, never quite sure why they succeeded or failed, academically or socially.

When I recently spoke to some of these pupils in their mid-teens, their reflections were interesting. Pupils from the top group tended to have remained friends in the secondary school. Pupils from the disruptive group were reported to be just the same, hanging around with each other – a thoroughly bad lot. Pupils from the large middle section had moved around the most. More of them were dispersed into other secondary schools by dint of their parents moving, and those who remained seemed to have formed smaller groups. There were no clear indications as to what they would or would not achieve. It is interesting to note the long-lasting effects of academic grouping on informal social interactions. A recent survey of the achievement of examination results within the pupil population also indicated a minority at the top and a majority in the middle (*World in Action*, Granada Television, 1989). I consider these figures have more to say about our *system* being inadequate than the innate capabilities of those being tested (Schostak and Logan 1984: 75–6).

I spent most of my school life in that middle group. During my periods in the lower end, I could not form friendships with my peers because I did not feel I had anything in common with them. I could understand the contented acceptance of one group (Biography, para. 8) and I had not the courage to emulate the disruptive group, though I much admired their spunk (Biography, para. 16). When I graduated to a top group, they could not accept me as one of them because they had come to perceive me as less able than themselves (Biography, para. 9). My ability really to achieve began to surface only when I had moved away from the school environment, where I had failed, to a new environment, where my peers had more reason to suppose that I was an able and intelligent person (Biography, para. 22).

The match or mismatch of pedagogy with pupils' learning processes and styles

The learning styles of pupils is a difficult factor to understand, largely because it is something that the individual discovers and develops, but also because it requires a degree of self-knowledge to be able to identify it in any way other than by stating a preference for doing things in a certain way. For a teacher to be faced with the problem of assisting pupils in identifying their learning style would be both difficult and time-consuming. Without, however, at least some recognition that all pupils are not happy with 'chalk and talk' as a teaching method we risk, at best, boring them and, at worst, denying them the opportunity to learn, thus laying them open to being labelled unintelligent.

Schostak and Logan (1984) recount the experience of a young pupil as reported to them by an education welfare officer. The boy had been given a dreadful reference from school because he was considered to be 'lazy' and 'a nuisance'. The officer concluded, 'He was a clever lad at the things he was good at. But, you see, all that sort of stuff wasn't in the school curriculum' (pp. 74–7). And a school report I uncovered recently stated: '. . . appears to have worked hard for these tests and, with the exception of those subjects in which she finds most difficulty, her marks are good'. I was positioned fifteenth out of twenty-one in a mixed age class of forty. In these two examples, there would seem to be no correlation between the means by which something is taught and the relevance of it to the learner's interest or learning strategies. Schostak and Logan call this 'a violation of intelligence' (p. 78), and further condemn schools wherein such examples are not uncommon by saying that, 'Schools for the cultivation and not the violation of intelligence have yet to be created'. (p. 88).

It may be argued that Schostak and Logan's condemnations are too dismissive of the good practice going on in schools, but for those pupils whose learning styles do not fit the pedagogy of the system, and who therefore fail, it may also be argued that it is no worse than the condemnation they receive as a consequence of such neglect. Many pupils go through life thinking that they are not able to address themselves to a vital subject, like mathematics, simply because of the way it was taught in the school which they attended. Such failure will prevent them from taking advantage of a number of opportunities of employment in later life. Ironically, the teaching profession is just one such example.

Woods, in his interviews with pupils, reports a number of examples of pedagogy stifling interest by the unnegotiated pursuit of boring tasks.

> I don't like geography because it's all on the blackboard all the while and I can't stand the teacher.
>
> > (Woods 1984: 230)
>
> The metalwork homework was to copy 10 pages out of a book, and that took three to four hours, every week for a year.
>
> > (Woods 1984: 229–30)

Given these examples, then, 'violation of intelligence' does not seem too strong a term. In terms of our positions as teachers, these examples show an abuse of our captive consumers.

Pupils can sometimes see, only too clearly, that they are being prevented from both learning opportunities and the opportunities to exhibit and possibly gain credit for developing their own successful learning strategies. Trevor made this point very clearly:

> 'Maybe I don't solve it in the same way, but if I get the same answer and I can explain it to the students so that they can understand it, maybe helping someone who doesn't understand it, then let me do it.
>
> > (Thiessen 1989: 29)

Conclusion

The discussion presented in this commentary has addressed the issue of the impact upon pupils' experience of the lack of consultation in schools. The effects of this upon the individual pupil are also identifiable on a larger scale. The experience a pupil has of being a consumer in our education system seems to bear little relation to the quality of the education that the system has to offer. In terms of academic success, it fails eighty-six per cent of its consumers (Schostak and Logan 1984: 88). Thus fourteen per cent of pupils attaining success at the cost of as much as eighty per cent of the budget does not indicate success. (*World in Action*, Granada Television, 1989). If it is aiming to educate all pupils up to a certain baseline from which they will then be able to exercise choice as to the direction they take thereafter, then this aim too seems to fail on a number of counts.

In terms of it preparing pupils for work and assisting them in the development of relevant skills, then the daily complaints from business and industry alike does not reflect well on the education system either. Even in terms of it nurturing pupils to continue to work within its own system, as teachers, it is not overwhelmingly successful, given the present shortage of teachers and the disillusionment of many of those already within the profession. Overall, it seems effective only for the minority.

Our education system, based as it is on the achievement of academic success for the minority, is managed largely by its own successful products – that is, the academically successful and professionally qualified. As education has come more and more into the ownership of these professionals, it has developed a system which sieves, selects and refines those who learn successfully and can reproduce information in the same mode and manner as it is taught. A consequence of this is that only a minority of parents and pupils can use and are able to manipulate the system to their own advantage, while the needs of the majority of pupils have become more and more marginalized. The majority of parents are, for the most part, merely informed of some of the proceedings that go on within the school via the medium of school reports and parents' evenings. For most parents, the information they receive on these occasions is presented as past history or as a description of the pupils' performance and attitudes with some prescriptory comments; for example, 'clever but lazy – needs chivvying', 'intelligent and a pleasure to teach', 'slow but tries hard'. The question of how much the National Curriculum, SATS and Records of Achievement will improve this mechanism is highly debatable in the light of who was and will be consulted about the aims, their content, method and evaluation.

It could be argued that the deficiencies in our education system discussed here are about to be remedied. The concept of consumerism is much in evidence these days. In most successful businesses, a great deal of market research goes into finding out what the market requires. The market is made up of consumers who have the power to accept or reject a product. In this highly sophisticated format of supply and demand, the true consumer is very carefully identified and targeted in order to maximize the financial rewards. With the arrival of the National Curriculum and Local Management of Schools, we in education are told that we have something to learn from the world of business and industry and we are encouraged to adopt some of its principles (Goodchild and Holly 1989).

In education, we have many perceived consumers who are identified in various ways. Many schools perceive their consumers to be parents and go for the hard sell on a parent-friendly curriculum, good discipline and above all good academic results. Other schools are more concerned with industry and tailor courses and exams accordingly. Few, if any, schools however identify and target pupils as their major consumers. In fact, the education system almost forbids them to do so.

The Secretary of State for Education introduced the need for a national curriculum by referring to 'The overall picture [being] one of disappointingly low standards of achievement' (National Association of Head Teachers 1989). He declared that, 'A national curriculum will guarantee that all pupils will receive an education which is broad, balanced, relevant to their needs . . .' (ibid.). It is the final part of this statement that is perhaps the key to the problem. The experience of the vast majority of our pupils is that of being within a system that is not in effect geared to their needs. What the Secretary of State seems to be saying is that, given what he and his colleagues in this matter deem to be appropriate educational content, formally (taught by teachers who have good practice, working with successful learners), this should be duplicated by every teacher, for every pupil in order to achieve an acceptable level of success and that this will be 'relevant' to the needs of all. My question is this, following the guidelines of good market research and business acumen to carefully identify and target the consumer, who was consulted about this? Was it the pupils who have been failed, or the pupils who succeeded, or the parents of either or both? Indeed, were the experiences of the consumers in this case taken into account at all?

Editor's note

Even if the range of interest groups is widened to include pupils alongside parents, teachers and schools, it is unlikely to produce an administrative system or a set of curriculum proposals which will meet the diversity of perceptions within each of these interest groups, let alone their competing and contradictory agendas. If the prime purpose is to develop the individual pupils, perhaps our best hope seems to lie in the selection and training of teachers who will be sensitized to such needs and how to meet them rather than to rely on global or national solutions. To do this would require that teachers be granted a more generous measure of autonomy than current policy allows.

References

Goodchild, S. and Holly, P. (1989) *Management for Change: The Garth Hill Experience*. Lewes: Falmer Press.

Hughes, T. (1988) Foreword, in Brownjohn, S., *What Rhymes with Secret?* London: Hodder and Stoughton.

Meek, M. (1988) *How Texts Teach What Readers Learn*. Stroud: Thimble Press.

Meighan, R. (1986) *A Sociology of Learning*. New York: Holt, Rinehart and Winston.

National Association of Headteachers (1989) *Guide to the Education Reform Act 1988*. Haywards Heath: NAH.

Rogers, J. (1977) *Adults Learning*, 2nd edn. Milton Keynes: Open University Press.

Schostak, J. and Logan, T. (Eds) (1984) *Pupil Experience*. London: Routledge.

Thiessen, D. (1989) Curriculum as experienced: Alternative world views from two students with learning disabilities, in Franklin, B. (Ed.), *Learning Disability, Dissenting Essay*. Lewes: Falmer Press.

Tobias, S. (1978) *Overcoming Math anxiety*. New York: W.W. Norton.

Willis, P. (1983) The class significance of school-culture, in J. Purvis and M. Hales (Eds) *Achievement and Inequality in Education*. London: Routledge and Kegan Paul.

Woods, P. (1984) Negotiating the demands of school work, in M. Hammersley and P. Woods (Eds) *Life in School: the sociology of pupil culture*. Milton Keynes: Open University Press.

5

What do I do next?

Doreen Littlewood

Editor's introductory note

Mrs Littlewood attended classes at the Department of Education (Liverpool) and, as part of a group of teachers interested in education biographies, wrote a personal education biography in which she recounted her experiences as a pupil and how she became a teacher with a particular interest in, and concern for, those pupils with special educational needs. Following that biography, she went on to keep an education *journal*. This journal had as its focus those everyday events, personalities and interactions in her classroom for which her customary or routine responses were perceived by herself as inadequate and which required reflection. These events, etc., had the informal title of 'What shall I do next?' A very brief note of a particular incident was made at the time and in the evening a fuller description was entered into the journal. Upon reflection on these accounts, it became apparent to her that such responses were linked to her education biography and she openly makes a direct connection between her coping style as a pupil and some of her responses to pupils.

Such journals are not only of great value to student teachers, they can play a valuable part in the continuing professional development of experienced teachers. One of the dilemmas of such journals and biographies, however, is that the writer becomes very exposed and vulnerable, and that the group and group leader receiving such confidences are required to establish clear and consistent ground rules for discussion, confidentiality and above all trust.

I am personally convinced that the use of education biographies and journals is one of the most effective devices to aid dialogue between student and tutor and critical reflection upon practice, especially the intimate intertwining of the personal and the professional.

Background

As a shy four-year-old, I started my educational journey in the nursery class of a large urban primary school. My early years were spent as a 'passive observer' avoiding confrontation or undue visibility. I worked quietly and steadily, completing the tasks set for me but unwilling to ask for more. My social interaction was limited to a small circle of close friends.

At the age of eleven, I transferred to a secondary modern school, having failed the eleven-plus borderline test. In retrospect, this 'failure' was one of the most valuable experiences of my personal and educational life. My self-esteem received a boost when I found myself a 'high-flier' instead of an average pupil. The ethos of this school was to develop the 'whole pupil', making each pupil responsible for her own learning.

As my confidence increased, I began to believe that I could achieve my ambition of becoming a primary schoolteacher. I moved from this school into the sixth-form of the local grammar school and onto teacher training college.

On the successful completion of the course, I started work in a school in an educational priority area. It was in the early years of my teaching career that I realized I needed more practical knowledge and training in order to help the high proportion of less able children in the school. I was granted secondment for a year to study for a Diploma in the Advanced Studies of Education (DASE) in the 'Education of the slow-learning child in the ordinary school'. On returning to school, my role changed to Special Educational Needs (SEN) teacher.

After a short break working as a supply teacher in primary mainstream schools while my daughter was very young, I returned to full-time teaching in a special unit attached to a mainstream school. This was the biggest challenge I had faced, working with children assessed as having mild to moderate learning difficulties, all of whom were given a 'statement of special educational needs'. I saw my aims as trying to build their self-esteem, develop their academic skills and help them integrate back into the very system in which they had experienced failure. After two years as teacher-in-charge of the special unit, I was given the added responsibility of being the SEN coordinator for the mainstream school with a roll of over 600 pupils.

In order that I might meet the needs of all these pupils, I felt I needed to further extend my knowledge and skills in the subject and so enrolled for a modular MEd course at the University of Liverpool. It was during these studies that I developed a growing interest in 'reflective teaching'. I started consciously looking at 'what I did', 'why I did it', 'how I did it' and 'how I could improve on it'. This interest developed and became the subject for my dissertation.

My dissertation involved looking at situations or events which caused me to reflect before action rather than react by instinct; for the purpose of the study, they were classed as 'dilemmas'. It aimed at determining whether my personal and professional history influenced my present practice. If this relationship existed, could a deeper understanding of 'self' help improve my practice?

Recording the dilemmas

I needed to find a method of recording the incidents or experiences which had caused me to reflect. I found there was not time within the busy classroom to record them comprehensively, so I made brief notes on a pad at the time. In the evening, I wrote a more detailed report in a daily journal. I tried to analyse why the specific incident or experience had caused me a problem and why I had dealt with it in a particular way.

I collected the data over a period of twelve weeks, divided between two periods, after which I categorized the 'dilemmas' looking for common strands. While looking closely at my professional practice, I found there was a close relationship between my personal and professional history and my present professional practice. An example of this relationship was to be found in my awareness of the needs of quiet children, and a desire to meet their needs in a sensitive manner while helping them realize their potential. Other examples of this relationship were the need to build self-confidence, develop self-esteem, and the overwhelming desire to solve problems while avoiding confrontational situations.

The following excerpt from the daily journal shows an example of how the views of quiet children can be overlooked by their peers when a more dominant member of the group expresses an opinion:

Monday 21st September – Rain gauges

We discussed where to put the rain gauges we had made so they would be safe from vandalism. The suggestions were, on the roof, in the car park, behind an air-raid shelter and in the wild garden. As the garden has a pond it is locked and pupils can only enter if accompanied by an adult.

As the discussion went on, it soon became apparent that the decision would be made as a result of personalities rather than the most suitable place. Billy was very vociferous in his choice of the car park. Karl and Sara defended their choices of the roof and the air-raid shelter respectively, but were eventually swayed by peer pressure to follow Billy. However Dan, who in my opinion had chosen the safest spot, did not pursue his view. Rather, he moved to the back of the group, his body language signalling retreat whilst apparently accepting the group view.

I gave each of the four a team point for their contribution and then took a more active role in the discussion, leading it towards the safety angles and away from personalities. We looked at the advantages and disadvantages for each site. I involved each pupil in turn in this process and then tried to get the children to make a more informed decision. This led the children to decide to put the rain gauges in the wild garden.

This dilemma had been two-fold. First, how could I get all the children to make their choice by using logical thought processes rather than by being influenced by a popular dominant member of the group. I recognize it is difficult for many children to resist peer pressure; however, this difficulty seems to be compounded in children who have a poor self-image in relation to their academic achievements. Second, how could I encourage all the pupils to express their opinions and realize they would be valued. In particular, how could I help Dan, a pupil lacking in self-confidence and displaying introvert characteristics, to continue to be an active participant. I could empathize with Dan and recognized his need for invisibility while deep down wanting to have his good idea recognized.

Having written up the notes into the daily journal, I then tried to analyse my actions. I had given the four contributors a team point in order to show the whole group how I valued the view of each pupil, rather than just awarding one to the pupil whose suggestion had been selected. Having seen Dan's reaction when his suggestion had been ignored, I was sure if he was always out-voted without any serious consideration having been taken of his ideas he would decide not to participate in future. Hopefully, this strategy would not only help Dan but encourage all pupils to contribute the next time the opportunity arose.

The move from an informal discussion to a highly structured one was, as I saw it at the time, the only way of giving everyone an equal chance to take part. It was certainly not ideal: the discussion became more stilted and the outcome could be judged as contrived. In defence of the method, it did involve all the children allowing no-one to be marginalized and possibly it helped develop the self-esteem of those rarely listened to.

As a result of this critical analysis, I realized that if I had put stricter parameters on the task the problem may not have arisen. There needed to have been more discussion before they were asked for suggestions and a need for a list of reasons for the choice to be given.

During the analysis, it became apparent that an area which stood out as a concern was interpersonal relationships. These interpersonal relationships extend beyond pupil–pupil and pupil–teacher to teacher–colleague. The following excerpt from the daily journal concerns my interpersonal skills when trying to advise and support a member of staff:

Monday 18th May – Staff support

An SOS arrived on my desk from a colleague asking for advice. She explained that she felt that she was failing a child who was experiencing learning difficulties in the basic subjects. After I had looked at the programme she had devised and assessed the child, I felt the programme was both well-structured and relevant. However, as usually the case in such programmes it required a high level of teacher–pupil interaction.

With a class of thirty children, three of whom exhibited behavioural problems, she was finding the time factor a problem. She had asked if a nursery nurse could be timetabled to work with this child; however, her request had been turned down. I suggested that we found a parent who could follow the programme with the child.

This she readily agreed to, but as I turned to leave she burst out that this would not help with the others! It was soon obvious that although concerned about this particular child, that was not the root of the problem. It was more a feeling that the whole class was being 'let down', while her time was taken 'containing the few' with behavioural problems. The problem was exacerbated by her feeling that she was alone in thinking there was a problem.

At the end of the lesson, we sat down to try and work out strategies for dealing with her dilemma. We started by discussing the three children and their specific problems, one of whom was being assessed by the educational psychologist with regard to his emotional and behavioural disturbances. In this case, although the problem was recognized, she felt she had received little support by either the school or the psychologist. The other two cases, although less disruptive, still exhibited very challenging behaviour. I had no ready answer, so went away promising to try and find a way of helping.

The dilemma in this situation was not within the first request for extra help for the child with learning difficulties, but rather the second problem of finding strategies, which were not too time-consuming, to deal with the disruptive pupils. Alongside this problem was the need to reassure the teacher that her difficulties were recognized and were real. It was necessary to not only give moral support but provide practical help and support. The moral support was relatively easy to arrange: I offered to be a 'sounding board' whenever she wanted to shout at someone or just talk things through. The fact that I also taught children with challenging behaviours and experienced the same frustrations helped. She felt she could reciprocate and play the listening role when I needed similar support.

However, the practical help and support was more difficult to arrange. In a large, busy school, there are rarely extra bodies available to put in classrooms in support roles. So I started by holding meetings with the parents and class teacher where we tried to devise programmes that we could all work on as a team. I asked for advice from the School Psychological Service on practical strategies we could employ and used my non-contact time to help the teacher implement them.

This action can only be seen as a beginning; there was and still is a need for greater reflection to see how similar situations can be avoided. If it is impossible to avoid such situations, we need to have strategies ready that we can put in place quickly in order to overcome them.

I am sure that the time I spent as a child being a 'passive observer' helps me now when a situation demands an ability to stand back, watch and listen.

Many of the dilemmas I recorded could be categorized as pedagogic dilemmas and were concerned with the motivation of a specific pupil or meeting curricula needs. Most of these dilemmas occurred suddenly, as a result of non-understanding of a part of the curriculum being taught or a pupil reaching a ceiling level in a subject. However, some of these dilemmas were as a result of a slow build-up of concerns over a period of days or even weeks, which finally demanded action being taken. This was the case in the next excerpt from the journal:

Thursday 26th March – 'can't or won't'

Shaun, an eager pupil who possibly needs to curb his enthusiasm to complete tasks in the interests of accuracy, has recently changed his attitude to new tasks. He now approaches new tasks negatively saying 'can't' before he tries. When observing him at these times, he appears to completely shut off and gives the impression rather of 'won't' rather than 'can't'.

Today he was presented with a piece of work which involved him using non-fiction books to find the answers. The reading level of the non-fiction books was within his capability; however, he did not even open the books before refusing to start the task. The reason he gave was that the task was too hard. This was the first time he has utterly refused to complete a task.

The dilemma was to determine why his attitude had changed and what strategies could be employed to rekindle his enthusiastic approach to his tasks.

I approached the dilemma by looking both through his books and at the incidents related to Shaun in my daily journal. This led me to the conclusion that the problem had grown from the time his integration had been increased. The possible strategies appeared to be that I could reduce his integration time, reduce the difficulty of the work set, or try to increase the support he received while working in his integration class. After reflection, I decided to employ the last of the three strategies. In order to implement this strategy, I decided to discuss with the class teacher how we could utilize the help I received from students from a local college to give added support to him in her class. Also, I changed the timetable of the part-time teacher for a period until his confidence was restored.

The reasons for this decision were two-fold. First, as we had been working towards moving him back into the mainstream in September, it could only have been seen as a retrogressive step to reduce his integration. Although it is obvious that a child should not be forced into an integrated situation before he or she is ready, most pupils need to be weaned from the protective security of the small class situation. It is often the case that many would happily stay in the small class for longer than is educationally necessary. In this case, I hoped that the added support would fulfil the weaning role.

Second, I felt if I employed the strategy of reducing the difficulty of the work set, it could act as a method of giving a quick boost to his confidence in his ability to complete tasks. However, in the long term, it would result in him rarely being given work that would challenge him or prepare him for fully integrated mainstream education.

The strategy I used in this dilemma was ultimately successful, although the time-scale did have to be altered. Instead of Shaun returning to mainstream education in September, it was January. Also, for the first term he had a higher level of support than we had initially planned. However, during his last term in the primary school, his support was reduced to that of his peers who were considered to have learning difficulties. At this time, he received help from Special Educational Needs Support Service (SENSS) for two thirty-minute sessions a week. As a result of the problems we had encountered in his reintegration into mainstream education, we recommended a review of his statement after one term in secondary school.

Throughout both my professional life and personal life runs a common theme of how to deal with or rather avoid confrontation. This showed itself in the journal in many of the situations which presented difficulties to me. It crossed the whole range of dilemmas. As a child I had developed avoidance strategies which I had successfully carried through into my adult life. In my early life I felt that if I became embroiled in confrontational situations I would become 'visible', the horror of the shy child, or that relationships could be irretrievably damaged. Therefore, the conscious avoidance strategies I used as a child became the unconscious reactions to confrontational situations in later life.

When I learnt to recognize these strategies, I found that what started as a weakness could be turned to a strategy of strength in both my relationships and teaching style. I now consciously avoid confrontation but am no longer afraid of it, and although it is always as a last resort I now face it whenever necessary. I now realize that relationships can be rebuilt with care. When studying the methods I employ when faced with such situations, I realize that I rely on quiet insistence rather than noisy confrontation when demanding conformity of behaviour or the completion of tasks. The following excerpt from the journal illustrates a situation when this methodology was used.

It involved a child with a communication problem termed 'elective mutism', which manifested itself in the school setting, particularly with adults. She had been a member of the group for two years and had slowly become more communicative. Although this was less evident at the beginning of a term and to a lesser degree after a weekend or half-term.

Monday 5th October – Confrontation

A problem arose during my ¾ hour non-contact time when Sonia refused to participate in a writing task set by another teacher. The teacher could not offer any reason for her non-participation; there had been no disturbing incidents in the session. She had tried asking, cajoling and demanding, but had received the same silent refusal to speak or work. The teacher was quite upset, as she felt that until this incident their relationship was slowly developing. Sonia had always completed work for her in the past, even if her body language had signalled a less than enthusiastic participation. The same support cover had been in place for over a year. I asked her why she had not started work, but she remained silent.

My dilemma was whether to let her put her book away and join in an activity with the others for the final part of the morning session or insist on her completing it.

My first action was to check that the task was within her capabilities, which was certainly the case. Then I had to decide whether to make her start the work. I could see no reason for her non-participation: the teacher was not an unfamiliar adult, the work was not beyond her capabilities and there had been no disturbances which could have upset her. As a result of this, I decided she should at least attempt the work or give a reason for not doing so. I was sure that if I did not the same problem would occur again, making the task of the support teacher even harder.

When the morning session ended, she still had not put pencil to paper. I found myself faced with a confrontational situation. At this point, I felt I was committed to ensuring some work was done, so I requested she came in after her dinner and start work.

After the lunch break, the situation had not changed. So while the rest of the class worked together, she continued to stare at the paper. Later in the afternoon as the children got changed for games, I conducted another one-sided conversation, still unable to find a reason for her behaviour. As I could not leave her unsupervised, I had to leave it until the next day. She got changed for games with a small smile.

The next morning she seemed surprised to be confronted by the same work and stared at me with a sullen expression. I quietly and firmly told her she would do the work and left her to the task. The confrontation continued through the morning, play-time and onto lunch-time. Again I quietly and calmly told her to go and have her lunch then return. At this point, I began to wonder how long I could let this situation carry on and what strategy I could use to break the deadlock.

Much to my relief when she came in, she glared at me, grunted, picked up her pencil and started to write. By the end of the lunch hour, one page was written and she was well on her way to completing the task. On completion of the task I received the work calmly, not making a fuss and set about rebuilding our relationship. This had to be done slowly and carefully, allowing her to make all the first moves so she would not feel threatened.

Categorizing the dilemmas

Before analysing the dilemmas, it was necessary to determine a rationale for their categorization. I started by sorting them into two categories, those which were influenced by people or events within the school and those outside the school. This method of categorization soon proved to be too unwieldly to be practical. It was obvious that I needed to focus on narrower categories if the task was to be manageable. I then sorted the dilemmas into the following four categories: relationships with pupils, relationships with colleagues, organizational dilemmas outside the classroom and relationships with people from outside the school. During this process, it became apparent that there would be overlaps between the categories, which might necessitate the further refining of categories. This was necessary in all categories; however, it was particularly true of the first and largest category, relationships with children. Here the dilemmas fell neatly into four sub-categories: pedagogic dilemmas, management and control dilemmas, social and environment dilemmas, and moral and/or ethical dilemmas.

When it came to the inclusion of dilemmas into the text, I looked at each category and allowed themes to emerge. These themes were classed as macro- and micro-themes. The macro-themes were those which occurred most frequently and could be classified as interpersonal relationships with colleagues, behaviour, pedagogic and organizational skills. The micro-themes covered the types of dilemmas which occurred less frequently, thereby producing less evidence, but which had caused me such depth of reflection that I felt justified in their inclusion. They tended to be more sensitive issues, such as moral and ethical dilemmas or those connected with self-doubts on my professional worth.

Analysing the dilemmas

Having categorized the dilemmas, there followed the more difficult task of exploring the meanings which may have been attached to these categories and events. It involved questioning myself as to why these events stood out as 'concerns' and why I had chosen to respond to them in the ways I had. This involved looking closely at my professional practice and trying to analyse it. There are recognized difficulties in reflecting on oneself in practice, and in my case it resulted in a period when I become deeply self-critical and introspective. I started analysing the situations in minute detail as each part of the situation unfolded rather than as a whole. Instead of looking at how aspects of my personal characteristics had influenced my behaviour, I looked closely for faults or weaknesses in those characteristics. Also, instead of looking for 'good practice' in my responses and actions, I only looked for examples of 'bad practice'.

This led to a period which was unproductive as far as the study was concerned, while being self-destructive for me as both a person and a professional. I made the decision to take time to stand back and assess how to approach this analytical stage. I realized during this period that I was concentrating too fully on my reactions and not looking at the situations that had caused them. From then on I tried to be more open-minded, merely reporting all the facts before analysing them and determining the reasons for my actions.

Working in this manner I found I could be more objective about myself. I found it easier to say, 'Yes, I would approach that situation the same way again' or 'No, if faced with the same situation again I would try a different strategy'.

It was while looking for influences on my practice that common threads appeared both in what constituted a dilemma for me and in how I reacted.

I found that in most cases the reasoning behind my reactions or actions could be traced back to my personal history.

My recognition of 'avoidance techniques', the need for 'invisibility' and the need for a positive self-esteem, could be traced back to my very early school years. While reflecting on behavioural dilemmas, I realized that as I had been a shy child – always the conformist – I had no past experiences to draw on when confronted with overtly disruptive behaviour patterns, so I had to rely on past professional experiences to help me work out strategies.

The consequences of such a study

The main consequences of carrying out such a study I found to be three-fold: the construction of 'personal theories' about teaching and learning, a greater insight into both my personal and professional development and, most importantly, a better understanding leading to an improvement in personal practice.

When I looked at the analysis of the various dilemmas, I recognized the importance I gave to the development of self-esteem. I realized that I saw my teaching methods as a way of developing this, so allowing effective learning to take place. This 'personal theory' extended into my relationships with colleagues, where I found an awareness of always trying to maintain or build upon their positive self-image.

The second personal theory I constructed, which can be linked to the first, was the need for all children to be involved in the learning process. The dilemmas registered concerns for children who had become marginalized or had developed quite effective work avoidance techniques. I am sure reflective teaching methods have helped me recognize these children and made me devise strategies to overcome these difficulties.

I believe that to be an effective teacher and colleague one needs a sound knowledge of both developmental steps and available resources. If one has both of these, one can structure the programmes of work in order to help the pupil make progress and give practical advice to colleagues.

The consequence of having a better insight into oneself can only lead to changes as one recognizes areas of weakness that need to be worked upon and areas of strength that can be built upon. An example of this was my difficulty in dealing with confrontational situations. Once I recognized it as a personal dilemma and understood why I was frightened of facing a confrontation, I could begin to work on developing strategies to enable me to cope. Now although I still avoid confrontation if possible, it is for logical reasons rather than fear.

As a result of this better insight into my strengths, I have actively developed my use of the listening role. I am sure that my years of being a passive observer as a child are useful when employed as a positive strategy when using inter-personal skills.

The final and most important consequence of this work for me is my improved knowledge of good practice, which led to changes in my personal practice. I found that having to justify my actions, if only to myself, made me consider them more and if necessary devise new strategies to meet situations. As these reflective skills developed, I found that – unlike initially when I used to reflect at great length and in great depth – I was able to reach a solution quickly using a combination of instinct and experience.

Although I no longer keep the daily journal I do still have a notebook to hand in which I jot down dilemmas to be reflected upon later. In this way, all the time I am examining my practice and looking for ways to improve it. I have also used it as an aid in the preparation of individual education plans, as the specific needs of the individual often appear as part of a dilemma.

I see the future use of the reflective method in the analysis of my teaching and learning as a way of working out strategies to overcome specific types of dilemmas. I envisage highlighting a particular area of concern and concentrating on recognizing and recording dilemmas within it. I will use a similar method to that used here, starting by noting any dilemmas in the specific area before reflecting on them, leading to the forming of strategies which will then be implemented. After that, I will evaluate their usefulness with relation to building them into my practice. It will become a cyclical process until I have built into my practice sufficient strategies for the incident or event to no longer present a dilemma.

The final step forward for me is to return to my history; so far I have looked at my early personal life, and now I hope to look more deeply into my professional history. I hope this will help me further understand my practice and consequently improve it.

6

Autobiography, feminism and the practice of action research

Morwenna Griffiths

Introduction

This chapter is a reflection on some action research that I have been carrying out together with Carol Davies, a primary school teacher, over the past three years. During her professional life, Carol has been committed to the individual pupils in her care, while preserving a broad educational vision. I have always taken the view that action research should be both personal and political. I believe that individual researchers should focus on themselves as individuals and as part of wider political structures. Actions should be directed at improving particular, local situations, recognizing the broader, global repercussions. This is easier said than done!

We began the collaboration with the intention of focusing on equal opportunities in Carol's classroom. We had no preconceived ideas about the best action research methods to use. As time has gone by we have come increasingly to rely on the journals that we both now keep. For me, re-reading them is a pleasure: it is reading the story of part of my life. They are a kind of autobiography, a narrative of the last three years.

I shall argue here that the pleasure of the personal is an important part of action research. There is, however, a danger that the personal can be entirely individual and apolitical. I argue that certain criteria should be applied to any piece of work in order to judge if it is epistemologically sound. These criteria are extremely abstract. So I then go on to use the examples of my journals written during several cycles of an action research project in order to explain what I mean in practical terms. (I am not engaged in judging the soundness of the whole project. That would require me to explain it in full, with all the methods that we used. I am focusing only on the journals written by one of us, only on one strand in the process.)

I begin the chapter by aligning myself with those who consider that action research, properly conceived, is a critical, political movement. I continue by explaining the call to a wide critical perspective, in theoretical terms, drawing on a particular tradition of critical epistemology, feminist epistemology, to do so. The argument, at this stage, remains at a very abstract level. I therefore explain what I mean, in practical terms, by anchoring the discussion to autobiographical writing in an action research project.

Autobiographical writing is common in accounts of action research. Researchers make frequent use of diaries, logs and journals as part of the action research 'tool kit'. The final report often contains references to the writers' own lives: their professional development and personal experiences. Indeed, it would be odd if it were not so. One way of describing an action research report is that it is autobiography – writing about one's own story. Action research is, inevitably, a narrative: it is research into one particular situation, in one particular time and place. Moreover, it is research carried out into the researcher's own situation. Finally, it is research in which the self of the researcher is itself at issue. Action research requires the researcher's own attitudes, beliefs, perceptions and values to be brought into question.

I have argued elsewhere for this view of action research as one in which individuals research their own situations, and bring their own selves into the research process (Griffiths 1990). It is a view which is shared by – and springs from – a number of influential writers in the field, even though they might have serious disagreements in other areas (Zeichner and Teitelbaum 1982; Carr and Kemmis 1986; Whitehead 1989; Elliott 1991). However, there is a serious potential problem that arises out of the emphasis on individual stories and selves. The wider critical context can get lost.

In early formulations of action research, it was clear that the wider critical, political context was an essential part of the process and value of the new method (Zeichner and Teitelbaum 1982; Carr and Kemmis 1986; Pollard and Tann 1987; Elliott 1991). However, in practice, it was found that the criticism and the politics could easily get lost. There was a possibility that action research would become merely a cheap method of improving technique and motivation, rather than a critical challenge to the *status quo* (Griffiths 1990; Elliott 1991). In an influential article, Weiner (1989) pointed out the lack of a feminist perspective in action research. Recently, writers have been reaffirming the need for an explicit critical and political commitment. Elliott (1991: 56) states: 'Out of the still smouldering embers of the traditional craft culture the phoenix of a collaborative reflective practice arises to offer creative resistance to the hegemony of the technocrat'.

In his address to CARN in 1992, Zeichner restated his commitment to the struggle for greater social justice:

> I think Weiner is right in her call for a focus in action research on both personal renewal and social reconstruction ... We need to become, or to stay connected to larger social movements that are working to bring about a more social, economic, and political justice on our planet. Although educational action research can only play a small part in this broader struggle it is an important part.

In this chapter, I will show how the personal and particular, as expressed in autobiographical research methods, can also be political and critical. My claim is that the story of our action research is both autobiographical and critical. The journals that we have kept are 'critical autobiography'.

My claim is dependent on (1) the view that, to be epistemologically sound, a method needs to be critical and political, and (2) the view that, to be epistemologically sound, a method needs to be personal, and also to be revisable over time. I argue for these two views, using feminist epistemology, in the next section. The claim would be hollow if it were not possible to convert abstract requirements into actual methods. I demonstrate that this is possible by (3) considering the method of autobiography in general, and 'critical autobiography' in particular, and (4) examining my own autobiographical writing using the criteria developed in (1) and (2).

The first part of this chapter, where I argue for particular epistemological criteria, is highly abstract and theoretical. It is sketched out in the next section. The conclusions to the argument appear at the end of the section.[1] If the epistemological argument is not something you want to read, it is possible to skip to the conclusions, which underpin the discussion of the way we have used critical autobiography in our research.

Feminist epistemology and methodology

Feminism is an important voice in the chorus of challenges to the neutrality of traditional epistemology. The feminist philosopher, Anne Seller (1994: 45), summarizes the argument thus: 'The apparently objective, neutral, rational voice of philosophy surreptitiously privileged the viewpoint of the middle/upper class European male, rendering invisible all other perspectives, experiences, voices ...'. Seller (1994: 45) goes on to point out that these perspectives cannot be easily incorporated into existing knowledge:

The way in which they [other perspectives] are developed is not in the form of adding a piece of knowledge in the appropriate form to the heap. Like Kuhnian paradigms, they constitute a revisioning of what is to count as a problem in knowledge, and a solution to it.

The feminist challenges are addressed to everyone: the challenge is to find an epistemology which is suitable for both men and women.

A number of very different, and disagreeing, feminist epistemologies were developed during the 1980s. (The number and range of them will surprise those who persist in talking of 'the feminist view'.) For instance, Irigaray provides a critique of the masculine imaginary, arguing that it generates a rationality preoccupied with dualism (Whitford 1991). Seller, on the other hand, argues from a very different position. She begins with a criticism using feminist insights, but goes on to widen the focus to include other manifestations of oppression. She argues for a democratic epistemology: knowledge based in communities of resistance, in which attention must be paid to every individual's subjective experience (Seller 1988). Other examples of feminist epistemologies are provided by Donna Haraway and Sandra Harding, who disagree over post-modernism. Haraway, as a post-modernist, embraces particularity and difference (Haraway 1991). Harding, arguing against post-modern fragmentation, proposes a stand-point epistemology in which it is acknowledged that all knowledge has social causes, related to gender, race, sexuality, etc., which can be taken into account when dividing beliefs 'into the false and probably less false' (Harding 1991: 8.).

Despite the depth of disagreement in the feminist epistemologies, there is a thread running through all of them. They all emphasize the subjective consciousness or the self of an individual. None of the feminist epistemologies assume or argue that the perspective of individual human beings can be superseded by the 'objective view from nowhere' or by a 'God's eye view'. All of them assume that the self or subjectivity is a starting point – though almost all of them go on, quickly, to point out that individual 'experience', 'perspectives', 'consciousness' or 'position in a discourse' are only the first step in a collective enterprise of formulating a feminist perspective. Thus Irigaray argues for the necessity of fostering a female community in which to discover a feminine subjectivity, different from the one created by males. Seller's work explicitly starts with particular individuals in particular situations. Both Haraway's and Harding's epistemologies depend on taking individual perspectives and combining them, politically, into group perspectives.

The metaphor of a 'thread' indicates that the agreement is no more than thread-like: the differences are indeed significant. I have had to use the phrase 'self or subjectivity', although the terms are each used to mark the different traditions which give rise to them. Very roughly speaking, post-modernists are more likely to talk about 'subjectivity' than the 'self'.

There are two other connecting threads. One is power or politics, and the other is theory, abstraction or structure. The thread of 'power' appears because all feminist theory is predicted on the significance of power. Necessarily so, because feminism arises out of a concern with the oppression of women. The various epistemologies vary in how they take notice of power differences other than those of gender, especially differences of 'race', class and of the 'First/Third Worlds'.

The connecting thread of 'theory' is there because feminist theory must, logically, also be predicated on the importance of theorizing. As I stated earlier, all the epistemologies depend on the existence of a collective enterprise in which a collective perspective is formulated. There has to be collective enterprise – but who makes up the collective? Black and working-class women have drawn attention to the sheer variety of 'difference': gender, race, class, disability, First/Third world, and so forth. 'Women' are a diverse group of people. The same is true, for example, of black men or white, working-class people. Such fragmentation can continue almost indefinitely. Increasingly, there is a recognition that most people will not identify one hundred per cent with any group in which they find themselves. The answers are being sought in a celebration of hybridity, fluidity and impurity, and in the recognition of a network of languages relying on multilingual abilities in the population (Haraway 1991; Richardson 1991; Said 1993). Paradoxically, perhaps, the emphasis on political and group affiliations and their diversity has increased the importance of individual experience in improving knowledge and understanding for all.

To summarize, the epistemological lesson for everyone – both men and women – is that knowledge can be gained only if the following are included: the subjectivity and experiences of individuals and groups of individuals; power and politics; and a dialectic of theory with individual experiences. Therefore, knowledge can only be gained using a method which allows for reflection on experience, using theory, in a number of different group/political perspectives, which will bring that experience into question. This indicates a process of returning to old knowledge using the new perceptions and then using the result to rework the new perceptions.

In brief: for reliable knowledge to be gained, a method needs to include (1) individual experience; (2) theory; (3) time for a process of reflection and rethinking; and (4) the perspectives of various groups chosen on political grounds.

Critical autobiography

Autobiography is a good candidate for a method which conforms to the principles for gaining reliable knowledge. Not only does it focus on individual experience, but also it is possible to apply the other principles. Therefore, it should be possible for autobiography to be a good source of knowledge for the teller and for the listeners.

At this stage, I need to say something about the concept of autobiography. We, in the West at least, share an idea of autobiography. It is not always realized how specific the idea is to our time and culture. It is likely that someone asked to use 'autobiography' will assume that the result should be personal, confessional, individualistic, atheoretical and non-political. They would, in fact, produce exactly the kind of writing which is not so useful in the production of knowledge. However, there are other forms of autobiography. For instance, autobiographical writing can be expressly political, as in the autobiographies of freed slaves in the USA, or in the 'Testimonies' currently being written by South Americans struggling against oppressive regimes.

It is the argument of this chapter that an autobiography will add to reliable knowledge if it makes use of individual experience, theory, and a process of reflection and rethinking, which includes attention to politically situated perspectives. This is a 'critical autobiography'. Autobiography as simple narrative is just a first stage, and of only limited use, for the purposes of gaining knowledge.

Individual experience. A situation is described from the perspective of the writer. This contrasts with the description of a situation as an 'objective account of reality'. Note, however, that individual experience need not be confessional or focused on the author's feelings (though it may be).

Theory. Theory may be reinterpreted in the light of experience, and experience in the light of theory. Examples are Walkerdine's (1990) exploration of educational and psychological theory in a series of articles, and Jackson's (1990) discussion of masculinity in the light of his remembered life, including his career as an English teacher. Each of these examples use autobiographical writing to aid in the reinterpretation of theory in light of experience and experience in light of theory.

Time for a process of reflection and rethinking. In a non-theoretical autobiography, time may just appear as the linearity of the narrative. However, a process of reflection and rethinking will undermine such linearity. In a single piece of theoretical work, the passage of time, and its effect on the understanding and theorizing of the experience, needs to be exhibited.

Perspectives of gender, race and class. Very often these perspectives are implicit. This makes the work of use but only of limited use. Gender, race and class should be organizing categories. In the critical autobiographies mentioned, Walkerdine and Jackson discuss both gender and class. Their construction of their own gender and class is part of their own experience, and it appears as part of the theorizing.

Examples of critical autobiography in our research

I have defined criteria for a critical autobiography. In this section, I give examples from the journals that I have kept as part of the process of our action research.

The action research has been continuing for three years, in an inner-city primary school which I chose for its social and ethnic mix, as well as for its long-term commitment to equal opportunities. I work together with Carol Davies, who is a highly experienced and competent class teacher. I have visited the school regularly over three years, staying for at least half a morning each time. When I return to the university where I teach I write the journal, and send it to Carol. She has also been keeping a journal, which I read from time to time.

The result of the collaboration has been a series of action research cycles of equal opportunities in the classroom. When we began, the focus was on groupwork, but it swiftly moved to 'learning to learn, individually and as groups'. The second year we started with a focus on 'support and challenge'. This developed into a focus on 'pressure', after a discussion with the children. In the third year, it became a focus on 'teacher effectiveness as a facilitator of children's learning'. All three projects involved the children in reflecting on their own learning strategies. A feature of the project has been the way that we have involved the children in formulating the research questions, in observations, and in evaluation and action plans. It may be necessary to reiterate here that this chapter is not a description of our research. The journals were just one strand in a process that also included the use of observation schedules, field notes, video, tape-recordings and questionnaires. Descriptions of different stages of the research can be found in Davies and Griffiths and Davies (1993).[2]

Individual experience

For a piece of work to count as a critical autobiography, the individual experience has to be there. This means a personal view, but it does not have to be confessional or about emotions. For instance, this entry is very much my own experience of a classroom activity:

(a) An afternoon spent mostly helping the children fill in the 'all about me' forms for their records ...

The question about friends, together with 'What makes me sad?', was very interesting for me, because it allowed me to ask questions of the kind that would usually be difficult to approach, e.g. about bullying. One set of children I asked were A, P and J, all of whom seem to be rather on the fringe of friendship groups at the moment; 'Everyone gets bullied' was their thought (expressed by P with agreement). They were unable to say whether everyone was a bully or whether it was just a small group of people. They immediately volunteered the names of bullies though, including N and T (with the evidence that T was in his socks, for kicking). I also spoke to S and K [who are best friends]. S said he didn't like being called names. On being asked 'Why?' (a difficult question for anyone to answer!), he said he didn't like being called a Welsh rabbit. He's proud of being Welsh, but clearly thought he was being 'racialized' (to use Elinor Kelly's term, from the Day Conference, last Saturday). K was indignant when S suggested he used the term, agreeing that he said 'rabbit' but *not* 'Welsh rabbit'.

This next entry was made after a class discussion about the action-research project. Again, it is very much my own perspective, rather than an 'objective account'. The children had been asked to think of action plans:

(b) The discussion was much better than I thought it was going to be. I thought it was going to die the death at first, especially given the degree of wriggling in some quarters, not to mention the presence of a number of children who had not been in on the project at the start (I, D [new children in class], Class C's [children whose teacher was absent]). It's encouraging that they are still so involved.

I notice that we may again [i.e. like last year's project] get stuck at class strategies for distributing rubbers and sharpeners rather than moving on to *individual* needs to improve learning. Though this may be a kind of precondition. For instance, they may need to feel they have made a concrete difference to the conditions of the classroom, in order to trust the processes of the project at all. And they may not be able to get on with *individual* needs if some of the *class* problems are not dealt with. I do realize that some of the children are dealing with individual needs, as you say in your write-up, but this is still very unsystematic, I think.

Theory

Theory can be seen entering in (a) above, in the mention of Elinor Kelly's theorizing of harassment and bullying. Theory also appears as a way of thinking about the curriculum of the classroom:

(c) One of the dilemmas that this topic [surrounding a visit to Warwick Castle] illustrated very well for me is one that is important for the future of multicultural/cultural diversity/anti-racism debates. It is the dilemma between: (a) multicultural (etc.) teaching as a *common culture* for all children being educated in this country (in rural Nottinghamshire as well as inner-city Nottingham, for instance), and (b) multicultural (etc.) teaching as a way of making sure that children can relate to the education they are being offered – that it does not require them to forget who they are at home – an *acknowledgement of self*.

I was conscious that when the children are asked to go back in time, only the ones with white parents would imagine that it was their own great, great, grandparents that they might encounter. For the Asian ones, they were being asked to go back in time, keeping the place the same. Fair enough, but it's a different exercise. And for anyone with mixed parentage (most of us?), only parts of the parentage are acknowledged. This was made more obvious because of the initial exercise in which they asked their own older family members to reminisce, which was, I thought, a very valuable introduction to a historical topic.

Would the Anglo school children in rural Nottinghamshire be asked to fly back in time, ever, to a place where everyone looked different, and they had no relatives? Well, yes, in themes of 'Romans', or 'Plains Indians' perhaps. But it would not be an analogous exercise, unless they could feel in some way that the exercise was to do with their own British culture.

Time for a process of reflection and rethinking

The process of reflection and rethinking can be seen in (c), where I am making connections and rethinking my views on the meaning of multiculturalism. The entry continued with reflections about gender and class.

(d) Imagining that you are anyone who counts in history tends to mean imagining you are a boy ...

[The children had been designing shields for themselves] I remembered how much I had enjoyed them as a child. I became very knowledgeable about them – knowledge which has since melted away. But this raises all the social class issues. Did it do me any good to imagine that I was part of the ruling class, rather than the peasantry (where my own family must have come from)? On the other hand, part of the pleasure of history is imagining yourself to be very different people, and for me, part of the pleasure of places like Warwick Castle is exactly that ordinary people are no longer excluded from the beauty and riches of such a place, including all those beautiful heraldic symbols. Ordinary people need access to all the curriculum of the rich as well as at the same time redefining what is important. Back to the dilemma I started with! [in c]

In noting how the particular excerpt illustrates reflection and rethinking about equal opportunities issues, it is important to note also that equal opportunities is a central question of the action research as a whole. The journal is providing a chance to return to this question over time. Over the three years of the project, this theme recurs, as do the other emergent themes of learning to learn, support, pressure and children's participation in research.

Perspectives of gender, race and class

Perspectives of gender, race and social class have been taken into account all through the journal, partly just because of the focus on equal opportunities. This is clear from the excerpts above. Early on in the project, it was apparent that the children would not fall into neat categories by gender, race or social class. During the project, we have taken care to listen to individual voices, and also to the voices of various groupings of gender, race, social class, ability, friendship, etc., in the class. These groupings are shifting: individual children belonged to now one, now another. We noted how some children apparently chose their own gender, 'race' and social class identities, which were not necessarily the ones expected by 'objective' measures. For instance, some children chose to sit with others of the same race, gender and social class, but these factors were not equally salient for all the children. Since political categories depend on the interaction of self- and other identifications (Griffiths 1992), gender, race and social class were used to question the evidence rather than as hard and fast categories.

The journal includes some reference to my own social position. This is clear in (d). However, such references are rare. It is difficult to see one's own perspective: this is exactly why we need research based on auto-biographical writing. In so far as I can make my own social position clear, the partiality of my perspective can be taken into account. But how to do that is a question that I have not resolved. Blanket statements about my own social class, race and gender are probably not helpful. If children do not fall into neat categories, why should adult researchers?

Conclusion

Autobiographical writing is often thought to be subjective, anecdotal or descriptive, in comparison with other research methods, such as question-naires or observation schedules. The argument of this chapter shows such a view to be mistaken. In writing the chapter, I have shown that, like other research methods, autobiographical writing can be done well or badly. In order for it to be valid and rigorous, it has to meet the criteria for reliable methods of gaining knowledge.

Autobiographical writing is demanding and can be painful. It is also a pleasure to write – and to read. Action research, likewise, is both deman-ding, painful and also a pleasure, both to do and to hear. The personal story is central to both. Learning from the stories of others is, I argue, an excellent way of improving one's own vision and practices.

Notes

1 A more detailed version of the argument can be found in Griffiths (1993).
2 The research has also been used and disseminated in a number of other ways, too. Our professional concerns, like our particular strengths, are different. I regularly use aspects of the project in my teaching at the university, as well as integrating it into other parts of my research work. Together, we have both given talks to other groups of teachers, country wide. An equal relationship has been built up by recognizing our different professional needs and concerns.

References

Carr, W. and Kemmis, S. (1986) *Becoming Critical: Education, Knowledge and Action Research*. Lewes: Falmer Press.
Davies, C. (1994) 'Twenty-eight children, five adults and no chairs'. *Education 3–13*. (Spring), 41–8.
Elliott, J. (1991) *Action Research for Educational Change*. Milton Keynes: Open University Press.
Griffiths, M. (1990) Action research: Grassroots practice or management tool? in Lomax, P. (Ed.), *Managing Staff Development in Schools: An Action Research Approach*. Clevedon: Multilingual Matters.
Griffiths, M. (1992) *Self-identity, Self-esteem and Social Justice*. Nottingham: Nottingham University, Education Publications.

Griffiths, M. (1993) Auto/biography and epistemology. *Philosophy of Education Conference Papers*, New College, Oxford.

Griffiths, M. and Davies, C. (1993) 'Learning to learn'. *British Educational Research Journal*, 19(1), 43–58.

Harding, S. (1991) *Whose Science? Whose Knowledge?* Milton Keynes: Open University Press.

Haraway, D. (1991) *Simians, Cyborgs and Women: The Reinvention of Nature.* London: Free Association Books.

Jackson, D. (1990) *Unmasking Masculinity: A Critical Autobiography.* London: Unwin Hyman.

Pollard, A. and Tann, S. (1987) *Reflective Teaching in the Primary School.* London: Cassell.

Richardson, R. (1991) 'Empowerment, access and the legal framework'. *Multicultural Teaching* 10(1), 5–9.

Said, E. (1993) *Culture and Imperialism.* London: Chatto and Windus.

Seller, A. (1988) Realism versus relativism: Towards a politically adequate epistemology, in Griffiths, M. and Whitford, M. (Eds), *Feminist Perspectives in Philosophy.* London: Macmillan.

Seller, A. (1994) 'Whose knowledge? Whose post-modernism?' *Women's Philosophy Review*, 11, 41–53.

Walkerdine, V. (1990) *Schoolgirl Fictions.* London: Verso.

Weiner, G. (1989) 'Professional self-knowledge versus social justice: A critical analysis of the teacher-researcher movement'. *British Educational Research Journal* 15(1), 41–51.

Whitford, M. (1991) *Irigaray: Philosophy in the Feminine.* London: Routledge.

Whitehead, Jack (1989) 'Creating a living educational theory from questions of the kind 'How do I improve my practice?' ' *Cambridge Journal of Education* 19, 41–52.

Zeichner, K.M. (1992) 'Action research: Personal renewal and social reconstruction'. Keynote address to the *International Conference of the Classroom Action Research Network*, Worcester College, September.

Zeichner, K. and Teitelbaum, K. (1982) 'Personalized and inquiry–oriented teacher education'. *Journal of Education for Teaching* 8(2), 95–117.

7

Making the private public

Waltraud Boxall

If you think till it hurts
    you can almost do it without getting off that chair,
scare yourself
within an inch of the heart
at the prompt of a word.
How old are you now?
This is what happens –

(Duffy 1993)

Popularity of journal writing

In recent times, journal or diary writing has gained increasing popularity
with teacher-educators (Holly 1984). It is a tool for encouraging student
teachers into a culture of self-critical appraisal. It can generate views of
teaching and learning that transcend the mundane. If this happens early
enough, it might help to deconstruct views of teaching and learning as a
set of illusionary practices or, indeed, as practices marked by false consciousness (Engels, in Russell 1981). As a resource, the diary provides the
ground on which private and public experiences interact and where theories
of schooling are likely to confront principles of education (Hamilton 1989).
The constant pull between the two provokes a desire to comprehend
the social world of the classroom as an expression of its interplay with
the world outside: 'Through the reflective acts of talking and writing
about what they think happened, teachers can become more consciously
aware of why children, and they themselves, do the things they do' (Nixon
1981: 60).

Education, experience, training and contradictions

When reflecting, in the mid-1980s on the nature of students' feedback to the primary PGCE course they had just completed, I, the novice teacher-educator, was struck by the inherent contradictions of their experiences. The intensity of the contradictions these newly qualified teachers saw in action and had witnessed being practised in classrooms and seminar rooms, resonated in my own memories of primary schools.

At the time, seemingly natural contradictions between the theory and practice of education occupied a substantive space in the public debate, adding little but endarkenment. Student teachers, whose starting position for teaching in the primary school was comparable with the war cry of a defenceless, yet determined crowd not to surrender, were sooner or later to transform into the vitriolic losers also. It seemed pressing, therefore, to find a way that could avoid the inevitable paralysis which the persistent experience of contradiction forces.

Keeping a diary during the year the students were on course offered these possibilities. Though not a solution to the contradictions themselves, writing a diary or a journal while preparing for institutional life was to help clarify what neither talking nor thinking alone could do (Wilkinson 1986).

Diary and informal assessment

The intention was to use the diary for informal assessment during the PGCE year. Being pragmatic as well as pedagogic, the diary was to provide the source that could be consulted and used for formally assessed assignments such as the Child Study. Furthermore, it was to enable the student teacher to make sense of the primary classroom through recorded observations.

A strong sense of the private dominated the character of this important first-hand bank of thoughts, feelings and reflections about schools. If the diary was the tool to facilitate and generate informed action despite the constant experience of contradiction, it could not be exposed to public scrutiny. To help illuminate what students encountered in schools, they needed to filter what they saw through their own histories. The act of writing for no other audience but themselves was to encourage reflection on the political and historic nature of teaching, not least through a realization of their own shifts in thinking from the beginning to the end of the PGCE year. The cognitive processes stimulated through this intimate exploration of the social world around them were, at the time, envisaged by me as an essential part of becoming a teacher (Kohl 1986).

Glimpses of the private

Maintaining a sense of self, an identity that had personal rather than institutional features, developing a voice, resisting bureaucratization, learning to live with and face up to the contingencies and incongruities of teaching and learning, constituted the rationale for the diary. The diary would act like a sieve through which assumptions and commonly held beliefs would be filtered. To stimulate intellectual development, I thought at the time, the assumptions and common beliefs that were evoked by what the students saw in classrooms, in staffrooms, in corridors and playgrounds, needed clearing out after having been confronted. The process was delineated by turning Vygotsky's (1962) development of social discourse to verbal self-expression on its head and 'outside-in' through writing.

Unwittingly, this process would be painful because it would help to uncover unmentionable sides of human interaction, not commonly accepted in any discourse, let alone an educational one, either spoken or written (Jung and Staehr 1989). It would reveal layers of realization of how the student is socialized into the role of the teacher and etch into the human landscape the experiences rendered by the transformation from being the learner to being the teacher (Walker and Adelman 1979). The dilemma I experienced over the private character of the diary I solved by signalling to students early in the year my wish to be offered on three occasions during the year some excerpts. These excerpts constituted the interactive element of an essentially private activity.

What I have been seeking for many years was a model for diary writing which, while maintaining its private character, was opened up occasionally to allow glimpses into the undergrowth of reflective thought. My agenda was, first of all, to attribute pedagogical importance to the diary and, second, to explore the potential for social discourse. For this reason, I asked for self-selected passages under the headings of 'moving moments' (1986–87), 'some contrasting classroom observations' (1987–88), 'entries from your diary' (1988–89. 1989–90, 1990–1), 'something on equal opportunities' and 'the imagination' (1991–92).

Presenting the task to students

Having set the scene at the beginning of the PGCE year by presenting students with a rationale for this informal, on-going self-assessment, I was keen to find out the students' responses to these. I was informed by a range of sources (Ashton-Warner 1958; Skilbeck 1970; Armstrong 1980; Galton 1980; Rowland 1984; Neill 1986) which I introduced to the students. These I had offered as exemplars. The educational remit set by them made explicit my expectations. The most significant text to help illuminate reflection was to become Dewey's (1970) *Analysis of Reflective Thinking*. It was used to help explicate the theoretical cornerstones for learning to reflect on teaching. Diary writing I theorized implicitly through the previously mentioned examples. Accompanying this was a simplified outline of a chronology. It plotted the process of becoming reflective through several significant phases.[1]

The exemplars offered to students together with the chronology did not in themselves stir much obvious public debate or controversy, although it failed, not surprisingly, to convince everybody of the validity of the exercise. Since there appeared to exist no institutionally enshrined check-up for the diary, it would have little appeal to those students less inclined to critical self-analysis in addition to formally set and assessed assignments. However, the dialogue I had hoped for has received its initial momentum with more than half of the student body each year, and could even be maintained beyond the year with a few for whom diary writing became an essential vehicle for their self-realization as teachers.

It was, of course, not a conventional dialogue. Its nature was distinguished by students adjusting to a form of analysis ostensibly leading to reflective, critical and illuminative insights and actions through their own writing without any didactic or exploratory intervention on my part. My voice was subdued. The part I played in the dialogue was informed by my intentions to foster subjectivity and the imaginary, not objectivity and the regulatory. Unlike the conventional academic essay, the diary was unencumbered by obligatory reference to text. What was asked for was, in fact, an acknowledgment of the students' experiences of teaching and learning with authentic openness and frankness to themselves.

Suggesting any type of grading the diary excerpts would have been absurd. The only educationally acceptable form of response to this form of self-critical expression can only be non-judgemental in character. The dialogue offers this facility.

The motivating force for my commitment to see students develop a more honest and personally significant perspective of teaching and learning, was deeply interwoven with my own biography. As a German, born a month before the end of the Second World War, 'under the hail of bombs' as my mother used to tell me, I had been more than troubled throughout my adolescence by the historic events that led to German fascism. Its maintenance for twelve years gave sufficient cause for suspecting authority mediated through whatever institution. The desperate search for answers to the pounding questions gnawing at my conscience in the mid-1950s had kept me awake. Even now, after several decades of an attempted unravelling of a period in history from which I could not escape, I was dissatisfied with many of the explanations I had come across. My frustration had been deepened by reading the educational literature when being a student at a college of education in the mid-1960s myself. Many of the texts I had come across, inevitably, had unpalatable associations (Wilhelm 1967). These could often easily be detected underneath the thin veneer that covered up the exact detail of an author's professional involvement during the twelve years of Hitler fascism. When looking back now, I realize that few theories were capable of sustaining credibility *vis-à-vis* a tensely suspicious section in the young post-war generation.

The chilly climate of social, political and cultural scepticism began to heat up when the Frankfurter Schule started to disseminate Adorno, Horkheimer, Marcuse, Habermas and many others. Likewise, the Sigmund-Freud-Institut, also in Frankfurt, began to publish crucial writings (Mitscherlich 1963; Mitscherlich and Mitscherlich 1967). Critical theory as well as psychoanalysis offered new perspectives to comprehend the incomprehensible. The social sciences thus contributed to a reassessment of educational theories which, in turn, would have the potential to influence educational practices.

At this juncture, I became acutely aware of teachers as instrumental in bringing about a transformation which follows critical theory through to the everyday existence they share with pupils in classrooms. This process is otherwise known as praxis. Praxis always interfaces institutional with personal experiences. What I understood to have happened to teachers under the tyranny of national socialist ideology was a paralysis of conscience only possible in circumstances where reflection and critical interpretation, vital ingredients of all educative processes, were overtaken by the dogmatic and inhuman pursuit of the 'master race'. If this could happen once, it might happen again (Horn 1966).

One possible approach to challenging the social control function of school, I reasoned, was to imbue the student with a sense of urgency for questioning all social processes in action. The texts which had informed me suggested a more open exposure of subjective experiences. Without acknowledging deeply moving and disturbing events which took place in the professional sphere, students would neither learn to understand their personal significance, nor would they be in a position to relate these centrally to the growth of their own professional identity as teachers. This avoidance of significant acts would seriously impoverish their interactive repertoire with learners and ultimately blunt their teaching sensitivities.

Once this process had begun, their personal integrity was in danger of being sacrificed for the sake of an erroneously labelled quiet life. Writing these experiences down, however, the student would see new possibilities for human interaction arise through an intensive inner monologue. Like all inner monologues with a consequence, private thoughts and feelings need to be aired occasionally so as to avoid the ill-effects of internally locked-up coping strategies (Woods and Hammersley 1977).

In the examples that follow, I want to demonstrate the close links between thought and actions following on from reflecting on particularly disturbing experiences. These experiences, had they not been recorded by the students, might well have been drowned in the multitude of events thrown up each day in any classroom and then left to smoulder, their significance lost, the energy of their rage dissipating through the quicksand of memory. Being ploughed back unrecorded into an unreflected and instinctive subterrain, they might have prevented what appear to be illuminating insights. Even if the indications of subsequent actions are limited to simply sharing previously private notes, they suggest a number of encouraging motives.

Each example illustrates the intricacies of the social world of the classroom for the student teacher. They share in a desire for life outside the Weberian 'iron cage'. Furthermore, they signal a gradual realization on the part of the students of the range of sensibilities necessary to unlock such values from their assumed biographical fixtures (Goodson 1992: 241). Yet they make no secret of the difficulties of overcoming or, indeed, solving the outlined problems. This in itself is exemplary, since so much of teacher discourse reflects simplistic interpretations and would-be answers to the multidimensional tensions brought about constantly by teaching and learning (Bullough *et al.* 1991). They also touch on the ambivalence created by the fact that teaching is 'emotionally infused' (Liston and Zeichner 1990: 618), and therefore has consequences that emphasize the tension between private and public dimensions of teachers' work. The examples also suggest a need for an early orientation of teaching that facilitates a connection and constant interchange between its private and public dimensions.

Examples from diaries

Example 1: 1986 (female)

A great thing happened today – Richard and Gary constructed a tower out of blocks and cardboard cartons which was taller than Ms Z. I really felt that some of the children had actually learnt that it is easier to build with cuboids than with tubes or cylinders.

I am not really happy how things are going. I feel the days are so hectic. I haven't time to sit back and think what individuals need, and whether I am teaching according to my principles, e.g. today when Richard and Gary built their tower the girls in the group were rather left out – they were trying to build with cylinders. If I'd done it the other way round, I might have had the chance to swop – as it was, we decided to leave the tower up.

Example 2: 1987 (female)

Second visit to … I was really shocked to see the headmistress grab hold of a little five-year-old boy and really shake him quite violently while shrieking at him (she really reminds me of a witch). The poor little thing was sobbing his heart out. I don't know what he was being told off for but whatever it was I think she went over the top in reprimanding him. I'm hardly in a position to tell her, though!!

I feel convinced that the headmistress does not like the children one bit. She really reminds me of the wicked witch in Hansel and Gretel. Every morning in assembly she amazes me by how nasty she can be to the kids. One morning she pulled a little four-year-old boy out to the front in order to tell him off and she made him stand on a bench in front of the rest of the school in order to thoroughly humiliate him. Me and Ingrid were giving each other looks; my teacher obviously noticed, because when we got back to the class she began to explain how although it might have looked rather cruel, it was for his own good. I was speechless.

Example 3: 1990 (female)

This entry in my diary is very difficult to write. That's because it's of something I'd rather forget, let alone record for posterity.

Anyone that knows me will know that if I am writing about something horrific it can only be about one subject – art! However, I do think it's important to record good and bad in this journal, otherwise it isn't really of much use.

Unlike the last art lesson, I went into this one feeling quite positive. I was surprised in our last session at what I could actually achieve. So, I was prepared to give it 100%.

Everything started off quite well, drawing holding forms in our art diaries. We were drawing in pencil, so that was o.k. Then we went into painting with poster paints. My idea was not exactly inspired as some were, but that didn't really worry me, as I thought it was probably a good idea to keep it simple.

The problem started when the painting began. My picture emerged as the most hideous piece of art work I have ever seen. Everyone else seemed to think I was dabbling, but I tried, my God, did I try. I don't know if it's because I am colour blind or what, but I really have absolutely no perception of colour whatsoever. It seemed that the harder I tried, the worse it got. It was the most hideous experience I can ever remember.

After a while I started to get really upset. This just sounds so absurd, but tears were just rolling down my checks. This is so embarassing to admit – a 22-year-old crying over a painting. While I'm writing this now, it's happening again. Luckily no-one around me seemed to notice or if they did they had the decency to not say anything!

After a while I decided to give it another go, unfortunately without success. Things were now getting really bad. J. gave me bits of advice, but I don't really think she appreciated how bad I felt or how hard I was trying.

The lesson always concludes with a critical session, i.e. all the class having a good laugh at my picture. I knew this was coming so I gave it one last big effort. However, by now it was getting worse. In my mind I was thinking of all the excuses I could use that would get me out of the end of the lesson. The obvious one was what I wanted to do, screw up my picture, throw it in the bin and run out of the room in tears. I also considered a well timed trip to the loo, everything went through my mind! This sounds so pathetic when I write it down now, but at the time all of these seemed viable options.

In the end, I decided to brave it. I sat as far away from my picture as I could. I was hideously embarassed, but at least I hadn't chickened out.

I left the lesson in a foul mood. I couldn't even bear to talk to anyone. By now I felt angry more than anything.

So what lessons can I learn from today? This account of today probably sounds overdramatic, but I can assure you it is not. If anything, I have played it down. Now, I can really appreciate why children play truant from school. If a child had produced as little work as I did today, it could have been treated very insensitively. What reason has that child got to go to school? When I am teaching my own class, please let no child in my class feel as wretched as I did today.

This is probably one of the most important things I will learn all year – I won't forget it in a hurry either.

Example 4: 1990 (female)

'We want teachers who are risk-takers' [external examiner]. My first reaction was to whole-heartedly agree with this, but when I thought about it, I am filled with worry – have I got the courage? Have I got the ideas? What risks am I prepared to take?

Had shared reading when we read *Peace at Last*. The children had already read it, but that helped. We went in the library area for drama. Ms M. was there, so I took them into the playground. Felt quite daring, but it worked well and the children were pretty good as it was a treat to them.

Example 5: 1991 (female)

Maths again – children receptive but I was not pleased with the lesson – a bit aimless.

A wet playtime/lunch break followed by my first language group session – it was hell!! Sheer torture – in and out to the toilet they trotted, they pinched, they shoved, they glared and they snarled!! But the other half of the group were totally opposite : responsive, interested, contributing to discussion, wanting to take it further, borrowed my books after lesson. I really need to talk to J. about this – how do I evaluate a lesson that works badly for some and so well for others?

I feel very despondent today – I came in to teach and 90% of a teacher's time appears to be taken up by chastising and 10% is content. Some of the staff don't seem to like children very much – they all seem to be constantly nagging, yelling, belittling the children. I must add that my class teacher is much better than the rest, but my observation school was nothing like this.

Example 6: 1991 (anonymous)

I am beginning to appreciate the journal as a way of ordering my thoughts now that I have, so to speak, jumped in at the deep end. I have taken the whole class for language and dance. I have attempted to start learning and develop a 'class voice'. I do have a long way to go, I realize that, but I wish the class teacher could offer more encouragement.

I have been experimenting with different ways of organizing the groups for doing practical maths sessions with water as they are doing capacity. The first session with the Butterflies and Ants, I asked them to write in pairs guessing and measuring while other groups used conticubes and work cards. Most of the children on the Ants table seem to need one-to-one attention.

I tried it a little differently the next session with Beetles and Moths. I sat with the group using the language related to capacity, e.g. 'more than', 'less than'. They were asked to choose containers sensible in relation to larger containers when they actually were measuring. I asked someone to demonstrate the concept of a full cup and a half-full cup. I felt this form of organizing worked best.

The song I picked for the children to listen to and sing today was 'My Grandfather's Clock', which fits in with the topic of measurement. Before the children went home, I showed the children some of the other children's art work which had been done that day.

Example 7: 1992 (female)

There is a girl in my class, very developed for her age, who constantly delights in 'winding me up' and seems to enjoy insulting me. She approached me obliquely today and almost inaudibly called me 'dragon breath'. Since this was only my first visit I thought it wiser to pretend I hadn't heard her. I thought a confrontation at this stage unwise. But I decided I would monitor her behaviour towards me throughout the day. This way we both got a chance to get used to each other, 'suss' each other out. I subsequently noticed that the insults stopped, her tactics changed to ones designed for a different kind of wind up, She now leads me on with a deliberate lie masquerading as a truth, e.g. 'it's my birthday today'. When the ensuing conversation had lost its amusement for her and when she was convinced that I was convinced that it was in fact her birthday, she disclosed the truth in a sort of 'April fools' fashion. She had scored and this seemed very important to her.

The burdens children bring to school with them are distressing, alarming and difficult to comprehend. Many of them are from homes suffering all the ill-effects of unemployment in a moribund society and in a climate which nurtures and rewards the less attractive aspects of human activity. Poverty, bad housing, lack of facilities, decaying urban areas, broken families, on-the-streets prostitution, drug-dealing, abuse, racism – this, it seems, is most children's realities. The only time when some children are happy is when they come to school. It is so important that the school provides a secure and caring environment for children in order to ameliorate at least some of the debilitating effects their social conditions have imposed upon their young shoulders.

A little girl, who I shall call 'W.', has, I was told, been badly sexually abused. She shows no outward sign of this experience which the teacher expected she would. She is quiet, pleasant and cooperative, not withdrawn or introverted, nor is she pushy or aggressive. She had no problem relating to me nor in making the first move. As I worked with her neighbour encouraging her to make her own story, W. began to show an interest in what we were doing. She eventually asked me if I could help her make a story. I worked with her and while she was eager to produce something of her own, she lifted storyline and character line for line from *My Little Pony*. With some guidance and coaxing I got her to relate her own story to me and I wrote down the main points of her story to show her that what she had said was, in fact, a real story. It took her a long time to accept the idea that she was capable of real storytelling, but in the end I believe she did. We both worked diligently putting her story into a more detailed form. Later she decided to illustrate it. She looked very pleased with herself. I, too, was delighted.

Example 8: 1992 (female)

I had my first taste of racism today. While I was on playground duty, an Asian boy from another class was complaining about another boy (white) who called him a 'black git' every day. I feel so inadequate when dealing with a situation like this, my immediate reaction is to be angry and emotional and upset, but I would be much more useful if I could respond in a sensitive, calm and quiet way. Why it is wrong to judge people by their ethnicity and skin colour ... I find it really difficult to explain because I felt that even though young children have a racial awareness that discrimination and racism is an adult thing and I just don't feel competent or able to explain to a group of children from all backgrounds why some of them may be subject to racial taunts. Maybe I've got it all wrong, but racial awareness is one thing, putting it into practice is another. Anyway, I told the other teacher on duty hoping to see how she would deal with it. I made a reprimand to the boy but I felt that was totally inadequate. However, the two boys were taken inside and spoken to. Apparently, there is a procedure for situations like this and the comments are usually made a note of and the parents informed. But, once again, this procedure was not undertaken (as in the L8 school). I mean, maybe it is thought that it was not of enough gravity to make a note of. But why have a specific procedure if it's not to be followed? Not to follow the procedure to me seems to belittle the actual offensive thing done in the first place.

Example 9 (one letter, two extracts): 1992 (female)

Dear Waltraud, I enclose a page from my journal. It is pertinent to multicultural education although it may not appear so.

The incident that upset me occurred when I found myself using the teacher's form of discipline, which was to threaten children with black badges. I knew that it was wrong and yet faced with a difficult lesson and a problem of control that's what I did. The children that had black badges from me were Chinese and Iranian! The next day neither came back with them on, although the teacher had told them to (and six other children that she had disciplined). The Iranian child said (to his credit) that his mum had thought it was rubbish and thrown it away, and the teacher (to her credit) told all the other children to take theirs off.

As a result of this incident, I spoke to the headmistress two days later and explained what had happened and why I felt so upset; she was very sympathetic. I never felt confident enough to say anything directly to the classteacher. The headteacher said that I would develop my own style of control and was encouraging when I spoke about positive rather than negative control. The incident was not mentioned again, so I never knew whether she spoke to the classteacher; however, I didn't hear black badges mentioned again.

I thought this morning's lesson was OK, not brilliant, but OK. I wish Ms K. would be directly encouraging and tell me that she thinks I'm going to make it because I am seriously doubting that I will.

I got so upset at tea-time that the family sent me to see Felicity to talk it through with someone in the same boat. Sometimes I am having difficulty with the content and that creates a lot of difficulty with control and things can go from bad to worse. These children seem to respond to being shouted at as a kerb to their nuisance behaviour, and so being used to that it is difficult to do different and be effective. I'm still feeling incredibly guilty about what happened yesterday that I really can't commit to paper but which I had told Felicity about which helped a little. It would be a very big risk to talk about it at school, partly because I should have said something about it before, and I shouldn't have anything to do with it if I really believed that it was wrong, which I do. I also can't trust myself not to be upset; I wish I could get really angry instead of dissolving into tears, feeling weak and vulnerable. Supervisor is in tomorrow that I hope that PE goes OK but in the frame of mind I'm in I won't be surprised if I go to pieces.

My supervisor saw a very difficult PE lesson and talked it over with me afterwards. I knew it was going wrong and did try to pull it together. I know now that I should have gauged what the children wanted and done something that they enjoyed, instead of going back to something that was beginning to be resented last time.

I managed to pluck up courage to speak to the headmistress about what was bothering me and she was very understanding and reassuring. I hope that I will have more time with the children on timetable next week and pretend to be the classteacher. Which means that there will be lots of marking as well as preparation. Popped back to see Felicity but she wasn't there so she came up to see me. What it is to have a friend. I have been so selfish over the last few months, needing so much time for myself and studying. The children (mine) have been really great; lots of cuddles and positive strokes and a bit less disagreement since they realized on Wednesday how overwrought I am. Wondering how I am going to cope as a real teacher.

The extracts presented here are intended to illustrate the kaleidoscopic character of experience student teachers have of teaching and learning. If challenged to think about classrooms as they have known them in the light of new options, the process accompanying reflective thought might, indeed, accelerate different forms of action and interaction. This process, however, is slow and its maintenance depends upon the uninterrupted freeflow between privately lived facts and their interpretations in a social context (see footnote 1).

Making sense of contradictions

The phases characterizing the process suggest how to make sense of chaotic, oppressive, perplexing, troubling or confusing circumstances, without being seduced to accommodate them. They also implicitly emphasize a need for patience. Dewey makes the following observations:

> The five phases, terminals, or functions of thought, that we have noted do not follow one another in a set order. On the contrary, each step in genuine thinking does something to perfect the formation of a suggestion and promote its change into a leading idea or direct hypothesis. It does something to promote the location and definition of the problem. Each improvement in the idea leads to new observations that yield new facts already at hand or data and help the mind judge more accurately the relevancy of facts already at hand.
>
> (in Skilbeck 1970; 79)

Teaching is at all times asking for judgements to be made. The student on teaching practice encounters circumstances where taken-for-granted beliefs and values may be rocked into shattering insecurity. Discriminatory, oppressive, anti-democratic practices continue to find their expression in today's classrooms, staffrooms, corridors and playgrounds. They are more likely to persist as contaminating elements of human interaction if they are left to roam in the known, unquestioned and unchallenged. Pondering on such experiences as facts, the student is provided with the possibility to envisage right and wrong, good and bad classroom practices through 'the arts of the practical' (Holt 1987). This, inevitably, will take time and occupy spaces beyond the overtly practical. It will be messy because it brings together a multitude of histories, none of which is easily ordered, let alone categorized. The diary offers such a space, as does the dialogue arising from its reflected facts.

Instead of falling, like so many before them, into unreflected passivity, students who find themselves squeezed into narrow intellectual worlds imposed by educational institutions, may break through these and open up new areas in institutional landscapes once they are teachers themselves, willing and capable of transforming uncreative and inhuman social practices.

Acknowledgements

A version of this chapter was presented at the British Educational Research Association's Annual Conference at Stirling University, September 1992. Primary PGCE students are asked each year to select passages from their diaries for the author for research purposes.

Note

1 The phases were given the following labels:
- Level of description
  Familiarization: Where am I? Who are the actors?
  What are they doing?
- Level of personal viewpoint
  Subjective response: I like what I see because . . .
- Level of critical analysis
  Objective reflection: Why do I like what I see? Is it because I know . . . or is it because of something else?
- Level of research
  Hypotheses: If my analysis is correct, what are the implications for me, the teacher?

References

Armstrong, M. (1980) *Closely Observed Children*. London: Readers and Writers.
Ashton-Warner, S. (1958) *Spinster*. London: Virago.
Bullough, R.V. Jr, Knowles, J.G. and Crow, N.A. (1991) *Emerging as a Teacher*. London: Routledge.
Dewey, J. (1970) Analysis of reflective thinking, in M. Skilbeck (Ed.) *Dewey*. London: Collier-Macmillan.
Duffy, C.A. (1993) *Mean Time*. London: Anvil Press Poetry.
Galton, M. (1980) *Inside the Primary Classroom*. London: Routledge and Kegan Paul.
Goodson, I.F. (Ed.) (1992) *Studying Teachers' Lives*. London: Routledge.
Hamilton, D. (1989) *Towards a Theory of Schooling*. Deakin Studies in Education Series No. 4. Lewes: Falmer Press.
Holly, M.L. (1984) *Keeping a Personal Journal*. Geelong, Victoria: Deakin University Press.

Holt, M. (1987) *Judgement, Planning and Educational Change*. London: Harper Education.

Horn, K. (1966) *Dressur oder erziehung*. Frankfurt am Main: Suhrkamp Verlag.

Jung, H.W. and Staehr, G.V. (1989) *Historische Friedensdidaktik – Konzepte und Modelle*. Hamburg: BRD.

Kohl, H. (1986) *On Becoming a Teacher*. London: Harper and Row.

Liston, D.P. and Zeichner, K.M. (1990) 'Teacher education and the social context of schooling: Issue for curriculum development'. *American Educational Research Journal* 27(4), 610–36.

Mitscherlich, A. (1963) *Auf dem Weg zur vaterlosen Gesellschaft*. Munich: Piper.

Mitscherlich, A. and Mitscherlich, M. (1967) *Die Unfähigkeit zu trauern*. Munich: Piper.

Neill, A.S. (1986) *A Dominie's Log*. London: Hogarth Press.

Nixon, J. (Ed.) (1981) *A Teacher's Guide to Action Research*. London: Grant McIntyre.

Rowland, S. (1984) *The Enquiring Classroom*. Lewes: Falmer Press.

Russell, J. (1981) *Marx Engels Dictionary*. Brighton: Harvester.

Skilbeck, M. (Ed.) (1970) *Dewey*. London: Collier-Macmillan.

Vygotsky, L.S. (1962) *Thought and Language*. Cambridge, MA: MIT Press.

Walker, R. and Adelman, C. (1979) *Classroom Observation*. London: Routledge.

Wilhelm, Th. (1967) *Pädagogik der Gegenwart*. Stuttgart: Alfred Kröner.

Wilkinson, A. (1986) *The Writing of Writing*. Milton Keynes: Open University Press.

Woods, P. and Hammersley, M. (Eds) (1977) *School Experience*. New York: St Martin's Press.

8
Crossing borders for professional development: narratives of exchange teachers

Ardra L. Cole and J. Gary Knowles

Introduction

In this chapter, we illustrate a role for narrative as a tool for reflection and enhanced personal and professional understandings. To do so, we draw on the narrative accounts of two teachers who joined us in a study of their experiences when they traded classrooms, schools, homes and countries for one academic year as part of an international educator exchange programme. The broad purposes of the study were to: gain insights into the different contexts and cultures of the school systems of Canada and Aotearoa New Zealand, from the perspectives of the two exchange teachers; explore, in general, the concept of international teacher exchange programmes as a professional development experience; and to understand, in particular, elements of the experiences of the two exchange teachers and how the exchange programme and the related activities influenced their professional development.

In our efforts to better understand the teachers' experiences and the educative nature of teacher exchange opportunities, we adopted a research method that we thought would 'come close' to apprehending and representing the richness of their exchange experiences. Thus, we took a narrative approach to understanding and representing the time the two teachers, Grace and Sue, spent in each other's school, home and country. Following others such as Beattie (1991), Connelly and Clandinin (1990) and Witherell and Noddings (1991), we believe that narrative, both as a process and a phenomenon, has a central role in personal and professional development. As Beattie (1991: 77) suggests: 'Narrative [can] be used to illuminate the ways in which we understand ourselves as teachers, appraise ourselves and our experiences and evoke and bring to life the meaning of those experiences'. Furthermore:

> Through telling, writing, reading, and listening to life stories – one's own and other's – those engaged in [the work of teaching, consulting and professional development] can penetrate cultural barriers, discover the power of the self and the integrity of the other, and deepen their understanding of their perspective histories and possibilities.
>
> (Witherell and Noddings 1991: 3–4)

We present the teachers' accounts of their experiences as extensive, uninterrupted narratives (reorganized and slightly edited by us) – a format that, we believe, captures some of the richness and detail of the year's experience, respects each teacher's individuality, and maintains the integrity of their voices. It was not our intention to conduct an intensive analysis of Grace's and Sue's narrative accounts of their experiences in each other's contexts. However, as we interacted with them and their texts we were struck by two things: the similarity of the topics they chose to write about, and how they responded to or made sense of their experiences within and outside the classroom. From readings of interview transcripts, we were able to pick up thematic strands from conversations which we then interwove with narrative threads from their journals. Our commentary, which follows the two narratives, reflects only some of the themes that emerged through our reading of the narrative texts.

A note on the teachers and our method

Grace is a single, Anglo-Canadian woman. Sue is married to Peter and has two daughters, Helen and Joanna, and is also of Anglo heritage. She is *Pakeha*, a Maori word describing white New Zealanders of non-Maori heritage, usually European (see King 1985). Both women are in their mid-thirties and have about the same amount of elementary (or primary, as it is called in Aotearoa New Zealand) school teaching experience behind them. Grace teaches in a rural school in Ontario, Canada and Sue in an urban school in Auckland, Aotearoa New Zealand. As part of an international teacher exchange programme, they traded places for one academic year. When we approached them, before the school year began, asking if we could 'observe' their experiences, they eagerly agreed to join us in a study of their experience of teacher exchange.

Because our research project involved participants separated by great distances and international boundaries, we had to rely on telephone and mail for some of our communications and information gathering. We conducted extensive face-to-face and telephone interviews (all of which were audio-taped and transcribed) with each teacher over the duration of their exchange: in-person interviews with Grace, the Canadian teacher, took place prior to her leaving Canada and also occurred in Aotearoa New Zealand; in-person interviews with Sue, the New Zealand teacher, all took place in Canada. The telephone interviews were shorter, limited by budgetary concerns. The interviews took the form of informal conversations between each of the teachers and the two of us. In our initial interviews, we invited Grace and Sue to talk about their background in teaching, how they came to participate in the exchange programme, and their expectations for the year they were to spend in each other's context. We also encouraged them to provide a sense of themselves as teachers by including descriptions of their classrooms, schools and educational programmes. Once in their respective new settings, our conversations focused on their day-to-day experiences within and outside the school – routine and special activities, highlights and challenges. Their accounts ranged from purely descriptive to reflective interpretations of their experiences.

Both teachers agreed to keep a journal of their experiences, which they delivered to us by mail at regular intervals. Although both women were experienced journal keepers (and had already planned to keep a journal for the duration of their exchange), we initially gave some suggestions as to how they might organize their journal writing and make regular entries for the purposes of the study. We also provided an excerpt from Holly's (1989) *Writing to Grow* on the form and purposes of journal writing. The journals provided a forum for the teachers to chronicle events as they happened; record impressions, thoughts and reactions to events and experiences; and to 'work through' and make sense of their experiences both within their classrooms and the broader cultural contexts. The journals were the narrative thread that gave continuity to the patchwork of experiences represented in the intermittent interviews and mail correspondence.

The two teachers wrote their journal entries in very different formats and styles. Sue initially elected not to use the wide-margined loose leaf paper that we supplied. She wrote in a predated, lined, commercially printed diary which had three days to each page. Thus, right from the start, her writing was defined by the preprinted page and tended to be abbreviated and direct, even sometimes staccato-like, because of the restricted space. The form and her writing style did not allow for extensive reflection on any topic. She wrote for her own record of the exchange experience, recording family activities as well as school experiences. Only after the pages of her preprinted diary were filled, at the end of the calendar year and half-way through the exchange period, did she begin to use the less restrictive format of the loose leaf paper. She told us, then, that she had changed the focus of her writing somewhat and that she was no longer placing as much emphasis on issues outside of the 'business of teaching and working'. She also told us that, from this time, she also kept another, more extensive, 'family' journal complete with memorabilia from travels within Canada and the USA.

Grace, on the other hand, wrote more flowing, extensive and reflexive accounts unbounded by pre-set page limitations. Like Sue, she also wrote for herself, recording her many and varied exploits out of the classroom. More than Sue's record, her journal recorded intricate details of life in her temporary homeland. These she photocopied and mailed to us. All in all we accumulated some 800 pages of written and transcribed narrative text, which we then read and re-read to identify emergent themes, and organized and edited for re-presentation in a cumulative narrative format.

A note on the New Zealand and Canadian contexts

The social and economic contexts of Aotearoa New Zealand and Canada, though vastly different in some respects, are remarkably similar in others. In the broader social context, at the time of the study, New Zealand was grappling with serious societal issues that were directly reflected in the schools and the curriculum: high levels of unemployment which have spiralled over the last decade; a depressed economy; a serious erosion of the general standard of living over the last three decades; questions about the role of the welfare state, the underpinning of New Zealand's infrastructure; the place of the indigenous Maori culture and language within New Zealand society; accommodation of immigrants, especially those from South Pacific Islands and South East Asia; deteriorating race relations; and serious law and order issues.

Ontario, where Sue spent her exchange year, is described by the rest of Canada as a 'have' province, home of the majority of the country's population, commerce and industry. Because of the province's large size and economic and political significance, the sociopolitical issues prevalent in the greater Canadian cultural context are magnified there. The issues facing Ontario at the time of the study were similar to those with which New Zealand was struggling. As in New Zealand, the economic climate was fraught with rising unemployment (a dramatic turnaround from the latter years of the 1980s), rising costs and lowered productivity, and questions about political foundations and universal welfare services were in the forefront of the provincial news. At the time, both New Zealand and Ontario had recently seen changes in governments, and were heavily affected by the widespread, global recession. And, in the year following the teaching exchange, the Ontario government began modelling many of its economic strategies after those of New Zealand.

While Canada and Aotearoa New Zealand have similar European colonial settlement and cultural roots, they have, structurally, quite different education systems. And both countries at various times have overlooked, to varying extents, the educational needs of their indigenous peoples, although probably to a lesser degree in New Zealand. New Zealand has had a centralized national education system (with strong regional nodes) that only recently has been fractured as efforts to decentralize and initiate strong local control have been put into effect. New Zealand has also experienced the effects of changing organizational structures and administrative control, and a serious erosion of the financial base for education. A state of flux and uncertainty within the national curriculum are partly evidence of this. Although the national curriculum often has been recognized for its innovative practices, performance in national examinations continues to direct students away from universal university education. Strong vocational and community education programmes also exert powerful influences on the preparation of New Zealanders for the workforce.

Education in Canada is under the jurisdiction of the individual provinces. Each provincial ministry of education is responsible for the development of educational policy, oversees school programmes, establishes curriculum guidelines, approves educational resources, sets guidelines for the operation of school boards, defines roles and responsibilities of teachers, principals, officials and trustees, and provides financial support. A board of trustees assumes local responsibility for the implementation of policy and programmes, staffing, funding through local property assessment, and overall management of the system in each school district. There is a current trend towards school-based management; however, this is a discretionary practice with guidelines set by provincial authority. In the province of Ontario, as in Aotearoa New Zealand, schools were (and are) in a state of transition as government agencies and educational institutions attempt to keep up with the changing social, political and economic climate. Reform and restructuring in public education and the education of teachers were just underway at the time of the study. In New Zealand, major organizational and structural changes were also beginning as the colleges of education and universities joined in the preparation of teachers.

The collective voice of classroom teachers is heard in different intensities in the two countries. In Aotearoa New Zealand, the teacher's voice has been recently somewhat muffled. While, traditionally, teachers have been of strong voice, primarily through their direct participation in decision-making associated with the administration of schools and curriculum, their status shows signs of change. Reliance on teacher secondment as a means of filling national, regional and local administrative and field service positions within the system, and broad and direct participation by classroom teachers in other aspects of school governance and professional development, are long-standing. Classroom teachers have played significant roles within the system as evidenced, for example, in the design and implementation of in-service or professional development programmes, curricular design and implementation, the administration of the education system, the preparation of new teachers, and in their community standing and recognition. But, flux within New Zealand society and the education system is changing the status of teachers and the conditions under which they work and develop.

Teachers in Canada are professionally organized in a national federated body which has provincial associations and regional affiliates. The Teachers' Federation and affiliates in Canada are strong and vocal, their influence on government and school board policy and practice clearly apparent. The teachers' voice in Ontario is heard loudly and clearly as new roles and responsibilities for teachers are defined. In a difficult economic and political climate, with increased pressures for teachers to do more for less, the Teachers' Federation asserts its influence to defend its members. At the same time, they attempt to promote an image of the teacher which reflects concepts of professionalism, empowerment and leadership. Working conditions, such as planning time, class size, teaching assistance and support for increasing responsibilities, and respectable salaries – considered to facilitate professional growth – are among those receiving renewed attention. In the face of fiscal restraint and demands for restructured schools and classrooms, there is an attempt by the various Teachers' Federations to design in-service education and professional development activities with an emphasis on long-term professional growth and ongoing renewal.

Thus, it was to these complex national and provincial contexts that Grace and Sue were introduced. Each teacher brought to their new contexts particular frames of professional and cultural reference, benchmarks, expectations and personal conceptions. They also carried with them well-established understandings about teaching, learning and schools, and about themselves as persons and professionals. They used their personal constructs as a basis to observe and make sense of the experiences and events they encountered in their newfound settings. Exposure to, and participation in, the different settings challenged some of their understandings, and provided opportunities for them to extend their thinking and construct new meanings. In the following accounts, Grace and Sue describe and reflect on elements of their exchange experiences. Following their narratives, we present a brief commentary about various aspects of their experiences, with particular attention to the ways in which the narratives reflect how the boundaries of their thinking and practice were extended both personally and professionally. We conclude with a note on narrative as a form of professional development.

Grace's narrative of experience in New Zealand

I grew up in a family of teachers, my mother was a teacher before she had children, and my father was a principal of a high school. I have always been kind of interested in education, and have always enjoyed children and been fascinated with how they learn. [I have enjoyed] going to different countries and just watching children, even if it did not involve schooling – just talking with people and observing people on the street, and just kind of being involved in their lives. All of those [experiences] have really helped me grow as an educator. [Observing in other contexts] makes you stop and think about the way you do things. You don't go to a new place to decide who is doing 'it' right and who is doing 'it' wrong. You go to get new ideas, to question what we are doing here [at home]. You may not be able to do anything about [the problems here] because one person is not going to change the whole [system], but travel does change you in a way because you get to think in different ways.

Teaching in Canada

I have taught for ten and a half years. I started teaching at a little country school with three teachers. Then I moved to [my present school], where I have been for about ten years. I have always taught Grade 1 or Grades 1 and 2.

[In our school] we have moved towards an individualized programme, especially in Language Arts. We got rid of the basal readers and the phonetic approach, and developed a more 'whole language' approach. I think it's wonderful. The kids are doing great things. My kids in Grade 1 are able to express themselves and write pieces of work that I don't think I could do when [I was] in Grade 4. It's so exciting to see what they are doing.

I have a new reading loft which is very exciting. It's square, made out of wood, and the kids can climb up onto a top platform. It has railings and indoor–outdoor carpeting – so they can go up there and sit and read quietly or they can go underneath. It's got two big windows that they can use as a puppet theatre or, when we are 'doing money', they can use as a store and people can go and buy things. [It was built by] our Parent–Teacher Association which is very strong. I tried for three years to get this thing made, so I was really pleased when I got it. I saw something like it in Denmark (on a much smaller scale). When I came back I said [to the principal] 'I have to have a loft', so I drew it up and he helped me with the dimensions because it had to be made so that it would come apart to go through the door.

Reading is a very, very important highlight of my classroom. Almost all of the kids love to read no matter what level they are at. They love the loft because they can just get up there with a book. They have 'buddy work', too, . . . [where] they read with children from another grade.

The kids do a lot of writing [on their own] also. In environmental studies, we usually do units, using sandboxes or water or research, where the children become involved in different things. This year, when we did a unit on dinosaurs, the kids were divided into groups and they were able to get a book and use the table of contents and index, find the names of the dinosaurs, and write down [information] about them. I thought, for six-year-olds, it was pretty good.

I'm really excited about the way language [teaching] in the classroom has developed since I started [teaching]. Right from the beginning I did not like the traditional programme in the school. It was very phonics-based. The kids learned to read but they really didn't understand what they were doing. They spent a lot of time just sounding out words. [With] this [new] way, even the poorest, most immature student is able to get a book and read it. He or she is not held back by the fact that she cannot remember what this letter says. They 'read' by context instead of letter by letter and word by word.

The children are also involved in discovering concepts of maths. They used to learn only by rote . . . [for example], '3 + 4 = 7'. Now they work with manipulatives so that they understand what 3 + 4 is. Instead of giving them a ditto sheet of number facts to complete, you might give them a blank ditto and say, 'Your number is 8. See how many number facts you can give me for 8'. And, the kids will give you more number facts than you ever thought of. It's exciting what they are doing.

My kids are probably freer [than students in other classrooms]. As long as the children are moving in the direction they are supposed to be moving – if you can put a lot of fun into learning and maybe take away a lot of the structure that we used to have, where they had to sit there and be very quiet – 'Why not?' if the kids are enjoying it. I have kids who don't want to go on summer holidays and don't want to go home on weekends because they like [school] so much!

Usually when the [children] start [in my class] they are anywhere from mid-kindergarten to about Grade 2 in ability [range]. Maybe I have two or three children who can read simple books and the rest [do] not [have] even a general knowledge of language and how it is made up. Home background varies also. [In the community] there are a lot of single parents and parents where the father is not home a lot. There are all different income ranges and a lot of [marriage] separations. It is not a multicultural community in any way.

I have done a number of [extracurricular] things in the school: helped coach basketball and volleyball, [organized] the Jump Rope for Heart

Programme, and the milk programme. This year I helped direct the musical Alice in Wonderland. [In New Zealand] I would like to be involved in sports – I have never taken responsibility for sports activities by myself.

The primary wing of our school is very cohesive. We work together. Sometimes we will have five teachers involved [in planning and presenting a unit] and all of those students will rotate [among the teachers]. We do a lot of things together so that the kids not only know me but they know the other teachers too and they feel very comfortable with them.

Settling in to the New Zealand scene

I was surprised at how 'at home' I felt among my new surroundings. I don't think I could have gotten a better exchange. The staff here is very helpful, warm and friendly. During my first week, they called me up, dropped in for tea and asked what I needed. They are a very supportive group and I'm sure I will enjoy working with them.

Even though I'm half-way around the world, I feel quite at home here. Many of the routines and expectations are the same. From the second I stepped off the 'plane, I've never had any feeling of being alone. I always knew I had someone I could call if I wanted to talk. I knew if I wanted to do something, there were five or six people I could go to and say, 'Do you want to do this?' As everyone told me, in New Zealand when they say, 'Drop in', they mean it. Very often I go over to Sue's parents – I drop in and end up staying for dinner. They have become my New Zealand parents and I feel very comfortable with them. I also feel very comfortable with the staff, especially a couple of them. You don't ever really feel alone – everyone is interested in what you are doing.

Relatives of my exchange family have certainly gone out of their way for me. I feel as if I have known them all my life. I felt very good about coming to New Zealand, but I never expected it to be THIS wonderful.

I am so busy that every day just seems to fly by because something new happens. The school is exciting because it is new, and the kids are very eager, in some ways, to do a lot of things. There is always something [social] planned. Usually by Monday I know what I am going to be doing next Saturday. It got to the point that, at school, they thought they should have a social calendar up [on the wall] just for me.

Many of the children spend their day in bare feet. Even though it's cold and rainy they don't seem to feel it. Since it's third term [and Spring here], they've turned off the little heat the school has. The rooms are so damp and cold it makes me think of the warmth of home. If the schools were this cold at home, the furnace would be running. I've never felt so cold inside except in Scotland. It's something I'm beginning to get used to though.

The things you hear on the news are kind of scary. You know things are happening out there and that maybe you should be more cautious. I feel very different about the way this house is locked up and [how] you would never put Christmas decorations outside because they would just [disappear]. They say, 'Always make sure the car is in the garage and the garage is locked and the gate is locked'. There seems to be a real uneasiness about what is happening in New Zealand [with respect to crime] and that, I must admit, surprised me when I first got here. You always hear only all the good stories.

At school in New Zealand: Reflections on classrooms, curriculum and teaching

I have twenty-six Standard 1–2 student – seven- and eight-year-olds. Because [the class is based on] vertical grouping, I end up with extra children – like [children from the] lower 3 and 4 [Standards] come into my class for mathematics – so that makes it really interesting. I have students from China, Fiji, Samoa, Tonga, as well as New Zealand Maori children. It's a real mixture. The multicultural aspect is probably the basic thing which really sticks out. Each one of those cultures brings very interesting twists to the classroom. Some of the [students] are very quiet. A lot of the girls from the Pacific Islands tend to be quiet, and education is maybe not their main aim in life. And the boys are very domineering. A lot of the Maori boys are very loud. I have some ESL (English as a Second Language) children, and they struggle to grasp the [English] language itself, as well as the content we are teaching.

The classes are large, and rules and regulations seem much more relaxed than in Canada. The atmosphere overall seems far more relaxed. The kids are able to come in and go out at their own free will. The classrooms don't seem to be as rigid. The kids don't line up to come in or they don't walk quietly down the hall like they do at home. They are supposed to walk in the halls but it takes a lot to get them to walk in a line. I guess little things like that make me feel more relaxed than at home. The students and staff tend to dress very casually here in New Zealand. No-one is afraid to participate [in sports activities] because they're dressed in frills. Girls very, very rarely wear a skirt to school. Boys come dressed in various ways, but always very casual – no real dress up. Bare feet is something that you see a lot of, even though it is cold out. [At first] it made me shiver but you get used to it. There are some days when I wanted to be in my bare feet too. It doesn't bother anyone to see a teacher in bare feet, whereas, at home, a teacher would not take off her sandals and be in her bare feet. Here, I would.

We start every morning with Fitness. When the bell rings, the [senior]

kids (that is, Standards 1–6, about grades 2–6) know to get into their
Fitness groups. We do [Fitness] for about ten or fifteen minutes and then
they come inside. They always do some kind of physical activity. It may
be jogging which we do every Monday and Friday when we go for about
a mile run. On other days, we do aerobics to music, or something called
Circuits, which are twelve different physical activities involving push-ups,
stretches, skipping, bench-stepping – various activities like that – and the
children change activity every two minutes.

[Then] we all go into our own classrooms. Basically, we set up so all
the seniors do vocabulary development and writing, and story writing and
spelling. Then they have 'play' from 10:20 a.m. until 10:45 a.m., and then
we have maths. All the seniors have maths at the same time because they
change classes with some of the [other] children. Then, in the afternoon,
we do reading. They have a five-minute 'small play' and then we do
'themes'.

On Wednesdays we have a sports afternoon from 1:00 p.m. until 3:00
p.m. The children divide into groups for games. There might be four or
five different activities going on, like paddle tennis, baseball, netball or
softball. The Acquapath we are doing now is definitely different from
anything we would do at home. Acquapath is a swimming programme that
is geared to make the kids more confident in water. It is an interesting
programme because the [classroom] teachers are [also] the teachers of the
Acquapath [programme]. Whether you have any swimming experience or
not, you are in charge of the twenty kids, and you are marking them on
different things. It is a big responsibility to have that many children in a
pool at a time. At home you would have the life-guards teaching [a
programme such as this] because they have the qualifications to do it.
Having that many [students] in the water at the same time is really hard.
We need a lot of parent involvement.

It is interesting to see all the volunteer helpers in the school. In Canada,
we're lucky to get one or two for the school. It's wonderful that [here] so
many are willing to give up free time to help the children. Basically, I have
been involved with the parents through my ESL children. [The parents]
take the [students] out and work with them on reading, vocabulary and
writing – anything I am involved in that I would like them to work on a
little more. I have also been working on a parent reading programme. The
parents are the ones who take the poor readers, or the ones who are
having a little bit more trouble with reading, and read with them every
day. These children are getting an extra dose of reading to help them
bring up their reading levels and skills. Some of these parents have actually
taken a three-hour course on how to help children in their reading, or on
how to be a parent volunteer. They really seem to enjoy working with
kids and it is wonderful to have the extra help.

I was surprised to find the children sitting in groups according to abilities. I changed that because I don't like them sitting like that (although we still do a lot of our reading in those groups). I've always tried to mix up ability levels – I think the students learn a lot from each other. That way the slower ones learn from the quicker ones. [I was also surprised that] some of the kids left my room for maths. At home, we usually keep the same kids all of the time. The other thing is that these kids are all different ages because they start school on their fifth birthday – or they have up until last year. At home, everybody starts in September of the year they are five; therefore, most of the kids are within a certain [age] range. With these kids, there can be almost a three-year spread between them when you have a Standard 1–2 class, even a four-year spread with some.

There seems to be far less emphasis on manipulatives and far more on memorizing. Children, even at my level, are encouraged to do formal homework every week. They seem to stress academics more, although the children do not seem to be more advanced. You tend to give the children more questions to do in a book instead of having them work with [concrete] things. Because you don't have the resources to work with, maybe some of [the children] move into the abstract level before they are ready.

When we are doing maths in Canada, we always have manipulatives right there ready to use. Here, there are basically no manipulatives. There are a few blocks that have to be shared among the seniors. These are senior classes, so it is a little bit different from [my own class] but [for example], there are very few measuring tapes. For geometry they had two sets of tiny geometric figures from which we were supposed to teach 'shapes'. You can get things from around the classroom or you can get things from the environment, which is good, but you need something to start with. I think a lot more of their work is done abstractly because they don't have the things to work with. I think that is a disadvantage to a lot of lower ability children who need to have the concrete materials with which to work.

[We] Canadian teachers have far more supplies [available in our schools]. We also have many extras – corrugated paper, bulletin board edging, lots of construction paper, bristol board, glue, paper bags, paper plates and envelopes. New Zealand teachers have to be far more creative. They have white and black paper, crayons, pastels, powder, glue and small packages of coloured paper that you handle like gold. New Zealand teachers and students are not as likely to waste paper because it's not so easy to get. Students also pay for pencils, notebooks, rubbers [erasers] and rulers. They pay a small school fee too. This money, plus a small grant from the Ministry, pays for the running of the school.

In our school [in New Zealand], we have three computers for the whole school. In Canada, we have at least one computer in every classroom, and there are a lot of programs you can get through the resource centre and which you can use for a month or however long you want. Here, there are so few [programs]. We have had one [computer] in our classroom since the [computer] course [I'm taking] started – probably only by taking the course were we able to get one into the classroom through a lot of wheeling and dealing. It has been in the classroom now for six weeks and the children have had a chance to use it for their writing but, because it is there for only such a short time, they don't get as many chances, and their time on it has to be limited. At home [in Canada], very often, I will let the children work on a computer until they say that they are finished.

New Zealand teachers get no preparation time unless teachers agree to combine classes for subjects such as physical education or music. Canadian teachers don't know how lucky they are. It's not that conditions are bad here, it's just that [in New Zealand] they lack some of the things we take for granted.

In both places, I have always spent a lot of time at work. At home, I spend most evenings doing work which leaves me free on the weekends to do other things. Here I spend a lot more time planning because you have to be so careful that you have the equipment that you are planning to use, whereas at home I know what is available. I also know where I can get my hands on it or where to go [to access it]. Here, you don't have a learning resource centre. You have to look and see what you have and plan around that – or you go to the library and find books on [the topic]. But, you don't have a lot of those resources right at your fingertips. [Even so], if something [else] comes up on a week night, then I can manage to do it because I feel that is part of the growth and education of being here.

Both in Canada and in New Zealand you have to [keep student] records. You have to keep track of the children's daily work as well as any formal testing you give. Here, in New Zealand, you have a folder that follows the children from the time that they are new entrants right up until at least Standard 4. [It] is very useful because you can look through and see a child's [development]. If they are having trouble in Standard 3, you can look through and kind of see that, 'Ah, yes, they were having trouble in Standard 2 in this area and they are still weak here, so maybe this is the area we should be focusing on instead of going on and on'. In [Ontario] Canada, we also have to do record-keeping. We have the report cards which are very thorough. A copy of the report card goes into the OSR (the Ontario Student Record). That OSR follows the child through from the time they are in kindergarten until they complete high school. The [administration] doesn't want little bits of the children's work in [the OSR]. They just want official documents. I believe we did talk, at one time, about having something that would follow [a student] through, but it has never actually been set up. Here it has. They also have [a different system of] reporting here. For the junior reporting, a written report only goes out once a year; for the seniors, it goes out twice a year.

Professional relationships

Because of vertical grouping, teachers must work together more closely than at home where each room is an isolated, independent unit. This seems to create a better understanding in the school – creating fluency and familiarity from one level to the next. The teachers here are warm and friendly. [At home] we do some group teaching, but not enough. I think the teachers in New Zealand (this school anyway) communicate better with each other, which gives the school a sense of 'oneness'. The lack of communication back home is something we have noted and discussed several times throughout my teaching career.

I think the 'working together' is wonderful. It is a great advantage that teachers do work together more. We tend to work together in the primary wing at home but most of the time one teacher will instigate it. For example, I might say, 'Let's all do a unit on something', but it would only be once or twice a year that all the primary teachers would work together.

Experiencing New Zealand

New Zealand is absolutely wonderful! The people are really friendly. I have just been doing a lot of New Zealand things, like going to Karaoke parties (the 'in' thing at the moment), going for walks on the beach with one of the teachers, eating out with different people at their homes, and kind of getting to know everybody. The staff at the school is very friendly and very accommodating and I am really enjoying that. I am just kind of 'living a New Zealand life'.

Sue's relatives have kind of adopted me as part of their New Zealand family now. It feels rather nice. During the weekends I have been doing a lot of New Zealand things: a lot of it has to do with the out-of-doors and involves the ocean – like eating fresh mussels [that I] actually collected; sailing on yachts; and swimming in the ocean – much to everyone's disgust because it was so cold. Cooking over an open fire is my favourite thing to do. We also had a good time tramping through the woods (or the bush). The bush, with the pohutakawa trees and the large tree ferns, was very interesting for me because it is such very different vegetation than our woods. I went to the ballet and am going again on Saturday [to see] The Nutcracker Suite. I have been getting to know what New Zealand is like, and loving every minute of it. Just studying the different things is just great. And the weather is a New Zealand thing!

On Sunday, December 29, 1 joined forty-nine others on a twelve-day [organized] tour. As New Zealand tends to be an 'outdoors' country, most of [the activities] involve excitement outdoors. I went up in a helicopter, zoomed down rivers in a jet boat, white-water rafted, went parasailing, climbed Fox Glacier and went trail-riding. I also had the thrill of seeing four sperm whales, over a hundred dolphins and some seals in their natural environment.

New Zealand is an ever-changing landscape of plains, hills, volcanoes, rivers, oceans, forests, dairy lands, rugged sheep lands and mountains. The North and South Islands are very different but equally as beautiful.

After the tour I spent three nights with a cousin of Sue, and then went south to Timaru. I spent four nights at a sheep station with another cousin of Sue and a wonderful time feeding the pigs, moving cows from pasture to pasture and sheep from hillside to hillside. Driving along make-shift roads in a four-wheel drive truck high in the hills with the drop to the valley about a metre away is something I will never forget. The view from the top will also stay in my mind long after I leave New Zealand.

[Then] I headed for Dunedin [where I] stayed with Sue's great aunt. I made my way back northward again stopping at the sheep station for one last night. Then it was train and ferry to Wellington. I'm glad I had people to visit after the tour because, then, I had someone to talk to about my new adventures. After Wellington I took the bus to Taupo and spent four nights on a dairy farm near Reporora. I went to Mt Tarawera (a volcano that last erupted about 106 years ago), climbed with others to the top, and then slid deep into the crater. It was eerie but beautiful standing on the crater's floor looking skyward.

I am getting used to driving on the left side of the road. It's fun to wind up into the hills as the scenery changes before you. I really like the beaches and the chance to be by the ocean. Walking along the sandy beach while the waves crash at your feet and the wind blows through your hair gives you a real sense of freedom. I have always liked to be near water, and New Zealand has only deepened that desire. I feel far more relaxed with water around than in a city of concrete.

[Being in New Zealand] has really allowed me to open up a little bit, whereas I have not had that chance in Canada. I don't think that anyone in New Zealand would ever think that I was shy and quiet, and yet, that is probably the way most people in Canada think I am. I think because I have always lived in a small town [where] people have known me, I have always been a little more reserved than I am here. Just basic things [have happened] that have really helped me to, maybe, broaden my own thinking about things or broaden my own needs, and [have] allowed me to be me.

Time continues to speed by. The staff often says they wish I could stay; sometimes I wish I could too. Although it will be difficult to settle back into a small community, it *will* be nice to be back with family and old friends.

Teacher exchange

When I heard of these exchanges, I thought it was the ideal time to go [to New Zealand] because I would be working in their system but I would also be able to see their country and meet the people, the sheep and everything else. I expected [to find] a system much like ours, and very friendly people.

A very important part of an exchange is to 'fit in'. It was important to me to 'become a New Zealander'. [It's important not to] impose your ideas on your exchange country. [You need to] enter an exchange with an open mind and expect everything to be different. (If you want the exact same situation as home, why did you exchange?) Some of the things that have stood out are working with these children – which is always a joy for me no matter where I am – getting to know them, and seeing them develop. I have especially enjoyed working with the ESL children, watching how they progress and how they really get excited when they understand something and want to go on [learning].

I think, in just working with another staff and another administrative system, getting a chance to talk to the different teachers and the headmaster here, you get a better feeling of the education system. I think my growth as a teacher has [come about by] working with a different culture of children [which has] helped me to think about things, or look at things, a little bit differently, especially in relation to who these children are.

Probably there are a number of things that I will take back home. I really enjoy their reading programme. Ours is something like it but they do have the New Zealand *School Journal* that they work with and the stories are all catalogued by age level and reading interest level. I think those are a good thing. In fact, I will take a few back with me. Other things I like are all the senior teachers getting together every week and discussing what is going on. I like the planning. That would not happen in Canada because our curriculum for Grade 8 is different from Grades 7 and 6, and so there is no sense in getting together to plan it; although once a year our whole school gets together. We take two or three weeks and plan a whole unit that we all do, from Kindergarten to Grade 8. The idea of doing fitness, having a sports afternoon, I think that is a great idea for the children. I have learned assessment methods used in New Zealand, what they call reading records and running records. I am not sure whether I totally agree with them but I have learned how to do them.

I have developed as a teacher, I think, just with the experience of a change. A chance to go to a new country and be part of that different education system has helped me to become more confident in myself. I am not an outgoing person. I would rather fit in than be the leader, and that will not change. I don't like to stick out, although I may when I get back home. Probably it helped me to meet and talk to people.

I feel good when people call me a Kiwi. It makes me feel as if I have accomplished a goal – to fit in and live in 'their' world. I find that I see many things differently than the way Sue saw them. It's interesting!

Sue's narrative of experience in Canada

I have been teaching for about twelve-years. I did a year in Auckland and a year and a half in a country area. When we got married, I could not get a [regular teaching] job in Auckland, so I just applied for any [teaching] job. The one I got turned out to be special education in a handicapped school and it was really wonderful. Then, I took special education [courses] for four years, had the girls, and went back [to teaching] part-time. When I was teaching part-time, I had six- and seven-year-olds for two years. Then, I applied for the job I have now with ten- and eleven-year-olds.

I have been involved in professional development programmes, doing Advanced Studies for Teachers after school and at night at Auckland Teachers' College. You can do just [about] any subject. I have taken courses in teaching art, communication, social development, social studies, all of the curriculum areas. I do it mainly for the new ideas and the practical things that I can bring back to the classroom, and because I feel I want to move more within the teaching profession. I don't want to stay in the same job forever.

Teaching in New Zealand

My school [in New Zealand] is from [the equivalent of Grades] 1 to 6 [with] nine [classroom] teachers, a teacher of special needs, and an itinerant teacher of special needs on a programme we call the 'Edmonton Scheme'. We are one of about four schools in the area that takes very slow children and puts them with a teacher and a teacher's aide.

My school is quite low socio-economically, so we pick up an equity grant which makes up for financial differences that might otherwise occur. Many of the children's parents are either unemployed or have low incomes. We have a high Polynesian [student] intake and a high non-English-speaking language group of children so that we need this assistance, the extra money. [There is a] very big multicultural group – [children from] Maori, [Pacific] Island [Polynesian], Fiji Indian, Korean and Chinese families.

My children in New Zealand were a Standard 2, 3, 4 [about Grades 2 and 3] vertically grouped class. We had two parallel classrooms [i.e. two classes of Grades 2 and 3 split], which means that no classroom gets overloaded with children. Having two classrooms also means that personality conflicts between students and teacher can be avoided because we can split the children up.

The principal makes the decision [about placement], but invariably teachers are involved. At the end of the year, we sit together to collate the rolls and [strive for] a balanced group of children on each roll – some smart ones, some below average and some average. Then we total up the roll and say, 'I will swap you for so and so' because you just know the kids you are going to clash with. We end up with what we each consider to be a fair group [or distribution].

In [my New Zealand] school, we exchange ideas and plan units together. We sit down as a junior school or as a middle school (which is where I teach) and look at all the topics and units we need to cover for the term, and pull out the ones that are timely or interesting, or whatever. Someone will go to the library and get all the resource materials we need. I might get the *School Journals* [a New Zealand Department of Education publication] and plan the art [activities]. And we bring all that together for one unit. Then, from that unit, we each take out what we want to teach. It ends up with the whole school teaching the same thing at the same time. It is a three-year plan and the children never repeat [the same content material].

Settling in in Canada

[I knew] nothing at all about the [Ontario] school [before I came]. I believe the school is quite strange. The county people tell me that it's different. I asked one of the teachers, 'Do you ever go out socially?' (In New Zealand, for example, all the teachers would maybe go to a movie.) She said, 'Why would I want to go out with some of them?' So, actually the staff don't mix well together. There are divisions, in other words.

I had been at the school a couple of times before [school began for the year]. I was really surprised, because the first day, after we had our children for about an hour, there was a school assembly. At home [in New Zealand] we would put on a show and do some great things and have some singing. Then someone would talk, and there would be a few more songs – it would be a fun time. [Here it] was very formal. The children sat on the floor and the new teachers were introduced and they stood up, said 'Hello', and then sat down. And that was my introduction to the school.

[In New Zealand] if we had a new member on staff (or a visitor like Grace) there would be songs of welcome and a morning tea. [Here] I walked into the staff room at recess to find no lights on and nobody else there. The morning tea is our social time [in New Zealand]. Everybody goes for morning tea time, and there is a little jar out and you pay twenty-four cents if you want a cup of coffee.

It has been my experience in every school that I have been in that the staff room is the hub of activity, especially at lunch time. Part of the ritual is to bring special treats and someone makes coffee and tea. It is usually a welcoming, inviting environment. It's homey. That's where things take place and where all of the socials are planned. This has not been my experience [here]. That's why I am finding all of this surprising.

[I relied on] the children to tell me who was who because I hadn't had any social [contact with faculty], whereas in New Zealand for the two new staffers and the assistant principal, they actually had a barbecue party on Saturday night before school started so that staff could get to know other people.

It has taken us a long time to make friends with the people here. I don't think it takes so long [to make friends] in New Zealand. I guess it depends on the sort of people you are. I'm quite an outgoing person, and I like to have people around. I enjoy other people's company. I got a real shock coming here. I'd been warned that it would happen but we [still] got a real shock that nobody bothered to include us in things until we made our own friends. I don't think that would happen in New Zealand.

At school in Canada: reflections on classrooms, curriculum and teaching

In New Zealand [schools], we have big windows and the classrooms [are arranged so that] to get to my room I have to come in through [other teachers' rooms]. There are outside doors, but once you get in [the building], the only way a teacher [in an inside classroom] can get to her room is to walk through [other teachers' classrooms]. So she trots through [the other rooms] where the teachers are working [conducting conversations on the way such as], 'Hi! How are you? Oh, I like what you are doing. Can I borrow that?'

Here [there is a] concrete wall [between the main building and] my classroom. I don't know what it's like outside because I have opaque glass on the windows and then wire on the other side of the wall. My room looks over the black top area so that it is all protected with a wall and wire window, so I don't know what the weather is like if I haven't been outside. I can't see.

The way I teach, the type of classroom I run, and the type of teaching I do is very, very different than the image teachers [here] have of [good teaching]. Lots of people have told me that, and I can just see it. [In other teachers' classrooms] the children all sit in rows. They are totally quiet. I cannot believe how quiet they are! In the Grade 2 class next door, at lunch time they all sit in seats to eat their lunch. In my class, they sit wherever they like to eat their lunches – that's private time. They chat and, if they make a mess, they clean it up. If they spill a drink, they clean it up.

I am different. [The other teachers] all wear very formal clothing. I don't wear my jeans to school, but I usually wear my corduroy pants and a sweatshirt. And I sit on the floor.

I think [the teachers] are really frightened of what the children [in my class] are going to be like when they get them next year. I really think they are frightened of how loud and boisterous and noisy [the children] are going to be. They [think children] should be quiet, sitting and working at a desk. [One of the other teachers] said that she had written to Grace. The teacher said, 'There is a lot of play in [Sue's] room'.

[In my school in New Zealand] we had a powerful [challenging] group of children. They were naughty, but really neat, and they did some great things. They wrote letters to me the other day and [when] I got them I felt strange and distant. A month ago, it would have meant a lot more but the kids here are 'my kids' now. When I was in New Zealand they were 'my class', but they're not my kids anymore; they are [the other teacher's] kids.

The bell rings at ten to nine and [the children] come in, sing 'O Canada', we take the roll, and then I do a news time with them. They have time to share their news every morning. If they don't want to share, they just pass. We do a bulletin – 'Today is Wednesday and the weather is . . .', and then I write somebody's 'news' – it's actually story writing. I also have two helpers who come in and [work with] groups of children. The other children have a choice of activity in the room. They can choose activity centres, sand, blocks, or a related activity which might be [something like] lists of other children's names. They like to make lists – people's names, things they study, colours. In another corner I have a colour centre with yellow, blue and green food colouring and eye-droppers. They mix [the colours] to see what they get.

During that time, I don't want to know what the others are doing. They are all busy but it's a choosing time for them. I just hang my head down and work with one group at a time – I rotate them. As the children finish their story, they go over to a table where there are coloured markers, and [they] start doing a picture to go with their story. I call up another child and then they do a story with me. That takes us up to the first recess in the morning. We stop about ten minutes before recess for sharing time.

We sit in a circle and [the children] show all of the things they had done that morning, or their story if they have written one. Some days we don't get through everybody's story. If someone had written a story and didn't have time to share it, then [that person] would be first to give a story tomorrow. All the kids listen as they read and 'finger-point' to the words. I have a kiwi stamp, which I put on the page and hand, which tells me immediately who has read and written a story.

When they come in from recess [the children] automatically get a book. I have 'shared reading' out of Big Books that I make in the classroom. It's so much fun – they come and read with a pointer, and they love it. We [work with the Big Books] for about twenty minutes and they have a choice of reading activity [such as] poems or word games. My room has lots of reading activities situated around so they can read with a pointer. They walk around with big long pointers and read. We have about six Big Books in the room now. We also do lots of [word games]. That takes us to lunch time.

[After lunch] we have a story and a song, about ten minutes of printing, more singing, and then [after recess] we do environmental studies. It's quite a social time [where] we make and do things [such as] Hallowe'en activities [in October].

I have physical education [scheduled] every day but I only teach it three times a week so that I can work on reading [instead]. [The principal] came in one morning to watch me teach. He said that he really liked what I was doing, and so he has given me a free hand to do what I want. He is quite happy with my work.

[The principal] keeps inviting people to come and see this 'strange new way of teaching'. I asked not to have more than three visitors at a time, but today he tried to push for five people in one day. I explained that three extra people was really too much, and that I certainly didn't want five people. I also asked him not to book people on a Friday, but he asked if a special friend of his could come on this Friday.

Last week I had eleven people through my room – eleven people! [The children respond], 'We've got some more customers'. [I have the visitors] sit on a chair to watch and, after that, they are given a pencil and paper and asked to help the children with their programmes. I need the help in my room.

This is my children's first year of writing. My [whole language] pro-gramme works. It comes from New Zealand – it is not mine personally. I think [teachers here] have had the theory [of whole language] thrown at them and they just didn't know how to put it into practice; then, all of a sudden, there is somebody who is putting it into practice and having a lot of success (people tell me that they would be happy if their Grade 2 students wrote like that, and this is only half-way into year one).

I have decided to write out my story writing programme with all my ideas and work cards and [put them in a] kit to sell. [The principal] has found out that there is no reason why not. I have so many visitors, and they all want my ideas, so I shall try this idea. I have the 'OK' from the Board office. [The principal] wondered if the Board may want to buy it.

My school in New Zealand does badly [as far as parental support is concerned], because we have a high proportion of working parents, but we do get very good support when there is something on in the school. Here, there is hardly any support. When we went down to [my daughter's] Science Exhibition at [her] school, there was only one other family looking. In New Zealand, it would be standing room only. You can hardly get in the door of the intermediate school to see the Science Fair.

[In New Zealand] from the time the children start school, the parents are encouraged to be part of it. They're in and out of school, on [field] trips, and so on. Here, the children go to kindergarten in the morning and the parents say 'Farewell' at the door. Even when picking up their children, they wait in the car park; they're not allowed to come into the corridor.

At home I would be outside much more because of the space, the land, and the area in the playground. I do a lot of maths and science outside. Teachers think about education differently.

The difference between the Canadian and New Zealand curriculum is that [in New Zealand] it is all taught together. It is not taught as Grade 2, for example. All the juniors [K-2] would be having the same experience at the same time. [For example, once they completed a unit on the zoo or the beach] they would never repeat that unit again. I use my resources over and over but I always write a new unit [plan].

We really thought that [schools in] Canada would be like we hear [schools in] America to be – so far ahead technologically. [There is] a lot of money, much more money in Canadian schools than we have [in New Zealand], and I expected better equipment. But [for example] the story books are boring and dull in comparison to what I am used to having. There is an amazing amount of funding to spend on the schools and you wonder where [the money] goes. When I asked for something at school – like a maths book – I got it. It just arrived. Now, in New Zealand that would be '$60 dollars out of a $200 budget' and I would feel really naughty asking for it. I would probably borrow somebody else's and try to copy it. [In New Zealand] my art budget [for] the whole school was $2000 – for the *whole* school. [Here] I will probably use that [much] in my classroom this year. [In New Zealand] our budget to replace physical education equipment was $800 for the whole year. Here, there is just so much stuff. Wonderful! The resource room is like Aladdin's cave – so much equipment and no accounting for its use! Children don't even provide their own stationery. Everything is provided!

The difference in the amount of equipment in the two settings makes

[New Zealand teachers], I think, more resourceful. We make far more things, whereas Canadian teachers will go out and buy [teaching aids] and then put them up or use them once, [such as] pretty bulletin boards that are up all year have fancy edging all the way around, and they are up as a teacher-made display. [My bulletin board] is a child-like display and it probably looks gaudy to [the other teachers] – it has kids' paintings on it. But it's like, 'if you can buy it, then get it'. [The teachers] asked [the principal] to buy all of these manuals – the same for all the classrooms!

I get 120 minutes of preparation time for every six-day cycle (something I never get in New Zealand). In New Zealand I would be in school at 8:00 [a.m.] and I would leave about 5:00 p.m. And I would probably go in for an hour on the weekend usually to frame our pictures [with] coloured paper. (I do art on Friday and I like to have [children's work] on the wall for the kids when they come [in on Monday].) Here, I leave [home] at ten to eight [in the morning] and I am home at 4:30 p.m. – and I have a fifteen-minute drive. So I am not spending as much time at school here as I did in New Zealand. Here, I work during my lunch time [because] there is nothing else to do. I eat my lunch [in the staffroom] and then I go back to the classroom. There is nobody else there – [the other teachers] eat their lunch and then they just leave. A couple of them go home for lunch.

[One of the other teachers] came in to see my running records today. She is very interested in [finding] a tracking/monitoring system for juniors. I have shown her how to evaluate the running record and [how to] teach from it. I heard something quite strange today, though. [The teachers who attended a session on a new student evaluation system] told me that New Zealand bought the programme from Ontario to initiate in New Zealand schools.

Professional relationships

At home, [the teachers] are quite different – they are much more relaxed, much friendlier, much easier to speak to. It is all very formal and very rigid [in this school], and the people are like that too. They portray different images. The image they [present] at school is totally different from the image they [present] at home. [For example], one [woman teacher] drove [to a neighbouring town] fifteen minutes by car to buy alcohol [for a dinner party she was having]. She did not buy it in town because that is not the image of a teacher [that she wishes to present].

[At home in New Zealand] I know most of the staff, their children, and I am interested in what they do. The teenagers come into the school when there is a day off and we chat. There are no boundaries [between home and school]. [Here] there are boundaries. [Here the attitude is] 'That's my private life and nobody knows about it'. [At home] you know what is going on in other people's homes so much more.

On New Zealand Day, a Saturday night, we had a potluck dinner. It was the first function we had as a staff. I thought that was really interesting – the first social function, and it was here at our house. Nobody else would have one [not even] at Christmas. The reason people don't bring their spouses [to any social functions] is because [the spouses] get sick of the teachers 'talking shop'. [At home] we don't 'talk shop' even at lunch time – unless it is something urgent.

Nobody infringes on your personal self. [The principal] doesn't ask me [anything that] is not 'his business'. Unless I volunteer the information, he will not ask me. He has been really good when I have asked for things. He is really helpful but very, very formal. He does not intrude upon me at all. And that is how it is. It's very formal.

'Personal rights' are really strong here. If somebody asked you something in New Zealand and you did not want to answer you could quite politely tell them to 'mind their own business'. But here, nobody would ask you anything personal. I even had to sign a form [before] my 'phone number could go on a [public list]. Somebody explained to me that nobody would confront me if they thought I had done something wrong in the school. They would have to put it in writing. At home, if somebody thought I had done something wrong they would tell me that what I did was stupid; we would talk about it, and that would be it. Here, it is all written down, and it goes to the Board office, and then comes back – the process is related to the Human Rights legislation.

I have become very friendly with the other Grade 1 teacher – who teaches part-time – and with [another one of the other teachers]. We do lots of things together. We actually plan our units together all the time now. [One of us] brings a whole lot of books, I will bring something else, and we write the objectives and evaluate together. That is something that is not typically done here.

I discussed with [two other teachers] the possibility of them joining [the Grade 1 teacher] and me for a junior school assembly once a week – to sing, celebrate birthdays, present certificates, show work, and so on. They said they would try it once to see if they like it.

[One of the teachers] is coming regularly to my room [to observe]. She is trying lots of language-centred activities that I am using and is delighted with the results. She has taken a copy of my day book [too]. She is surprised at how much we share in New Zealand. I showed [another teacher] who was having problems with a low-ability writing group how I would set up a remedial programme.

Experiencing Canada and the USA

The first six weeks, I didn't really get to know anybody here at all, and we [the family] depended on each other. Maybe we didn't give it a chance because we were away most weekends. We travelled [a lot].

[During spring break] we enjoyed a wonderful two weeks in the [United] States. We spent a week in Florida going to all the tourist attractions and travelled back through Washington, DC where we spent two great days. [On the way] I made a mistake of going right through the middle of Cincinnati [Ohio] because I missed the bypass. It's a pretty big place to go right through the middle of. We went through so many enormous towns – a lot of them were kind of scary. For example, it was scary to go through Macon, Georgia with the state troopers all around the place. We were told that if we did anything wrong to really watch out, because if you couldn't pay your fine on the spot, you'd be locked up. We heard all sorts of things like that.

We drove to Niagara Falls. They are magnificent! We went on *The Maid of the Mist* [tour boat that goes under The Falls]. We were so close to The Falls, it was unbelievable. And the noise was so loud! We also went up in the [viewing tower] and, again, the view was unbelievable!

We're getting really good at travelling on the subway [system in Toronto]. [On this trip to Toronto] we drove to [a city outside of Toronto], had lunch with some other [teacher] exchangees, and then took the [commuter train] into Toronto. Then, we travelled by subway to see the Ice Capades [a professional skating troupe].

We were planning on going to Quebec [a French-Canadian city approximately 800 km away] but we just couldn't get ourselves together to make the arrangements. It's really stressful living in another country. At home everything I do is easy for me. I know where to shop, where the doctors and dentists are, and how to get from place to place. [Here] every time I want to go somewhere I have to ask directions, and so on. So given that and the fact that we were hit by a blizzard when we were supposed to make our bookings, we just said, 'Forget it'. We felt sad in the end, though, because we would have liked to have gone.

We have had a terrific week with friends at their cottage in Port Loring [Ontario]. The cottage is on the edge of the Pickering River about an hour from North Bay. The sky is blue! We enjoyed doing 'winter things' with them – snowmobiling, cross-country skiing, sledding, and so on. We went to visit a hermit who has 100 acres on the other side of the river, accessible only by water in summer and ice in winter. He has all sorts of gadgets to improve his situation as he has no power. The wildlife is so friendly they feed from your hands. It felt really great to be part of an extended family again (all in all there were twenty-one of us in three cottages). We will be going back in July to do 'summer things'. We are so lucky to have made such good friends.

Usually we feel pleased to be coming home at the end of a holiday but this time we returned reluctantly. I guess it was great to be part of a family again. Reading this again, I now realize the things we miss the most – family times. Today is the first time I have really felt homesick.

Being New Zealanders in Canada

We watched the opening of the World Cup Rugby on television – such patriotism! Pete sat up late watching New Zealand and England [play], [and a few nights later] we watched New Zealand walk all over the United States [team].

[The whole family] watched the opening ceremony for the Winter Olympics [and later in the week] we watched the slalom and downhill racing, and the bobsled teams. The girls were very patriotic when the New Zealand girl won the women's downhill event.

We have become very patriotic since we left New Zealand. We don't make a big fuss [about patriotism] at home but, here, if we see anything about New Zealand, we really perk up.

My parents send a lot of cuttings from the newspaper and some magazines. I don't buy [Canadian] magazines, although I sometimes get them from people. I never really read them; I just flick through them. When a New Zealand magazine comes here [however] I read it from cover to cover.

I seem to be a bit behind in my correspondence. We have been out more I guess. I write every week to my family, but friends get rotated every couple of weeks so there is always a letter on the go. I love getting mail from New Zealand.

Teacher exchange

People say that you shouldn't go back [to your old job after you have been away] but that you should grow and regroup from that job. Somebody else filled my position and took over all of the responsibilities that I had, so it would be difficult to go back to start again in the same school. As someone said, 'It's better to start again in another school'. I have applied for a deputy principal job [in New Zealand]. [Because] I got out of the country and did something different, I probably have increased my chances of promotion.

The perception is that I would bring back something new to the school, something good and interesting. I have learned from [the exchange] but, really, I don't see that I have learned a lot from other people [in the school] here. To be fair, though, even the principal said that this wasn't a good example of what most schools are like. You get so much out of this exchange, but not necessarily academically for your classroom. I think New Zealand is quite a lot further ahead than the system here.

There are courses offered [through the School Board], however, and every night of the week there is an opportunity for people to get further training. I am going to computer courses at night. [And, on one professional development day] I went to [one of the Board's secondary schools] to visit one of the best art departments in southern Ontario. Art has been my field, so that was really interesting for me. I also spent a day with a 'mentor' who is also at our school. I go in and out of her room quite a lot now. She has been teaching me [to work with] pastels, which I have never been able to use successfully myself or in the classroom.

[You need to think about] expectations [for the exchange]. I haven't been disappointed. Everything that we've wanted to do, we've been able to do. We've been lucky. We've had some amazing experiences and the experiences the girls have had [have been] wonderful. I guess the travelling and the living side of it is what we will always remember. And the good friends – because they really are very special now.

Ardra and Gary came this afternoon. I find that after talking with them I have to question some of my own attitudes. It is good to get other perspectives as you can become very insular and see things in a one-sided manner!

Commentary

As we read and re-read the narratives of Grace and Sue, we were struck by the similarity of the topics they raised in their writing and conversations, even though they were speaking of and from each other's home environments. Of course, they also had similar issues and tasks to face as they landed, met new people, adjusted to climatic differences, prepared for school, taught daily, and so on. The fact that both teachers had preconceptions of their entry into their newfound home environments may well have had a profound effect on their materialized expectations and the recordings of those experiences. Much of their descriptions or explanations of their new environments and circumstances rested on comparisons between 'home' and 'here'. At first glance, this comparison appears focused on judgements about the new contexts. Yet, we sense, these comparisons represented efforts to make sense of their new situations.

For Grace and Sue, contrastive experiences in each other's classrooms and schools presented a challenge to their conceptions of their own situations. For example, in their initial descriptions of their home schools and classrooms, it seemed that Grace and Sue had similar classroom pro-grammes and approaches to teaching, and yet Sue was seen by the teachers in Grace's school as having a 'strange way of teaching'. And, whereas Grace described her classroom as activity- or play-centred, a colleague in her Canadian school reported in a letter the apparent anomaly of Sue encourag-ing 'a lot of play' in Grace's room. Similarly, what Sue described as an equitable way of working with children of different abilities, Grace found to be just the opposite. Also, Grace's description of the Aotearoa New Zealand curriculum as one placing more emphasis on memorizing and 'academics' than on concept development through manipulation of materials was in direct contrast to Sue's description of teaching in her New Zealand school. We see these as examples of how experiences in unfamiliar settings provide opportunities for the ongoing reconstruction of knowledge. Grace and Sue also made sense of their new settings (and, we expect in the process, gained insights into their home situations) by comparing and con-trasting professional relationships in their respective contexts.

Before leaving Canada, Grace commended the way in which the teachers in the primary wing of her school worked together. On reaching Aotearoa New Zealand, she realized that, although at home they did 'some group teaching', it was 'not enough'. Whereas she initially described teachers in her Ontario school as 'cohesive' and indicated that they worked together, she had an opportunity in New Zealand to broaden her perspective on pro-fessional relationships and experience new possibilities, wanting to adopt similar practices on her return to Ontario.

Meanwhile, Sue, on exchange at the Ontario school, was initially almost overwhelmed by the isolation and apparent rigid boundaries between teachers' classroom territories, evidence she thought represented teachers' unwillingness to collaborate or work together. Over the course of the exchange, perhaps with Sue as a catalyst, the teachers in the primary wing began working together quite closely, at least around the tasks that Sue and they defined together. And, no doubt, this way of operating reflected Sue's approach in her home school in Auckland, Aotearoa New Zealand.

Travel opportunities also provided an array of experiences that had strong influences on Grace's and Sue's personal and professional identities. In Canada, Grace's physical and cultural environments were bounded. She grew up, lived and worked in a small rural community – a relative speck on a continental land mass with large commercial and industrial cities in relatively close proximity, the Great Lakes nearby, and the Atlantic Ocean over 1000 miles to the east. Continental North America dwarfs Maritime New Zealand in sheer size and population. Climatically, she was used to being in a cool temperate, continental zone. In contrast, Auckland, with its warm temperate, almost subtropical, maritime climate and easy access to a variety of landscape forms made possible a different kind of lifestyle – one that was less structured by the extremes of weather, distance and the pressures of large populations. These conditions formed a context for Grace to 'be me'.

Aside from the professional aspects of the experience, being 'on exchange' provided opportunities for Grace to extend personal and psychological boundaries. In a strange, new and vastly different place, unshackled from familiar surroundings and expectations, she was able to explore elements of her psyche: her identity, self-concept and interpersonal orientations.

Sue's experience of 'becoming patriotic' was not a surprise to us. Indeed, numerous recent New Zealand authors have written about the place of the 'OE' (Overseas Experience) in the process of 'becoming *Pakeha*'. And further, King (1985, 1991), for example, argues that, for New Zealanders, a sojourn in a foreign country has the place and role of establishing more firm appreciations of the peculiar New Zealand culture and lifestyle:

> The effect of my travels . . . was unexpected. I felt more, not less, a New Zealander. I became more deeply conscious of my roots in my own country because I had experienced their absence. I missed physical things, like empty land and seascapes, driftwood fires, bush, New Zealand birdsong. And I missed common perspectives with Maori and Pakeha New Zealanders . . . With the perspective of distance, New Zealanders seem to have gone much further towards developing cultural traits than they had at home.
>
> (King 1985: 171–2)

Thus, King suggests, such distance from home as represented in foreign travels or sojourns induces thinking about the relationships of *Pakeha* to Maori and insights into one's nationality. (This is particularly relevant, since it is only a few years ago that New Zealanders typically described an 'OE' to the UK as a trip 'home'.) Likewise, the experiences of Spoonley (1991), Ireland (1991) and Laidlaw (1991) attest to a kind of bold patriotism that strikes when individuals (in these cases, New Zealanders) are out of their country.

These thoughts withstanding, 'the experience of being foreign has the potential for working a significant transformation at the deepest level of an individual's sense of being' (Lewis and Jungman 1986: xvi). And: 'No matter how strong the attachment to one's native land, one cannot live away from it very long and still resist what is seen every day' (Miloz, quoted in Lewis and Jungman 1986: xvi).

Narrative as professional development

Looking back over Grace's and Sue's narrative accounts of experience, we are reminded of some of the many educative qualities of narrative inquiry, both for the narrators and those with whom the narratives are shared. Sue's

150 *Ardra L. Cole and J. Gary Knowles*

comment that talking with us about her experiences induced her to question some of her attitudes reflects one educative purpose of narrative inquiry: to encourage reflection and reconsideration of one's understandings and practices. Connelly and Clandinin (1985) refer to this as 'giving back a story', so that it might be re-lived and re-told. We expect that through the process of articulating their experiences and in the reading of the narrative texts, both Grace and Sue engaged in an ongoing reconstruction of their understandings. In this way, we see narrative inquiry as a form of professional development for those involved.

Grace's observation of how differently she and Sue saw things reminds us of another educative quality of narrative, what Connelly and Clandinin (1990) call narrative's 'invitational quality'. Drawing on Crites (1971) and Peshkin (1985), Connelly and Clandinin suggest that narrative accounts invite readers to vicariously participate in others' experiences. In so doing, readers are provided opportunities to assess and reassess their own understandings. The qualitative differences between Grace's and Sue's narrative accounts reflect their individuality – how differently they interpreted and reconstructed their experiences. This difference, along with the richness and detail of their accounts, invites readers to imagine how *they* might interpret similar kinds of experiences. In this way, narrative inquiry encourages others to engage in a process of reflection and re-imagining. As Clandinin and Connelly (1991: 277) suggest, shared narratives 'help readers question their own stories, raise their own questions about practices, and see in the narrative accounts, stories of their own stories'.

Finally, we see narrative inquiry as a form of professional development at a broader level. Narrative accounts such as those by Grace and Sue provide in-depth knowledge of teachers, teaching and educational contexts. To quote Witherell and Noddings (1991: 8), 'Understanding the narrative and contextual dimensions of human actors can lead to new insights, compassionate judgement, and the creation of shared knowledge and meanings that can inform professional practice'.

References

Beattie, M. (1991) 'The making of relations: A narrative study of the construction and reconstruction of a teacher's personal practical knowledge'. Unpublished doctoral thesis, University of Toronto, Ontario.
Clandinin, D.J. and Connelly, F.M. (1991) Narrative and story in practice and research, in Schon, D.A. (Ed.), *The Reflective Turn*. New York: Teachers College Press.
Connelly, F.M. and Clandinin, D.J. (1985) Personal practical knowledge and the modes of knowing: Relevance for teaching and learning, in Eisner, E. (Ed.),

Learning and Teaching the Ways of Knowing. Eighty-fourth Yearbook of the National Society for the Study of Education, part 2, pp. 174–8. Chicago, IL: University of Chicago Press.

Connelly, F.M. and Clandinin, D.J. (1990) 'Stories of experience and narrative inquiry'. *Educational Researcher* 19(5), 2–14.

Crites, S. (1971) 'The narrative quality of experience'. *Journal of the American Academy of Religion* 39(3), 391–411.

Holly, M.L. (1989) *Writing to Grow: Keeping a Personal Professional Journal*. Portsmouth, NH: Heinemann.

Ireland, K. (1991) Echoes from a snail's shell, in King, M. (Ed.), *Pakeha: The Quest for Identity in New Zealand*, pp. 71–8. Auckland, NZ: Penguin.

King, M. (1985) *Being Pakeha*. Auckland, NZ: Hodder and Stoughton.

King, M. (1991) Being Pakeha, in King, M. (Ed.), *Pakeha: The Quest for Identity in New Zealand*, pp. 9–22. Auckland, NZ: Penguin.

Laidlaw, C. (1991) Stepping out from shadow, in King, M. (Ed.), *Pakeha: The Quest for Identity in New Zealand*, pp. 157–70. Auckland, NZ: Penguin.

Lewis, T.J. and Jungman, R.E. (1986) Introduction, in Lewis, T.J. and Jungman, R.E. (Eds), *On Being Foreign: Culture Shock in Short Fiction*, pp. xiii–xxv. Yarmouth, ME: Intercultural Press.

Peshkin, A. (1985) Virtuous subjectivity: In the participant-observer's eyes, in Berg, D. and Smith, K. (Eds), *Exploring Clinical Methods for Social Research*, pp. 267–81. Beverly Hills, CA: Sage.

Spoonley, P. (1991) Being here and being Pakeha, in King, M. (Ed.), *Pakeha: The Quest for Identity in New Zealand*, pp. 146–56. Auckland, NZ: Penguin.

Witherell, C. and Noddings, N. (Eds) (1991) *Stories Lives Tell: Narrative and Dialogue in Education*. New York: Teachers College Press.

9

Breaking tradition: the experiences of an alternative teacher in a rural school

Mary Jean Ronan Herzog

Introduction

For generations, children in the USA have learned a common and memorable history lesson. Immigrants came from many countries and cultures to their new home to blend in the 'melting pot'. In some ways, the melting pot theory worked. At the end of the twentieth century, travellers to any city from coast to coast or anywhere in between in the USA, can see the same films, eat at the same restaurants, and sleep in the same hotels.

Mary Lauren, the teacher who is the main character in this story, is a native of the Southern Appalachian mountains of North Carolina, an area known as the 'bible belt'. Although media images suggest that the region is unique, it has been permeated by mainstream American culture. With the encroachment of McDonald's, Motel 6 and cable TV, even rural Southern Appalachia has lost some of its individuality.

The public schools play a central role in Mary Lauren's community, which I will refer to as 'Mountainside'. There is a scarcity of employment opportunities, and schools tend to be among the biggest employers. The schools are used for meetings, community athletic events and functions such as fire department fund raisers. There is a lot of local pride in, and concern about, the schools, and the school board elections have higher voter participation than the national elections. The schools in Mountainside are an integral part of local politics. The forces of the *status quo* continually win over the changes of modernity.

What John Dewey (1938: 18) said in *Experience and Education* still holds true: 'The school is a kind of institution sharply marked off from other forms of social organization'. The public schools in Mary Lauren's community reflect the influence of the social efficiency movement of the early twentieth century. They also reflect American standardization. Children are divided by age. Classrooms are organized around rows of desks, textbooks, worksheets and seatwork. Mass-produced bulletin boards alert students to the proper use of subjects and predicates, and the correct way to diagram sentences and divide fractions. Student papers adorn the walls, and everyone can see who the 'smart kids' and the 'dumb kids' are. The teacher's desk is in the front of the room.

In keeping with its early twentieth-century roots, the curriculum in Mary Lauren's community is differentiated along social lines (Kliebard 1986). Although there are pockets of exceptions, students are usually sorted according to 'ability', and the resulting labels correlate with social class, race and parental educational background. 'Academically gifted' students attend special classes that encourage critical and creative thinking and problem-solving; they tend to come from the educated, upper socio-economic classes, and are often 'outsiders'. Special education students take classes where their abilities and self-concepts are also reinforced. By and large, they come from the lower socio-economic classes and the more isolated parts of the region. The average students, who have no labels at all, very often fall through the educational cracks.

The schools are typically organized around a paternalistic hierarchy in which the chain of command starts with the superintendent and *his* central office staff. The hierarchy continues with the male principal, female teachers and, finally, the students. Many of the male administrators come from the coaching ranks. Obedience is valued. Students obey teachers, teachers obey the principal, the principal obeys the superintendent. Teachers, like students, are rewarded for obedience and conformity to institutional norms.

Differences among teachers

A closer look in the schools, however, reveals that there are breaks in the patterns; they are not as uniform as they at first seem. Sometimes the differences are in the design of the school building. A visionary principal can make a difference. It may be that the community is active and works together for a different kind of school. But the biggest differences transpire in the classrooms of individual teachers like Mary Lauren. In any school in the region, it is likely that a small percentage of the teachers may in some ways be alternative. That is, they do not fit the traditional mould. In these traditional, rural public schools, these are the teachers who are different. They are the innovators, the dreamers and the rebels. They are often treated as outcasts by their more traditional colleagues regardless of their geographical roots.

This story about Mary Lauren, a pseudonym, is a story of a non-traditional teacher who works in a traditional rural school in the Southern Appalachian mountains of North Carolina. It is part of a larger qualitative study designed to examine the characteristics of teachers who push the margins of tradition back and design their own curriculum (for discussions of qualitative research methods and analysis, see Bogdaw and Biklew 1992; Miles and Huberman 1984; Lincoln and Guba 1985; Erickson 1986; Patton 1990). Mountainside Elementary School is in a relatively poor county of 30,000 residents. A state university and the public schools are the major sources of employment. The presence of the university creates a 'town-gown' atmosphere but, in this case, there is no town. There are hills and mountains, and people are either outsiders or natives. As a result of consolidation, some students travel as much as thirty to forty-five minutes down the mountains to school. Until a few years ago, they were in a little K-12 school high in the mountains. A substantial minority of the schoolchildren have parents employed by the university.

For the purposes of this chapter, the story includes a description of Mrs Lauren's classroom and her perspectives on several questions. It also includes an excerpt of an interview with a child who described what she does in this class. It is a description of a teacher who pushes against the margins, a teacher who is not bound by the traditions of her small, rural public school. The following questions guided the development of this story:

- How is Mrs Lauren different from other teachers?
- What motivates her to be innovative in a traditional educational environment?
- What kinds of problems does she face as a result of her approach?
- How does she relate to children?
- What satisfactions does she derive from her work?
- What can other teachers learn from her experiences?

Mrs Lauren

Mrs Lauren has been teaching for twenty-seven years. She has taught many different grades and configurations in several different schools throughout her tenure. As she nears retirement, she takes classes at the university, keeps up with the newest educational literature, has a constant stream of visitors in her classroom, and says that when she retires, 'I will do something for children'. She feels as if many of the structures in public education are harmful for children.

This story focuses on her classroom when it was a combination of kindergartners, first- and second-graders whom she was allowed to keep for two consecutive years. Mountainside Elementary has combination classes most years, and teachers take turns as they are generally considered undesirable. Over the few years since, she has repeatedly asked for a combination but has been refused. For Mrs Lauren, combining the classes was not the result of an organizational need, but her desire to break the age barriers that schools normally maintain. She believes that children of different ages have much to teach each other. She thinks the non-graded concept, and the combination of kindergarten, first- and second-graders in her room allows her the freedom to cross the grade barriers inherent in a traditionally graded school. She described her reasons for wanting a multi-aged group of children:

> I just thought it would be a wonderful thing to have that continuum to see how the children interact and work together. I felt that for my second-graders, it would give them many benefits, such as being leaders, developing a caring attitude towards younger children. Instead of this usual attitude we see in school between children. And then for the young ones, the modelling would be wonderful. One of my second-graders just taught a kindergarten child how to tie his shoes the other day.

Mrs Lauren's classroom

A long bulletin board and two long tables in the corridor at the entrance to Mrs Lauren's classroom contain contributions from the children. There is nothing uniform in the children's products. There are projects, pictures, poems and other writing. Invented spelling is the norm on written work. They are not graded; in fact, these items contain no teacher marks of any kind.

Mrs Lauren's self-contained classroom is small for her twenty-nine children. The room is divided into areas: carpet, projects, housekeeping, woodworking, creative play, clay, sand, puppets, books, etc. The carpet area is central; it is the place where sharing, planning and group discussions are held. Mrs Lauren wrote a grant proposal and received a new MacIntosh computer for the room; she was the only one in her school to submit a proposal.

The typical day begins with sharing. The children sit attentively on the carpet while the child in charge of sharing for the day calls on others, one at a time, to share. The principal's announcements of birthdays and faculty meetings are a brief interruption. The entire school body stands at attention to sing 'The Star Spangled Banner' and to pledge allegiance to the flag. After the patriotic traditions are completed, the children resume sharing. They share all sorts of things: a new toy, a visiting grandmother or baseball cards. A seven-year-old girl who read Judy Blume's (1985) *Freckle Juice* brings a container of freckle juice, the recipe and has freckles painted on her face. To close the sharing time, the children practise maths with the calendar activity. They learn about concepts such as today, yesterday, tomorrow, ones, tens and hundreds.

Mrs Lauren's children have more freedom of movement in her room than they do in other classrooms. They do not have to raise their hand to use the supplies – in fact, the only time they raise their hand is when they are all sitting on the carpet. When Mrs Lauren needs to call the class to the carpet for a group meeting or activity, she does not have to flick the lights, ring a bell or call out in a loud voice. She gently says, 'Listen'. The children stop what they are doing and look at her to find out what she wants.

There is no teacher's desk in this classroom; there is no area of the room which focuses on the teacher. The classroom is set up for children. They get continual practice in making choices and decisions. Mrs Lauren has a conference with each child every week to go over the child's work, progress and plans. Instead of telling the child what to do, she probes with questions.

She and her assistant work as a team. The children approach the assistant as much as they do Mrs Lauren. The classroom is a busy place, not only with the children's activities, but also with the visitors, observers and parents who are there each week. She keeps written records of the children's' work and progress and maintains a portfolio on each child. A typical day, described by a second-grade girl, illustrates how involved the children are in constructing the curriculum:

> Sharing is first. Then Mrs Lauren talks to us about stuff – like Halloween stories or any special plan for the day. Today she told us about how to do our new journal. We usually do our communications first. We write about what we plan to do and then on our conference day, she looks at it. Then we do our explorations – we can do measuring or graphs or shapes. I made a graph in my book. I went around and asked everybody in the class what their favourite colour was and then, when I was done, I wrote a summary. Second-graders have a little yellow book to record what we do in the morning at home. Right after lunch we do our reading. Then we go to centres like art.
>
> Also we do projects. I asked Molly if she wanted to do a project

on bees. We started by listing 'What we know about bees' on one side
of the page and 'What we want to know about bees' on the other side.
Then we did research and started to make books and pictures. Then
we made a bee in woodworking and painted it. Then we shared it with
the class.

Being different

Artifacts common in traditional schools such as basal readers, workbooks,
worksheets, chairs and desks, rows, ability groups and even the teacher's
desk are missing in this classroom. It feels more like a community than an
elementary school class. Mrs Lauren's reflections illustrate some of the
struggles she encounters by being different in a traditional school.

Mrs Lauren considers her educational approach to be non-traditional,
saying, 'My opinions are so far out and different from most teachers'. There
are several ways in which Mrs Lauren deviates from the norm in her school.
She does not like her children to be pulled out of class for special programmes, such as special education or academically gifted classes, because
of the disruption to the days' continuity. The physical environment of her
classroom is unique in the school. Mrs Lauren is less restricted by the
structural, institutional constraints of school than most teachers. She has
an evangelical spirit and hopes that through her children's' progress and
behaviour, the other teachers will eventually accept her methods. Her comments during our interview illustrate how she feels about these differences.
She said:

> Most of the teachers see school a certain way, and they already know
> that within my classroom I'm functioning quite differently from them.
> If I start coming on loud and clear, then they may feel like I'm attack-
> ing what they're doing. They will accept me more easily if they just
> observe from the sidelines and gradually see that my children are lear-
> ning and that they have good manners and good self-control. They
> will gradually develop respect for what I'm doing as they observe what
> I do – better than if I go trying to talk and explain or sell my
> programme.

Mrs Lauren sometimes has to use ingenuity to circumvent the strictures of school policy. She talked about how she needed a bulletin board
in the corridor outside of her room. There was, however, a policy pro-
hibiting nails and tacks in the walls. Mrs Lauren considers displays
very important, not for showing others how well her students are perform-
ing, but for helping develop positive self-concepts and pride in work.
She said:

In our school, we're not allowed to put nails or anything else into the walls. And there are no bulletin boards provided out in the halls in any way shape, form or fashion. It's just concrete blocks. The children began producing all this beautiful work, it needed to be displayed – to keep them producing, to keep building up their self-confidence and feeling proud of themselves. And there was no place to display it. So I started trying to figure out, how could I display their work?

She located special nails that would penetrate concrete and made her own bulletin board. She and her assistant put it up in the middle of the night when no-one was around. At the end of the school year, they took it down (also at night) and filled the holes in the wall with plaster compound.

Problems

Mrs Lauren says that other teachers in her school are critical. She is aware of the criticism and says she has to be able to defend her methods. She often feels isolated and not accepted by several of the teachers. Other teachers have expressed a certain resentment at the attention she receives from others outside the school. Isolation is not easy; it is stressful. In our conversations, she spoke of her experience of being on the outside:

When I agreed to do a K-2 combination class, on the third day I had at least three different teachers march into my room, turn around, put their hands on their hips and say, 'This is the *dumbest* thing I've ever seen!' And I just looked at them and said, 'Well, I really wanted to do it and it's working great'. And they don't say very much to me now. I guess one or two got the feeling I probably wasn't too happy about what they said.

Now they meet my assistant in the halls and continually ask, 'Well, how is it going?' Because they evidently think something bad is going to happen. But it's working beautifully.

Mrs Lauren said that she has to be careful about what she says. She perceives the school environment to be one which does not allow for the free exchange of ideas. She said, 'You really do worry. You have to be careful. I mean I have to be careful, because I would be offensive to so many teachers. And I can't just turn them off'.

For example, Mrs Lauren has heard teachers complain that her students spend all day playing, and she has developed coping strategies to deal with such criticisms. Thus, she carefully documents her curriculum and the children's progress. She uses the children's portfolios and holistic evaluation records rather than the standard types of tests. In this regard, Mrs Lauren said:

For several years I heard [through the grapevine] that the third-grade teachers said my children must have been just playing around last year. I had to find a way to deal with that. So I started portfolios on the children, and I kept them through the year with samples of their work. When the next year arrived and I heard these rumblings, I just went down the hall and said to Mrs So and So, 'I heard Chris or Michael is having a problem. Would you like to see the work that he did last year?'

And I pulled his folder and went down there and showed her what all he had done. And I did that about twice, and I never again heard anything from a third-grade teacher. The other teacher said, 'Oh, it just takes a couple of weeks to teach them to sit down and raise their hand to sharpen their pencil. They're always wanting to use the stapler'. You see, in my room that's okay and they don't have to have permission to do it.

She has often experienced conflict simply because of the way she sets up her room:

In the very beginning, when I first started setting up learning areas in the room, I was the younger teacher. There were three or four teachers at each grade level. After lunch, we would come back and these other teachers would have a break and they would come to my classroom and walk around my class and point out to me all the things I shouldn't be doing and why it wasn't going to work. These teachers didn't like my changing the physical arrangement of my room. That bothered them.

But despite being isolated, Mrs Lauren knows the system and has learned how to work within it. She uses the state course of study and the child development guidelines rather than textbooks as sources of guidance. She has learned that if she takes the time and effort to justify her approach in writing, she is usually free to use that approach. She described some of the ways in which she copes with the curriculum requirements:

I prepared a little notebook where I wrote down my philosophy, wrote down everything about my daily schedule and why I was doing it and what could be expected from the children. He [the principal] could read my book anytime he wanted to. This really came in handy when the evaluators came into my room. I used it with them, too, and it worked great.

I've had problems with my principals off and on. I found out one thing all principals like is a clean, neat room. My children are trained to keep a very neat and clean room at the end of the day. So when he comes through for inspection, he doesn't get upset.

Motivation and satisfaction

Why does Mrs Lauren continue to teach when she feels so isolated? She is committed and dedicated and believes that she is making a difference. She believes in children and in teaching and learning. Although many of the teachers in her school are not supportive, she has a strong support system outside her school. She receives a high degree of support from parents; many parents specifically request her as their children's teacher. She also gets professional support from the outside. She is often called upon by university faculty to participate in forums and classes; she has frequent visitors from other districts and even other states; and she has a close relationship with the regional education agency.

Even with this network of support, Mrs Lauren said she sometimes feels let down. She described one of these periods, when she felt criticism directed at her and was worried that her children's parents would get upset. Her comments also illustrate a missionary spirit that she takes to her work:

> And then, it seems like every time I hit one of these down places, somehow, something's provided. I came home, turned on the TV, and heard about schools for the twenty-first century, and I knew I was okay. And I was on target, and that gave me my self-confidence back. And I went right back to work. It was just like a miracle, because I walked in and there it was. It gave me back everything that I'd been thinking and feeling that I thought I knew. But all these people coming at me made me feel a little bit nervous.

Relations with children

Research on the conditions of teaching shows that one of the most important rewards of teaching is in the relationship between the teacher and students (Lortie 1975; Boyer 1990; Spring 1990). Mrs Lauren believes in the importance of early childhood experiences and treats children with respect. The atmosphere of the class, where the children are involved, active and, at the same time, well-behaved, is evidence that they are comfortable and productive in her class. Her curriculum and approach to 'discipline' are a natural outcome of a holistic, democratic, integrated approach. She is not authoritarian. She talks to the children when they have a problem, taking a responsibility rather than a punishment orientation. She talks about the importance of feelings 'that are built among people'. She said:

> You don't train children by saying, 'I want you to do this and you will do that'. It has to come from reading books and building up in them, 'Well, what are your goals for this classroom?' And 'How can

we all live in here and work and share together?' And letting them tell you, really, what you would be telling them. Anything they forget, you pull it out of them, instead of trying to put it in them.

Her curriculum is founded on authentic experiences that are connected with the world outside of school. She attempts to provide a cohesive programme and avoids frustrating experiences for the children. It is developmentally appropriate, child-centred, integrated and democratic. She says:

> You really can't embrace two programmes in one room too easily because it's giving the child two messages. If you set the room up in learning areas and you tell him he's going to get to use them, then at the same time, he's sitting down at a desk and you give him so much work that he never gets to use them, then it's like, the child is wanting to go there, and he's frustrated and you're frustrated.

Conclusion

Although Mrs Lauren is only one alternative teacher in one small, rural school system, her story illustrates many of the problems non-traditional teachers face. She seeks professional freedom in a hierarchical environment. She struggles with her lack of power. She does not feel free to voice her concerns to colleagues and administrators. She has developed coping mechanisms. She avoids other teachers who are critical of her. She keeps her classroom neat and clean to be above reproach. She documents her philosophy, methods and her children's progress. She seeks support outside of her school.

This glimpse into Mrs Lauren's classroom has implications for rural schools where traditions are strong. America's schools, like the country itself, were built as a vehicle for providing a common culture (Tack 1974). The drive for standardization is crushing the notion of individual differences. Being different today is risky. It is easier to conform to the customs and norms of society, the community and the institution than it is to go against the grain. Rewards tend to go to those teachers who follow tradition, who do not rock the boat.

Rural schools have not been exempt from American cultural homogenization. Indeed, schools are often the first in small communities to embrace standardized practices. Teachers in rural American schools are often subjected to the same requirements as their urban or suburban counterparts, regardless of the fit of those requirements to the place. Teachers using alternative or progressive approaches in small, rural schools face special problems. Institutions such as public schools place a high premium on conformity. Being alternative is by definition being different, and teachers who are different are often perceived as threats to the *status quo*, regardless of the quality of their work.

Mrs Lauren bases her curriculum on wisdom from child development and progressive, experiential education. Her curriculum ideas have been influenced by readings about the British infant school. She is pushing the walls of tradition despite the effort and trouble it causes her. While Mrs Lauren is unusual within her school system, she is not unique. Many traditional schools have teachers who take risks and who face many of the same problems. They need to be identified, and their stories need to be heard. However, they should be nurtured in ways that do not unnecessarily threaten their more traditional colleagues in the classroom next door.

The story of teaching needs to change. We need more stories of successful teachers whose emphasis is not on textbooks and obedient children, isolated skills and performance on standardized tests. We need to hear stories of teachers who use their communities and the experiences of their students as an integral part of their curriculum. Their stories should be shared, not as prescriptions for lesson plans, but to fire the imaginations of teachers who are looking for other ways of teaching.

References

Blume, J. (1985) *Freckle Juice*. New York: Macmillan.

Bogdan, R.C. and Biklen, S.K. (1992) *Qualitative Research for Education: An Introduction to Theory and Methods*. Boston, MA: Allyn and Bacon.

Boyer, E.L. (1990) *The Condition of Teaching: A State-by-state Analysis*. Princeton, NJ: Carnegie Foundation for the Advancement of Teaching.

Dewey, J. (1938) *Experience and Education*. New York: Collier Books.

Eisner, E. (1991) *The Enlightened Eye*. New York: Macmillan.

Erickson, F. (1986) Qualitative methods in research on teaching, in Wittrock, M.C. (Ed.), *Handbook of Research on Teaching*, 3rd edn. New York: Macmillan.

Kliebard, H. (1986) *The Struggle for the American Curriculum 1893–1958*. Boston, MA: Routledge and Kegan Paul.

Lincoln, Y.S. and Guba, E.G. (1985) *Naturalistic Enquiry*. Beverly Hills, CA: Sage.

Lortie, D. (1975) *Schoolteacher*. Chicago, IL: University of Chicago Press.

Miles, M.B. and Huberman, A.M. (1984) *Qualitative Data Analysis: A Sourcebook of New Methods*. Beverly Hills, CA: Sage.

Patton, M.Q. (1990) *Qualitative Evaluation and Research Methods*. Newbury Park, CA: Sage.

Spring, J. (1990) *American Education*. New York: Longman.

Tyack, D. (1974) *The One Best System: A History of American Urban Education*. Cambridge, MA: Harvard University Press.

10

Empirical authors, liminal texts and model readers

David Thomas

Introduction

This chapter arose out of reading Woods' (1993) most interesting account of one teacher's life-story. Independently of the intrinsic value of the account, I was intrigued because, like Woods, I too am in possession of a teacher's life-history. My teacher's story is very different from the one Woods relates, being one of great happiness as a pupil, of failure in teaching and of the abandonment of the profession. However, my main reaction to the account by Peter Woods is that, although sharing a common fascination with the possibilities of teachers' biographic work having a major impact upon personal and professional development, I have rather more problems than he appears to acknowledge in his paper, with the very concept of the interpretation of the biographic text.

For those who have not yet read 'Managing marginality' (Woods 1993), here is its main thrust. It begins with an account of the relationship between the paper's academic author and a primary school teacher, 'Peter', whose pupils had won a prize for the best children book of the year. This prize appears as a kind of professional epiphany; the culmination of his views, beliefs and ideals about teaching and learning. Through a process of discussion and writing, Peter's life-history from early childhood to the present is constructed. His educational philosophy is described, and from it, an argument is developed about the importance of life-history in educational research, the significance of the self, the concept of marginality, critical incidents, managing marginality and the grounded life-history as a research method and a resource for the self. The paper contains several extracts from Peter's life-history.

My aim is not to formally critique it – indeed my feelings about this particular paper are those of gratitude for having been introduced to a remarkable teacher – but to use it as an opportunity to engage with some personal concerns about the problematic nature of this genre and especially the biographic text and its possible interpretation[s].

Stories and interpretations

Having finished my boring tasks for the day, I turn to my shelf of novels and find there, as yet unread, Umberto Eco's (1990) *Foucault's Pendulum*. Even before opening the book and reading a single page, I am intrigued. 'Foucault?' Who is he referring to? Anyone with only a marginal acquaintance with European intellectual developments of the last two or three decades will wonder if Michel is being invoked – 'the primary unit of analysis is the discourse'. But no, we remember that Eco has been Professor of Semiotics at the University of Bologna since 1975 – the first Chair of its kind in Europe – and the Saussurian sensitivities embedded in his professional (and professorial) *langue* would hardly allow such a coarse jest; unless, of course, he is playing some special kind of double-bluff. Without having opened the novel, I wonder what it is I am holding, since it may well be that this is, given Eco's prodigious grasp of languages, one of his novels which was written in English and then translated into Italian. If so, then what is the relationship between my copy and the original text, and is the printed version a replica of the manuscript? In fact, this book was written in Italian. We know from Eco himself that like many (most?) authors, he makes last-minute alterations to the galleys, so that there are small but significant differences between his manuscript and the printed text. (Seeing Balzac's alterations to his page proofs alter permanently one's view of the text as a finished product.) Standing there, book in hand, I am confronted by the – certainly post-Derridian – problematics of text, authorial intention and the role of readership.

While these aspects are of central importance to literary criticism, they also resonate with some of our current concerns in educational and social science research. In the particular text which has provoked this Chapter (Woods 1993), we are given extracts from a longer 'text' (possibly a mix of written and taped accounts, not easily available to readers of this book for obvious reasons), together with a critical and interpretive commentary. In its structural features, Woods' paper is not very different from a number of similar studies (e.g. Knowles 1988; Butt and Raymond 1989; Clandinin

1989), in that 'readers' are faced with a number of interpretive dilemmas. There are, of course, two categories of readers: first, there is the *interpreter*, Woods himself; and then there are those who read his paper, whom I shall refer to as *over-readers*, and there are special problems for both.

Definitions

* *Empirical author*: the embodied person who created the text.
* *Empirical text*: the final unalterable text.
* *Authoritative text*: the fictive 'text of texts'.
* *Liminal authors*: the creators of possible texts.
* *Liminal text*: the other text which might have been created.
* *The interpreter*: the one who offers a guide to the text.
* *The over-reader*: the reader of the interpreter's account.

Empirical author and intentionality

Let us start by asking if, using Eco's own category system, we can say anything about the empirical author (the actual, *embodied* creator) of the original text (Collini 1992). With such an individualistic medium, it is quite natural to want more than an 'account', since we are invited to re-create a person. We wonder how old he is, what he looks like, how he speaks, whether we would like him, and so on? We may invent the empirical author (I refer here to the author of the text Woods uses in his paper), sitting at his desk, pen in hand; or crouched over a keyboard, his face illuminated by the green glow of the screen (I prefer to see him with a fountain-pen, probably a Waterman's); or sitting in the interpreter's study, glass of white wine nearby and the tape-recorder humming in the background. And as he writes or talks, we imagine him as having some kind of *intention* for these acts. Among the questions we would like to put to him would be: 'Why are you writing this?', 'Why are you writing *what* you are writing?', 'Who is your imagined reader?'

Of those things which he might have chosen to write, we would like to know why *did* he choose *this* event and not that one, why did he decide to include *this* person and to leave out others from his cast of characters (like lepers at a squint, those characters we can never know), and why choose one *word* over another. We see him pause, pen in hand, as we all do, making choices or having choices made for him. Between the empirical author and his empirical text are the shadowy shapes of an infinite number of liminal authors, making textual decisions before a final (?) text version is created. Between the empirical author and his produced text (the empirical text) are those other 'texts' which could have been written on the

basis of other intentions, through the exercise of other choices, under differing sets of motivation and within other relationships.

The available empirical text is what we *have*, but its status is, in one
sense, problematic, for who knows what else might have been written? If
such a text is, shall we say, provisional, then it produces a measure of uncertainty for interpreter or reader. Once it is acknowledged that the empirical
text is not necessarily the authoritative text – the extensive but theoretically
finite set text which can be produced (the text of texts) – then to offer
explications of more than a provisional character would be rash.

The empirical author is credited with an apparent command of authorial
intent. He knows what he is about and is rational in his choice of events,
personalities and language. What is then produced becomes the empirical
text. Except, of course, like all writers, there is something else at work.
An unsettled, itchy, mischievous imp from some unacknowledged region
inside the self, fuming up from the compost of discarded memories, or from
some even more inaccessible interiority, pushes the pen to write this word
and not another. The private, personal world of the text creator, is seldom
available to the reader or over-reader, and while this absence of knowledge
encourages speculation about covert meanings and unintended outcomes,
the text itself becomes the only reasonably secure foundation for inter-
pretation(s). Thus, paradoxically, the empirical text is both treacherous and
firm.

Authorial games and gamesmanship

When Eco (1990) introduces a character into *Foucault's Pendulum* called
Casaubon, the average English reader is placed on alert, and we feel we
must pay special attention to 'the old magus of Bologna' (Richard Rorty's,
1992, phrase), since he/we may be playing games of deconstruction here.
Has he selected a major character from *Middlemarch* with a particular
intent? Can this choice, in a work which can be regarded as if not a
knockout blow then at least a vicious upper-cut to the whole structuralist
enterprise, be a simple accident? He must *surely* have been aware, we
imagine, given his command of the canons of English literature, of the
intellectual task Casaubon had set himself – the ultimate structuralist
labour – to 'uncover the key to all mythologies' – a task he was obliged to
set down leaving it to Levi-Strauss as a still uncompleted labour. Are there
verbal plays here? Are we to respond with a Lacanian *glissade* into the
bilingual resonances of 'casa' and 'bon' as ironic, teasing allusions upon the
unhappy household of George Eliot's heroine and her unappealing husband
and his ultimately doomed quest?

In this case, Eco comes to our rescue, for as the empirical author he can state that he had quite another Casaubon in mind when he named his character and the Eliot connection did not appear, to his conscious knowledge, until he had nearly finished writing the novel (now the empirical text, at least, in English) and, as witnesses to his own actions, we can hardly do anything apart from accept his report as factual. However, the tingle of cultural recognition which such a name evokes in one reader, even though such reactions were not part of the authorial intention, illustrates the autistic quality of the text. Once generated and available, the authorial intention may be transformed by readers who bring to their reading their own translations – what Eco refers to 'the uncontrollable drift of its [the texts] future readings'.

Readers and over-readers

This leads to linking the authorial intention and the final (?) empirical text to the register of readers. The author of a text ·to be read, and especially where the text is then made available to everyone, takes a gamble. It may be imagined that each writer orients his or her text towards some 'model reader' or 'ideal reader'. Private letters, journals, diaries and accounts, ostensibly meant for a single ideal reader, or those other 'quasi-private' products (with a double intention of being initially addressed to a friend or lover but with a sharp eye upon posterity – like Cecily's diary, or Philip Larkin's letter) may have both a single ideal reader as well as model readers in mind. All writers, whose works are cast upon the public waters, know that, whatever their intentions might have been and the precision of their identification of a model or ideal reader, their text is at the mercy of readers, as differentiated individuals, with varying linguistic competencies and diverse cultural resources (this Eco terms the readers' 'world knowledge'). Those who provide autobiographical material for public attention are not naive and will have (consciously or otherwise) a sense of readership, and with it goes an awareness of an intention to create in the mind of the model reader a certain effect. As the post-modernists would have it, 'there are no longer any innocent texts', which implies that there are no virgin readers.

Most writers consciously or unconsciously identify a model reader who will bring to the task of reading an empirical text a 'world knowledge' which enables the interaction between authorial intention, the empirical text and interpretive readership to proceed with sympathy, understanding, delight and reciprocity. Like all really clever authors, Eco is pleased when clues, puzzles, conceits, references and allusions are missed, undetected or misunderstood, and this differentiates the model reader (perhaps we should refer to the modal reader?) from the ideal reader – who is most usually the author him or herself. If that is correct, then we should, as responsible social scientists, invite the empirical author to inform us of intentions, potential readership and their anticipated world knowledge. This implies a strategic role for the empirical author in assisting with interpretations. In Woods' paper, the role of Peter in assisting with the interpretation is not clear.

Interpreting sacred and secular texts

The problem of textual interpretation is a venerable one. In the Judeo-Christian tradition, the meaning of The Word was a central theological activity. This became a crucial enterprise with the Reformation, when every reader was capable of coming to his or her own interpretation. This led to a great concern to have the exact Word so that an authentic interpretation could commence from a sound footing. What would constitute the uncorrupted Word? The St James Vulgate came from a Greek source via a translation from the Hebrew (Old Testament) and from the original Greek (New Testament) translated into Latin. To understand it there was the need for learned readers and interpreters. It became possible to discover what those who had written the Testaments had written as opposed to what St Jerome said they had said and what the organized church said St Jerome had said. As Tyndale wrote:

> I had perceived . . . that it was impossible to establish the lay-people in any truth, except the scriptures were plainly laid before their eyes in their mother-tongue, that they might see the process, order, and meaning of the text.
>
> (in Trapp 1992)

The interpretation of sacred texts was, in Reformation Europe – and no less in our time with the emotions stirred up by the *Satanic Verses* – a matter of life and death, as well as opinion. I would advance a Protestant view on the interpretation of secular texts, that the text (ideally) needs to be placed before our eyes so that we can construct our own *process, order* and *meaning* without the pre-emption of a mediating agency. That is not to say that the 'Protestant' position allows one to say anything one likes about a text: there are limits.

Interpretations and over-interpretations

Among the issues Eco (1989) investigates are the limits to the *interpretations* which can be made of the empirical text. He seems to reject the notion that the empirical text, once out of the study and into the printing press, is sundered from the author's intention and is vulnerable to any textual diagnostics which can reveal aspects, themes, meanings and intentions of which the author was unaware. This is the heartland question of what constitutes plausible interpretation and the point where 'over-interpretation' begins:

> The classical debate aimed at finding in a text clues either what its author intended to say, or what the text said independently of the intentions of its author . . .
>
> . . . one can ask if what is found is what the text says by virtue of its textual coherence and of an underlying signification system, or what *addressees* found in it by virtue of their own system of expectation.
>
> (Eco 1990: 64, emphasis added)

Eco distinguished between legitimate interpretation and *over-interpretation*. Over-interpretation occurs when the interpreter transgresses by deconstructing the writer's own 'world knowledge' through imposing the interpreter's own world knowledge and by ignoring the writer's intentions (stated or obvious). We might consider not only the difficulties of interpretation of historical texts through the medium of fashionable sensibilities, but also 'readings' of contemporary life-histories over gender, race and class divides. For Eco, the internal coherence of the text stands in a defensive posture against the 'uncontrollable drives of the reader'. Some forms of modern literary criticism seem to take a perverse delight in denying the writer any valid claim to his or her own interpretation. Philosophers, like Rorty (1992), would argue that Eco's distinction between *interpreting* and *using* a text is unacceptable, since 'all anyone does with it (the text) is to use it'. Rorty (1992: 93) goes on: 'Interpreting something, knowing it, penetrating to its essence, and so on, are all just various ways of describing some process of putting it to work'.

Rorty seems to take the view that part of the process of interpreters 'going to work on a text' is to 'convince other people that we are right', and this involves a purely pragmatic condition of having to attend to the whole text and not to selected portions of it. In both interpretive and utilitarian approaches, it is possible for either to have the empirical author state that the interpretation offered by his reader is different from his empirical intention but which, on reflection, appears as a valid alternative, if unexpected, explanation which *is* warranted by the text taken as a whole. However, if the interpreter offers a sharply different view of the text from that offered by the author, how may such differences be debated? Here Eco takes the empirical text itself, as understood in the 'world knowledge' of the writer and his or her model reader, to be the decisive arbiter. That is, the interpretation should not go beyond the parameters of the text itself no matter how arcane, pleasing, intriguing or recondite the textual re-reading may appear to be; that is, there are limits to what may be said, and those limits are 'given' by the text itself. As a conceit to illustrate this point in 'Managing marginality', the empirical author is given the name Peter. We do not know whether this is his real name or pseudonym, but it would be in the spirit of deconstruction to link this choice of name with that of the interpreter's. From them we could proceed to elaborate a metaphysical connection between the empirical author and his interpreter as an exchange of identities. From Eco's perspective, this would be an 'over-interpretation', but not from that of Rorty. Its significance is that it challenges the 'taken for granted' assumptions by several researchers in the genre that their magisterial explication is, in any sense, the last Word.

Rhetorical flourishes

If we take the view that teacher narratives, like most narratives, fall into a category of text which is saturated with explicit and implied conventions, it is important to be sensitive to the deployment of these conventions in the accounts.

As Graham (1992) points out, it is necessary to pay attention to the textual characteristics of the narrative. One aspect, the 'poetics', is a part of the process by which we, as interpreters and over-readers, can perceive the cultural and literary codes which are drawn upon by our empirical authors. Among the prominent features of this approach is the understanding of how stories of teachers and teaching come to us already carrying a set of cultural and literary conventions which shape how the biographical work can be represented. Certain teacher stories are brought to us within a 'romantic' context, which may or may not be intentional. For Graham, the poetic form of the narrative may be a literary device through which the teller of tales seeks to move the interpreter and reader into accepting the legitimacy and plausibility of his stories. The basic pre-generic *mythoi* which have been identified as the archetypal narrative formats – tragedy, irony, comedy and romance – can be used as a way of identifying ways of telling stories which have a powerful impact upon those telling and hearing them, since these have been incorporated into our world knowledge of how stories may be told. Clearly, there is a danger here of over-emphasizing a kind of Chomskian narrative 'deep structure' for narratives. However, as a research strategy, I believe approaching teacher stories from the perspective of literary devices is worth considering.

In Peter's story, the romantic associations are evident as we read of his life as a journey (*Bildungsroman*) begun in dread and turmoil (he likens his early schooling to being caught in a fly trap or flattened by a mouse trap), through various experiences of a particularly nasty kind (abused and demeaned by his teachers), but despite or because of it, he trains as a teacher and is inspired by a couple of tutors and makes his journey towards a pedagogic philosophy which combines structure and support for pupils' learning with room for 'freedom, space, latitude and flexibility' and 'facilitating the experience of communitas' in his pupils. In places, the element of quest is overt, as he struggles for an identity and to find a route that is authentically his and not imposed by others.

For Graham (1992: 21), some stories by teachers have a romantic structure:

> Romance also allegorizes teaching as a quest: in particular, it foregrounds its spiritual and moral dimensions as a human endeavour whose ultimate direction lies in liberation from oppression and repression. In narrative terms, a romance plot characterises the drive towards human fulfilment and in this sense is implicated in matters of identity – creation. Understood in this way, an awareness of teaching as romance, assists in reconfiguring the utopian impulse within education as a human project, helps to cast fresh light on the Socratic principle regarding the benefits of an examined life, and draws attention to the aesthetic aspects involved in acting upon the idea of teaching as a moral craft.

Interpreters and over-readers

As Bruner (1992) notes in *Acts of Meaning*, there has been nothing short of a major revolution in many disciplines (anthropology, linguistics, philosophy, literary theory and psychology), centred upon the question of interpretation and meaning. In the 'new' cognitive sciences, notions of meaning are culturally located, and hence are shared and public. I want to suggest that interpreters' accounts, accompanied by partial text, limit the possibility of shared public meanings.

If a researcher has developed a warm rapport with a teacher who is prepared to communicate a life-history, it is difficult, and perhaps morally indefensible, to go 'public' with an interpretation which is other than celebratory. Therefore, the stance which the interpreter adopts in these cases is emotionally and intellectually distinct from that which would be adopted in more conventional research relationships. 'It has to feed into teaching', writes Peter Woods, and needs to find its own moral justification, which is right, but there has to be room for scepticism as well as celebration.

I do not know any outstanding examples (and would be glad to know of any) of interpretative-narrative work in which the empirical author and the interpreter are in conflict over the interpretation. There is a danger in selecting for public presentation those accounts which are permitted to be published by their creators, along with those interpretations which are authorized by the conventions of the relationship. For example, as a researcher who possesses teachers' autobiographies which may *not* be published, what is the appropriate academic stance towards the knowledge which these accounts may generate? Does there exist a negative universe of unpublishable accounts?

The role of the over-reader has to confront not only the selected excerpt from the empirical text, but also the interpreter's perception of both the (unseen) total text and the quotations from it. In a sense, the interpreter's account is like having a review of a play or novel which one hasn't seen or read and, in many cases, may never see. In essence, the over-reader has few options but to 'go with the flow' of the interpretation. The interpreter forecloses upon my options by giving me a version, supported by a judicious selection of quotations, which leaves me little to do except follow the surface logic of the resolution. It would be interesting to publish a teacher's life-history without any exegesis. The task for readers would be to provide their own interpretations of the empirical text, which could then be published together with some synthesizing commentary – preferably by the teacher him or herself. We would then see the range of responses which a single life-history might evoke. It would be worth trying.

If Bruner is correct, central to understanding how people behave is the relationship between action and saying (or experiencing) in the ordinary conduct of life, and this understanding is communicable through the act of interpretation. But it raises awkward questions for the researcher who has access to just one of these dimensions – but that is another issue.

Interpretation and trustworthiness

One of the tasks for the over-reader, presented with limited access to the full empirical text, is to ascertain to what extent he or she may be able to accept the interpretation offered by the interpreter. Mishler (1990) suggests one criterion for the trustworthiness of an interpretation would be the degree to which we would regard it as a satisfactory *basis for action*. Mishler is well aware of the difficulties of reporting research findings which are derived from voluminous sources such as interview transcripts. He sees the task of interpretation as one involving taking the text as datum, using it as an example of a more abstract and general type, analysing it through transparent methods of categorizing and coding and by demonstrating clear links between data, findings and interpretation. The analytic task is based upon the discovery of 'representative patterns' of ideas, behaviours and events within the text. For Mishler (1990: 249), the critical questions are:

What are the warrants for my claims? Could other investigators make a reasonable judgement of their adequacy? Would they be able to determine how my findings and interpretations were 'produced' and, on that basis, decide whether they were trustworthy enough to be relied upon for their own work?

These are the questions which over-readers of interpretations of narratives are required to address.

References

Bruner, J. (1992) *Acts of Meaning*. Cambridge, MA: Harvard University Press.

Butt, R. and Raymond, D. (1989) 'Studying the nature and development of teachers' knowledge using collaborative autobiography'. *International Journal of Educational Research* 13(4), 403–19.

Clandinin, D.J. (1989) 'Developing rhythm in teaching: The narrative study of a beginning teacher's personal practical knowledge of classrooms'. *Curriculum Inquiry* 19(2), 121–41.

Collini, S. (Ed.) (1992) *Interpretation and Overinterpretation*. Cambridge: Cambridge University Press.

Eco, U. (1990) *Foucault's Pendulum* (trans. W. Weaver). London: Picador.

Eliot, G. (1986) *Middlemarch*. Oxford: Clarendon Press.

Graham, R.J. (1992) 'Stories of teaching and the rhetoric of romance'. Unpublished manuscript, University of Manitoba.

Knowles, G. (1988) 'A beginning teacher's experience: Reflection on becoming a teacher'. *Language Arts* 65(7), 702–12.

Mishler, E.G. (1990) 'Validation in inquiry-guided research: The role of exemplars in narrative studies'. *Harvard Educational Review* 60(4), 414–42.

Rorty, R. (1992) The pragmatist's progress, in Collini, S. (Ed.), *Interpretation and Overinterpretation*. Cambridge: Cambridge University Press.

Trapp, J.B. (1992) 'Homage to Tyndale'. *London Review of Books* 17 December.

Woods, P. (1993) 'Managing marginality: Teacher development through grounded life history'. *British Educational Research Journal* 19(5), 447–65.

11

Keys to the past – and to the future

Peter Woods

Introduction

This chapter is a direct response to Chapter 10, 'Empirical authors, liminal texts and model readers', by David Thomas. The justification for this response may be found in that part of his text which reads, 'With such an individualistic medium, it is quite natural to want more than an "account", since we are invited to re-create a person'. The following notes are offered in the hope that they will facilitate such an act of re-creation.

After some introductory remarks, I have endeavoured to focus on selected extracts from David Thomas's text. The relevant sections are indicated by an asterisk.

*... in 'Managing marginality' the empirical author is given the name Peter. We do not know whether this is his real name or pseudonym, but it would be in the spirit of deconstruction to link this choice of name with that of the interpreter's. From them we could proceed to elaborate a metaphysical connection between the empirical author and his interpreter as an exchange of identities.

I have an old school photograph. Like an ancient scroll it has to be unwound to reveal the secrets of the past. At the moment it stands on one of my library shelves – a small white column separating the J's and the L's in that part of my library housing an ever-growing collection of novels. To the left is a paperback copy of Joyce's *A Portrait of the Artist as a Young*

Man and works by Kafka, Kazantzakis and Koestler. To the right are copies of Lawrence's *Lady Chatterley's Lover*, *The Rainbow* and *Sons and Lovers*, and Laurie Lee's *Cider with Rosie*. All are long-standing favourites. Although the choice of shelf was unconsidered, the location of the photograph is not without relevance. I have always felt a certain affinity with Stephen Dedalus, Paul Morel and the young Laurie Lee. The proximity of Lawrence's *The Rainbow* also reminds me that Lawrence, like another of my favourite authors, Leo Walmsley, turned away from teaching to devote their lives to writing. Each had difficulty in reconciling their enlightened views with the educational system of their day (Delavenay 1972).

If I reach up and take down the photograph and unwind it to its full panoramic extent, 313 boyish faces stare out at me, their features seemingly chiselled in stone and fixed for all time. The living, lively grin which spreads across the face of one of the youngest sits uncomfortably among the expressionless faces of his peers and older brethren. His animation would be more at home on a primary school photograph. A few rows behind is another, older pupil. His face exhibits all the philosophical resignation which comes with greater age and experience. The educational sculptor had not yet begun his work on his younger contemporary. The older boy is standing, whereas the younger boy is sitting cross-legged. The only things which link these two pupils are that they have the same Christian and surnames – Peter Woods – and they are part of the same school photograph. Centrally placed at the bottom of the print are the words 'NORTHTOWN GRAMMAR SCHOOL, MAY 1949' in small, dark capitals (a fictionalized name).

This photograph is the only tangible evidence of their childhood association. When these two students left school, they pursued their own careers and there was no reason to think that their paths would ever cross. However, Dame Fortune, eternally capricious, was to decree otherwise. Nearly forty years later, those same pupils were to become David Thomas's empirical author and interpreter. They were reunited by a series of remarkable coincidences.

At this point in the Introduction, I thought it might be helpful to the reader if I said something about my social background and family circumstances. I was born in 1936; both of my parents came from nonconformist backgrounds. Although they had each been part of a large family, they had enjoyed comfortable, lower middle-class childhoods. My paternal grandfather owned three drifters and spent the greater part of his life wresting a modest and sometimes precarious living from the North Sea. My maternal grandfather also had the sea in his blood. In his early years he had been a deck-hand on a tea clipper and in later life he became a coastguard. His reminiscences of his experiences in such exotic locations as the South China Sea fed the more romantic aspects of my personality. My subsequent love of travel and my early interest in such writers as Frank Thomas, Bullen, Joseph Conrad, William Clark Russell and Henry de Vere Stacpoole probably owed much to his lively accounts of the tea races, vessels like the *Cutty Sark* and life under sail in tropical climes. In the years immediately preceding my birth when the Great Depression was at its height, my father had to endure long periods of unemployment. A physical aversion to the sea made it impossible for him to follow in his father's footsteps and he obtained casual labour in one of the local timber yards.

Their experiences during the early 1930s left both my parents with strong feelings about the importance of a good education – specifically entry into the area high or grammar schools. It would be the passport which would ensure their children's return to their rightful middle-class background. Against all the odds, during the early war years, my mother paid for me to go to a private 'dame school' instead of attending the local council school, and when my adopted sister was not successful in gaining entry to a selective secondary school, my mother insisted that she should enter a private establishment. This was all paid for from a very modest working-class income. My mother's delight when I successfully negotiated the rigours of the eleven-plus examination – but only after a borderline interview – was obvious, but as the years passed I came to realize that my achievement was as important to my mother's longed-for process of social re-instatement as it was to my future. Her concern that I should enjoy the advantages of a formal academic education was akin to the middle-class perceptions prevailing at the grammar school. This was a view of education I found that I could not recognize and which I soon abandoned. Although I was not aware of it at the time, the seeds of naturalism and a kind of liberal humanism had already taken root in the fertile soil of my early experience.

Like my father, I inclined towards a more flexible and tolerant, a more sensual and hedonistic view of life. I came to believe that the educative process should involve the elevation of the senses and should include an element of pleasure and lasting satisfaction. My mother, on the other hand, appeared to have an innate fear of anything sensual, which even extended to shows of family affection and which probably reflected the more puritanical aspects of a strict, non-conformist childhood. My mother's upbringing and aspirations, however, could not conceal the reality of our present circumstances and provided little protection from the latent hostility – from both staff and pupils – which confronted me when I first entered the hallowed portals of Northtown Grammar School.

I was totally unprepared for the animosity which was directed towards me by some of the staff, the more established of whom clearly preferred their experience of teaching in a private grammar school unaffected by the changes which were introduced by the 1944 Education Act. I was not aware at this time that I lacked the mannerisms and the forms of speech which were inborn in many of my classmates. I was cheerfully unaware of my inferior social status. The alienation felt by the 'scholarship boys' at North-town Grammar School in the decade or so after the Second World War has been described by Peter Woods (1987) in his paper 'Life histories and teacher knowledge'. Gradually, as I began to consider the basis of my education at the grammar school and my rejection of much of its substance, I found myself beginning to question the feelings of guilt which I had about my marked lack of achievement and my parents' anxiety for my success. Knowing the sacrifices which my parents had made and the esteem in which they held formal academic education, I began to feel that I had betrayed their trust and could never make adequate reparation. A natural desire to realize my parents' expectations for me and a concern to be true to my own gradually emerging beliefs were in opposition. This gave rise to a guilt complex which manifested itself every time I achieved poor examination results and whenever I succumbed to the lure of the Norfolk countryside instead of staying at home to complete my homework. It is only recently that I have come to understand the duality of my mother's motives and the fact that social prejudice, in a variety of forms, was an important element in my adolescent feelings of isolation and alienation. This increased awareness has finally allowed me to come to terms with my guilt syndrome.

Northtown Grammar School was, at this time, an all-male preserve. Segregation was to continue for many years after I left. In such a male-dominated society, it was natural that the more physical pursuits of rugby and association football (followed by cold showers), and occasional fighting, achieved the kind of prominence which they might not have done in a more integrated community. Any form of transgression was punished by physical chastisement. When I was in the sixth-form, I was caned by the headmaster for slipping out of school at lunch-time to watch a group of little terns which were nesting on the nearby beach. This was regarded as a serious breach of discipline. I was told I was setting a bad example. When my peers left the grammar school it was expected they would complete their National Service and then go on to university (ideally Oxford or Cambridge). Many were destined for all-male colleges. Although I enjoyed being involved in more rigorous pursuits, such as cycling, birds' nesting and kicking a tennis ball around the quadrangle at lunch-times, my preference was for gentler activities. I was interested in the natural world, in lyrical and pastoral poetry, in ballet and music and art. While I would not go so far as to refer to these latter preoccupations as being of a more feminine kind, it is perhaps fair to draw an analogy with classical times when martial pursuits tended to be represented by gods and gentler activities by goddesses. While I preferred to dwell with Euterpe, Thalia and Terpsichore on Helicon and Parnassus, my peers seemed to be happier in the company of Aries and Heracles on Olympus. Perhaps the grammar school was seeking to preserve the distinctions of the ancient world.

While we were at school together in the late 1940s and early 1950s, contact between myself and the other Peter Woods was minimal. I soon became aware that there was another Peter Woods, but as he had embarked on his secondary school career some three years before myself, his world and mine rarely touched. Our orbits followed different trajectories. A couple of years so after the photograph was taken, the older Peter Woods became a school prefect. It was at this point that our separate worlds began to coincide. I can recall him seated at the head of our dinner table, choosing who should serve and who should clear away. I also remember him drawing attention to the fact that it was taking me an unreasonable amount of time to progress from the warm cloakroom to the winter playground. Sometimes, during lunch-breaks, he would be on library duty. I chanced upon the school library when searching for a warmer alternative to the playground. In the years that followed, this large rectangular room with its open shelves and glass-fronted bookcases was to become for me an alternative world of endless fascination. The rows of books, many handsomely bound, helped me to appreciate the variety and boundlessness of knowledge.

In one of the locked bookcases there was a fine collection of birds' eggs. I felt myself drawn to this part of the library. The delicate shells and beautiful mottled colours of the eggs evoked the freedom and spaciousness of the countryside, which was within cycling distance of my home in Gorleston-On-Sea and the fragileness of that 'other world'. I would half close my eyes and the mixed blues and greens and browns and whites would become summer skies with cotton-wool clouds, the open fields, the resin-scented forests and the lonely, wind-swept marshland of my childhood environment. In my mind, I used to imagine that I had discovered the hiding-place for the key to that particular bookcase and that I could remove the eggs from their cold, dusty surroundings and cradle them in the living warmth of my hand. To this day, that small zoological collection and its immediate surroundings are symbols for two contrasting aspects of education – one indicative of space and freedom, and the other enclosed and claustrophobic. They also help to explain why I had difficulty in coming to terms with those austere buildings and the system of education which had flourished there for generations. In 1951, along with the other pupils, I was obliged to participate in the school's four hundredth anniversary. I found this event both awe-inspiring and intimidating. It said so much about the tenacity (and sterility) of the system which was being celebrated and which I was beginning to reject.

When they left grammar school, the two boys in the photograph went their own ways. After two years National Service, the younger boy – the future empirical author – entered Loughborough Teachers' Training

College, married and moved to Northamptonshire. Many years later he was appointed headteacher of Brixworth VC Primary School.

One day in the summer of 1988, the telephone in my office rang. It was my secretary with the information that a Professor Woods from the Open University wanted to speak with me. Although I did not know a Professor Woods, the call occasioned no surprise as our school had recently been the focus of some media attention. When he was put through to me, the caller explained that he had been interested to learn, from reports on television and in the local press, that our school had invited a practising author to work with a group of children and had produced a full-length children's story called *Rushavenn Time*. He went on to say he understood that the school published this story and, in competition with some of the leading publishing houses, had won a prestigious literary award. He said that he was particularly interested as he was researching similar projects and he wondered whether he could talk to me about this venture. An appointment was made for the following week. At this initial meeting I was to discover that, not only did we bear the same Christian and surnames, but we had attended the same grammar school and had settled within ten miles of each other in the same county. This intelligence seemed to be stretching the bounds of credulity to their utmost limits. Other meetings were arranged and a relationship – an understanding – gradually developed.

Critical commentary

*There are, of course, two categories of reader: first, there is the *interpreter*, Woods himself; and then there are those who read his paper, whom I shall refer to as *over-readers*, and there are special problems for both.

*We see him [the empirical author] pause, pen in hand, as we all do, making choices *or having choices made for him* [my emphasis]. Between the empirical author and his empirical text are the shadowy shapes of an infinite number of liminal authors, making textual decisions before a final (?) text version is created. Between the empirical author and his produced text (the empirical text) are those other 'texts' which could have been written on the basis of other intentions, through the exercise of other choices, under differing sets of motivation and within other relationships.

*The empirical author is credited with an *apparent* [again my emphasis] command of authorial intent. He knows what he is about and is rational in his choice of events, personalities and language. What is then produced becomes the empirical text. Except, of course, like all writers, there is something else at work. An unsettled, itchy, mischievous imp from some unacknowledged region inside the self, fuming up from the compost of discarded memories, or from some inaccessible interiority, pushes the pen to write this word and not another.

I would like to suggest that there are not two but three categories of readers. There is also the 'subject' himself, the empirical author. I base this assertion on the belief that there is resident in all writers a number of literary daemons analogous to David Thomas's 'unsettled, itchy, mischievous imp(s)', and liminal authors, who are intent on subverting the empirical author's specific intention. Their intervention, which may manifest itself as a kind of subliminal spontaneity, can result in a lowering, or even abrogation, of the proper level of control over the authorial purpose. (This not to deny the possibility of legitimate liminal texts which would have a validity had the writer exercised a different choice or if he had had a different authorial intention.) To prevent this from happening, the empirical author has to assume the role of both reader and interpreter. During the course of his reading of the text which he has written, he may find himself saying, 'This is not me. This is not what I wanted to say'. To regain control over his material he has, through reading and interpretation, to suppress any liminal texts which do not accord with his precise authorial intention. It is against this background that the empirical author struggles to produce the uncorrupted or authoritative text.

David Thomas would probably be pleased to learn that I still have the Waterman pen which I used to compose texts in large, outdated diaries which were nicely bound and could be purchased quite cheaply. The crossings-out on the handwritten page represented either a failure of literary intent on my part, arising from fatigue or lack of inspiration, or – more comforting for the truly creative artist – a denial of the alternative expressions welling up from the competing liminal authors inhabiting David Thomas's 'inaccessible interiority'. When using a word-processor the denial may be more permanent, but the penned corrections were useful reminders of the presence of 'ghost writer'. This is why I still prefer to write in pen and ink rather than seated before a word-processing screen. Regrettably, convenience and lack of time mostly dictate that I adopt the latter *modus operandi*.

The real interpreter has to work in a similar manner, but we shall come to that later.

*Among the questions we would like to put to him [the empirical author] would be: 'Why are you writing this?', 'Why are you writing *what* you are writing?', 'Who is your imagined reader?'

*It may be imagined that each writer orients his or her text towards some 'model reader' or 'ideal reader'.

My decision to start thinking and (subsequently) writing about my earlier life experiences was certainly not prompted by a desire to create a work of literature. Thoughts of publication or appealing to an audience of potential readers never featured in my original intentions. The only readership which I had in mind was the ideal reader – myself. Thus there was no temptation to create a certain effect (other than that which I wanted to achieve for myself). In case this should appear to be just another example of literary indulgence, I should perhaps explain that one of the outcomes of marginality can be a failure of confidence. From childhood and adolescence I had become increasingly introspective. This stemmed, in part, from an awareness that my thoughts and ideas were not of the mainstream. Until quite recently, it never occurred to me that there might be groups of people – model readers – who would be interested in the thoughts which I was endeavouring to express in private diaries and notebooks. I was quite content to share my opinions with a few close and trusted friends – a farmhand, a gamekeeper and a Ministry of Works custodian. It was only when I went to Loughborough to train as a teacher that I was forced to become more outgoing and expansive. My two years' teacher training gave me the confidence to maintain and to talk more openly about my thoughts and feelings. An important element in this was the discovery of two very special lecturers – Jim Abraham and the author Ernest Frost – who not only shared many of my views, but actively encouraged me to hold on to my opinions. I never felt marginalized in their presence. Once I became established in teaching, I occasionally found that there were naturally occurring – not contrived – opportunities to test those beliefs. David Thomas is right in referring to the *Rushavenn* experience as a kind of epiphany.

In thinking about my life – and later writing about it – my overriding aim was to attempt to preserve a past which was particularly meaningful for me. One of the problems with any attempt to 'summon up remembrance of things past' is the discontinuity and transitoriness of one's recollection of past events. A particular sound or smell, walking into an unfamiliar room, the rounding of a corner and encountering an unexpected view are often sufficient to trigger the memory, but such experience can be as ephemeral as a dream. Perhaps no-one has expressed more beautifully than Proust, in the opening chapter of *Swann's Way*, the intermittent nature of these recollections, and the problems of re-establishing continuity and perspective:

> I would ask myself what time it could be; I could hear the whistling of trains, which, now nearer and now farther off, punctuating the

distance like the note of a bird in a forest, showed me in perspective the deserted countryside through which a traveller is hurrying towards the nearby station; and the path he is taking will be engraved in his memory by the excitement induced by strange surroundings, by unaccustomed activities, by the conversation he has had and the farewells exchanged beneath an unfamiliar lamp, still echoing in his ears amid the silence of the night, by the imminent joy of going home.

(Proust 1982: 3)

In my writing, I wanted to achieve some kind of continuity and permanence for those treasured, fleeting impressions. I did not want to have to continue relying on the intermittent occurrence of unusual combinations of circumstances as my route back into the experiences of my childhood.

There were other aims. I thought that an attempt to recreate the past might help me to define exactly who I was at a time when I seemed to be surrounded by people, sometimes with the best intentions – parents and relatives, Sunday-school and daytime teachers, ministers and other concerned adults – who seemed to be wanting to mould me into their own image. This appeared to be a kind of active narcissism or self-indulgence which would sometimes lead them to invoke personal philosophies to justify, or lend strength to, their actions. What I felt I needed to do – for myself, not for others – was to try to get below the surface and to find out who I really was and what I could have become without all these external influences. There was also the thought that if I could discover myself, this might help me to arrive at a better understanding of my peers.

I also believed that such thinking and writing might help me to form the basis of a philosophy of life which would not only be my own, and allow me to be true to myself, but which would help me to cope with my feelings of marginality. This would be necessary if I was going to survive and make the best of a life which, at that time, spread out to a distant, limitless horizon and beyond.

But the latter aims were always subsidiary to the first.

*I would advance a Protestant view on the interpretation of secular texts, that the text (ideally) needs to be placed before our eyes so that we can construct our own *process*, *order* and *meaning* without the pre-emption of a mediating agency.

*I want to suggest that interpreters' accounts, accompanied by partial text, limit the possibility of shared public meanings.

*One of the tasks for the over-reader, presented with limited access to the full empirical text, is to ascertain to what extent he or she may be able to accept the interpretation offered by the interpreter.

The following points are probably worth making:

- I would have been delighted to have made the complete text available, but as far as publication is concerned, it would not have been practical, as David Thomas recognizes, in this book.
- To fully understand the views of the empirical author, as expressed in his autobiography, would not the over-reader also need to have access to his other writings, specifically his work on *Rushavenn Time* and his account of the life and writings of the Yorkshire-born author Leo Walmsley? While all of this material has been made available to the interpreter, it is difficult to envisage how similar facilities could be provided for large numbers of over-readers. Perhaps there comes a point when certain things, such as the integrity of the interpreter, have to be taken on trust:

*If we take the view that teacher narratives, like most narratives, fall into a category of text which is saturated with explicit and implied conventions, it is important to be sensitive to the deployment of these conventions in the accounts.

It is perhaps important for me to explain that after I had produced parts of my initial text, these were subjected to a process of refinement. Such revisions, which are still continuing, have been prompted by a desire to produce as 'pure' a text as lies within my capability. By 'pure' I mean a piece of writing which is as faithful to the context of the original experiences as is humanly possible. While acknowledging that there can be no such thing as a definitive text where attempts are being made to recapture the past, what I have managed to produce so far is something which seems to have more in common with Laurie Lee than with James Joyce. Like Lee's *Cider with Rosie*, my narrative is written in the first person. The central character in Joyce's *Portrait*, on the other hand, is named Stephen Dedalus and is written about in the third person. Whereas I have tried to re-invoke the 'wholeness of my early environment' – specifically that of a localized area of East Anglia on the Norfolk–Suffolk border – and the interaction which took place between that location and myself, Joyce's principal concern (at least by the time he came to write *Portrait*) lay with his art rather than his surroundings. Joyce sought an internal route to an understanding of his environment. In my childhood and adolescence, I was content to expose myself to the external influences of the Norfolk countryside, to take large draughts from the bucket pulled up from the depths of the natural earth, and to allow those influences, like the purest well-water, to penetrate every part of my body and to nurture my developing personality. It is only now that I have set about trying to clarify and to understand the nature of the interaction and its lasting or temporary influences.

Like Joyce, I have endeavoured to evaluate the 'integrity', the 'symmetry' and the 'radiance' of my former condition and to utilize those very personal 'epiphanies' which have resulted from my exposure to the powerful influences of my native environment. My approach is far less esoteric than Joyce's. It is less concerned with aesthetics and meditation than with an honest attempt to recapture the essence of my early years through detailed research and thoughtful reminiscence.

Just as I had felt drawn towards the library at grammar school, so I became increasingly interested in literature. Perhaps one of the reasons why those who feel marginalized turn, like Lawrence, to books and writing, is that they are seeking to find elsewhere what they have failed to discover in the real world. Having found what they are searching for in a fictive, literary world, they then feel more able to set down their thoughts on paper. Gradually, literature became an all-absorbing, liberating force for me.

As I re-read some of my early drafts, I realized that I had made use of a number of literary analogies, the sources of which I could not have known at the time. My introduction to the authors referred to had post-dated the events being described. It became apparent that I had peeled back some of the superimposed layers, but by no means all. Perhaps this was why I became so interested in archaeology and why it was to become one of my abiding passions. There was a clear parallel between the archaeological and authorial processes – stripping back successive strata of occupation (equating to the contaminating effect of internal or external influences on the empirical author – the liminal texts) – and getting down to the natural subsoil (the arrival at an uncorrupted or authoritative text). Only at this lowest level, I had decided, would it be possible for me to be completely satisfied with my efforts to explore those influences which had shaped my world and myself in the intervening years. Later, I came to realize that life, like settlement, is a continuum; that the contemporary layers of occupation will at some time in the future form a new Middle Ages and later still the equivalent of our prehistoric era. My experiences would always be specific to myself and to the context of my life. From this remove of time, another analogy comes to mind. It is as though in the far distant past I had sat beside a pool of limpid water. The mirror-like reflection, which was the true image of myself, seemed perfectly preserved for all time. But then successive groups of outsiders had come along with pointed staves which they thrust into the water like spears, shattering the image into countless unrecognizable fragments of liquid glass. All I could do was wait for the muddied waters to settle and for the golden disc to re-assume its former position in the sky. Only then would the image begin to re-form. Joyce talks of 'paring back of the nails'. One of the problems of trimming nails, like pulling away the overlying skins of an onion, is to know when to stop. As each layer of onion skin falls away, there is the ever-present fear that the point might be reached where nothing remains in the hand. The autobiographer has the same problem.

*Certain teacher stories are brought to us within a 'romantic' context, which may or may not be intentional.

In my case, 'the poetic form of the narrative' is not 'a literary device through which the teller of tales seeks to move the interpreter and reader into accepting the legitimacy and plausibility of his stories'. This suggests the deliberate use of a contrivance to win over an audience. I had the good fortune to be part of a 'romantic' world and the language which I use emanates from the 'romantic' ideas and thoughts which arose within me at that time. The language is not inconsistent with the thoughts, the feelings and the background of my adolescent years. The greatest difficulty which I have had to overcome is to discover a form of language which not only expresses the range and complexity of those sensory responses, but which remains faithful to my thoughts and feelings at the time. I have not knowingly petitioned the muse of romance in order to promote a particular view of my life or of my teaching. The ideas which Graham (as quoted by David Thomas) expresses were not implicit in my narrative intentions. Nevertheless, they may be a valid interpretation to place on the views expressed in my writing.

*Eco distinguished between legitimate interpretation and *over-interpretation*. Over-interpretation occurs when the interpreter transgresses by deconstructing the writer's own 'world knowledge' through imposing the interpreter's own world knowledge and ignoring the writer's intentions.

*Rorty seems to take the view that part of the process of interpreters 'going to work on a text' is to 'convince other people that we are right', and this involves a purely pragmatic condition of having to attend to the whole text and not to selected portions of it.

Having addressed the issue of those circumstances which tend to confound the efforts of the empirical writer, it is now necessary to turn our attention to the role of the interpreter. It seems to me that the prime function of the interpreter is to identify the specific purpose of the empirical author and then to attempt to evaluate the validity of his writing (the empirical text) *in that unique context*. Liminal texts, as well as coming between the empirical author and his authorial intent, may also impose themselves between the interpreter and the empirical text. What the interpreter has to do is to try to ensure that he is in possession of an uncorrupted text, untarnished by the efforts of phantom liminal authors. To do this, he will need to undertake detailed research. As David Thomas warns, he will have to avoid the pitfall of over-interpretation, of going beyond the intrinsic purpose and meaning of the material at his disposal. Similarly, the over-reader will need to exercise caution and restraint. He, in turn, needs to operate as what we may term an 'over-interpreter' and attempt to determine, through careful reading, whether his trust in the integrity of the original interpreter is justified.

It is a particularly demanding role for the interpreter. He has to penetrate the author's didacticism. He has to become attuned to the writer's 'inner music':

> Civilised man has formed during the whole course of civilisation 'the habit of seeing first as the photographic camera sees . . . He sees what the Kodak has taught him to see . . . As vision developed towards the Kodak, man's idea of himself developed towards the snapshot . . . each of us has a complete Kodak idea of himself.' In literature we have not a snapshot but the total man. And we find him only if we go in to literature as literature. 'If we can't hear . . . we can look in the real novel and there listen in. Not listen to the didactic statements of the author, but to the low calling cries of the characters, as they wander in the dark woods of their destiny.'
> (Walsh 1959: 216–17, citing extracts from D.H. Lawrence's *Art and Morality* and *The Novel and the Feelings*).

I believe that my interpreter has achieved just that, not least because he enjoyed the advantage of having known many of the places and characters of our shared childhood environment. From my point of view, I shall rest content if my over-readers catch some of the notes of that inner music which echo the natural orchestrations of the highways and byways of my native Norfolk. But if the interpreter or the over-reader finds any disharmony in that music, then they have every right to be critical.

> *If a researcher has developed a warm rapport with a teacher who is prepared to communicate a life-history, it is difficult, and perhaps morally indefensible, to go 'public' with an interpretation which is other than celebratory.

> *There is a danger in selecting for public presentation those accounts which are permitted to be published by their creators, along with those interpretations which are authorized by the conventions of the relationship.

Although I can understand the nature of the concerns, I wonder whether we are being over-sensitive about the publication of non-celebratory interpretations of teachers' life-histories. Elsewhere (Woods 1991) I have postulated the view that every novel is, to a greater or lesser extent, an autobiography of its creator. If this hypothesis is tenable, then it could be argued that there is little difference between the novelist–literary critic and the teacher autobiographer–educational interpreter relationships. Many novelists' walls are papered with rejection slips. Why should teachers' texts be excluded from the possibility of adverse criticism? If they are fearful of a negative response, then their course of action is clear – they do not present their material for examination. A non-celebratory interpretation would, at its best and like any good critical commentary, be a carefully researched identification of those corrupting influences which the writer may not have been able to identify for himself. While it may be difficult for any author to accept that he may be subject to the malevolent attentions of imps or daemons, I cannot see that this raises any serious moral problems.

It is probably true to say that there would have been more likelihood of conflict between myself, as empirical author, and Peter Woods, as interpreter, if I had been intent on producing a text which had, as its prime concern, the purpose of promoting a particular view of the educative process. This was not the case. I was far more interested in finding a format for a prose account which would precisely re-invoke the sensations of my early years in Norfolk, and the attempt to discover how those early influences shaped my later life, my personality and my development as a teacher.

Admittedly, it is not possible to describe the effect which such influences had on my teaching career without some reference to a philosophy of education and how such thinking evolved out of those formative events. However, any possibility of conflict or tension between the empirical author and the interpreter was probably removed in our particular circumstances, because the didactic or promotional aspect of my recorded views on education were subsidiary to the other and, for me, more important preoccupations noted above. I have never felt the need, or desire, to actively promote my personal philosophy of education. It has worked for me and that has been sufficiently satisfying. If others have stumbled across my ideas and wanted to make use of them, all well and good. I prefer that this should occur *naturally* and not because I have sought to impose those views on someone else. Rigorous canvassing can lead to the creation of bandwagons and, in the most extreme circumstances, revolutions. There have been and continue to be, too many revolutions in education and too few opportunities for the natural evolutionary processes to develop. The original intentions of the authors of new ideas can easily become subverted to practitioners who, regrettably, enjoy only a partial understanding of the underlying philosophy, and a minority of others who seize upon any initiative primarily as a vehicle for their own advancement. Problems arise when ideas become ideologies. My lack of enthusiasm for educational evangelism may also stem from a belief that the seeds of pedantry are nurtured in the soil of pedagogy. But the absence of an inspirational stance should not be taken to indicate a lack of conviction in respect of the views which I hold on educational matters.

When Peter Woods first proposed that I should really push ahead with the writing of the autobiographical account of my childhood and adolescence, I gained the impression that he considered that this would be something very rewarding *for me* to undertake, and that it might be an interesting and worthwhile extension of the biographical writing I was currently undertaking. It certainly seemed to me, at the time, that my interpreter's suggestion that I should continue committing my thoughts to paper was prompted by philanthropic rather than selfish or premeditated motives – that the suggestion was made to further my personal development rather than to create a potential quarry for educational research. It was only *after* Peter Woods began to read some of my early drafts that he conveyed to me his feelings that these might provide the basis for some interesting research in the field of grounded life-histories. (This all happened at the time when we were having a dialogue about the Rushavenn project.)

Having produced the text primarily as a kind of literary exercise or exploration which might, or might not, give me further insights into the kind of person I was and those forces which had shaped my life and personality, I was quite content to allow my interpreter to make whatever use he wanted of the text. There was no expectation or requirement that his findings should be celebratory. While it has to be acknowledged that the whole framework for Peter Woods' study was a celebratory one (i.e. of critical educational events), I have endeavoured to show that this did not prevent a critical attitude being adopted. Had his interpretation been at odds with my own, this would not have produced serious problems for our relationship, as the potential source of conflict – his commentary on philosophy of education – was not concerned with the prime motivation for this particular literary undertaking.

Throughout my life, my ideas had been subjected to close scrutiny and adverse criticism. Those strategies which I had evolved to help me to cope with my feelings of marginality would not count for much if they could not now accommodate a few rigorous observations from an interpreter.

Thus, the two points which I would like to stress are that, as far as I am aware:

1 The particular circumstances of our relationship did not limit or influence the outcomes of the research or exclude the possibility of an adverse interpretation. I never had any fear that our relationship and shared background would somehow curtail or pre-empt the processes of genuine objective research.

2 I have always considered the views which I have evolved on the appropriateness or inappropriateness of our systems of education, and the strategies which I have adopted, as something personal to myself. If others found my ideas of interest I was happy for them to adopt and, if

necessary, adapt them for their own special circumstances. But if they disagreed with my views on life and education, I did not consider this to be a personal affront and certainly not a valid reason for restricting anyone from presenting – even publishing – a considered critique of my pronouncements. Although I might like to think that such magnanimity derives from an innate generosity of spirit, it probably has more to do with my early exposure, and reaction, to individuals who were bent on adopting a strongly proselytizing approach in their dealings with me.

I perhaps also need to emphasize that it was only my experience of educational establishments which was unhappy. Most of the other experiences of my childhood in the Norfolk countryside – my forays with my game-keeper friend, the excursions to the Saxon Shore Fort at Burgh Castle and the isolation of the farmland marshes shared with farm-hands and ornithologists – was idyllic. It was the kind of childhood which, sadly, few children will have the opportunity of enjoying today.

I would like to conclude with a confession and an affirmation. The time spent writing parts of this chapter should have been devoted to putting the finishing touches to *The Combined School Development Plan and Action Plan Resulting from the Recent Inspection*. I will leave it to my over-readers to decide which of these two exercises I have found more interesting and rewarding.

At the beginning of this chapter, I made reference to the search for a key which had the power to unlock not only a library bookcase, but my whole future. I am sure there are other teachers desperately searching for their own special keys. Despite the odds stacked against them, they should take heart. Those precious keys are there for the finding.

References

Delavenay, E. (1972) *D.H. Lawrence: The Man and His Work*. London: Heinemann.

Proust, M. (1982) *Remembrance of Things Past*. London: The Folio Society.

Walsh, W. (1959) *The Use of Imagination*. London: Chatto and Windus.

Woods, P. (1987) Life histories and teacher knowledge, in Smyth, J. (Ed.), *Educating Teachers: Changing the Nature of Pedagogical Knowledge*. Lewes: Falmer Press.

Woods, P.J. (1991) *The Honey-gatherers: Leo Walmsley and the Autobiographical Novel 11*. Woolaston: Arestos Publications.

12

'Composing a life': Women's stories of their careers[1]

Jennifer Nias and
Kath Aspinwall

Introduction

It is a rare experience, outside some forms of analysis, for adults to spend a considerable amount of uninterrupted time talking about themselves to an interested other. As Didion recognized: 'Only the very young and the very old may recount their dreams at breakfast, dwell upon the self' (Grumet 1981: 117).

Researchers who undertake in-depth interviews provide opportunity for, and legitimate, what would otherwise almost certainly be seen as an indulgence. This chapter is concerned with such interventions and draws upon our experiences of asking teachers to tell us some of their stories, their life-history or their biography. Far from feeling used for another's purpose, we have found that teachers welcome such involvement. For example:

Over twelve weeks I interviewed about 35 men and women in different parts of the UK. None of them talked for less than an hour and a half, and some for as long as five hours. They talked in their classrooms, at lunch time and after school until the caretakers shut us out, and then in their own homes, in pubs, restaurants, railway stations, parks. The hunger that they all showed to reflect upon their lives as teachers in the presence of a neutral but friendly outsider appeared almost insatiable.

(Nias 1989b: 392)

Such interviews or conversations have provided us with rich insight into other people's lives and we have used these data to make connections and draw conclusions of various kinds about teaching and the experience of *being* a teacher.

This chapter considers from two perspectives what this experience has meant for those to whom we talked. The first part is written from the researchers' viewpoint and presents an 'outsider's' interpretation, derived from teachers' stories of how and why primary teachers, particularly women, perceive and explain their career development. We suggest that by mid-career a considerable number have redefined the term, to mean the extension of personal interest, learning and development rather than vertical mobility. The second part of the chapter explores the way in which an 'insider' constructs her life-history as she shares it with a researcher. It extends our understanding of 'story' as the individual making of meaning to the whole process of reflecting on one's past and present, making sense of this experience and presenting it to another. Strauss refers to 'a symbolic ordering of events' and suggests:

> The sense you make of your own life rests upon what concepts, what interpretations you bring to bear on the multitudinous and disorderly crowd of past acts. If your interpretation is convincing to yourself, if you trust your terminology, then there is some kind of meaning assigned to your life as a whole. Different motives may be seen to have driven you at different periods but the over riding purpose of your life may yet seem to retain a certain unity and coherence.
>
> (Strauss 1969: 145)

Bateson (1990) refers to this process of making sense as 'composing a life' and argues that it is particularly significant for women, for two main reasons. First, the hidden nature of women's achievements, in the past and often in the present too, means that writing their biographies and reading other people's enables them to gain a perspective on their own lives and so to become increasingly empowered:

> Because we are engaged in a day-to-day process of self-invention – not discovery, for what we search for does not exist until we find it – both the past and the future are raw material, shaped and reshaped by each individual.
>
> (Bateson 1990: 28)

Second, as they tell their stories, they discover important continuities which are often hidden from them and others by the discontinuities of their lives, not least those imposed upon them by biological rhythms:

> Just as change stimulates us to look for more abstract constancies, so the individual effort to compose a life, framed by birth and death

and carefully pieced together from disparate elements, becomes a statement on the unity of living. These works of art, all incomplete, are parables in process, the living metaphors with which we describe the world.

(Bateson 1990: 17)

'Story telling', Bateson (p. 34) concludes, 'is fundamental to the human search for meaning', particularly for women who often live unrecorded, invisible and interrupted lives.

The first part of this chapter is principally based on Nias' longitudinal research into the subjective reality of 'being a teacher'. In *Primary Teachers Talking* (Nias 1989a), she examines teachers' lives and careers as individuals experience them and discusses the patterns which emerge. Central themes in the book are the extent to which teachers' sense of personal identity is invested in their work and the ways in which they establish, defend, maintain and support the integrity of this as they move through, or in and out, of their professional lives. The second part draws on a biographical study involving one woman primary teacher. 'Sarah' was asked first to reflect on her professional biography in five conversations and then to consider what contribution the process of recounting her experiences in this way had made to her understanding of herself and her career (Aspinwall 1985; see also Aspinwall 1986).

We suggest that both approaches contribute, though in different ways, to the understanding that the storytellers and their interlocutors and audiences have of women's careers. We conclude that, in Bateson's (1990: 234) words women 'are deeply concerned with effectiveness ... and yet their mode of action is responsive rather than purposive'; to an understanding of which both 'outsiders' and 'insiders' bring their own complementary perspectives and that this responsiveness is, paradoxically, an act of creation.

Career patterns

Women's careers as vertical mobility

As Nias listened to her interviewees talking, she at first assumed that when they used the term 'career', they were employing it in its conventional male-oriented sense, whether they were looking towards the future or reviewing the past (Huberman 1988). In particular, they were very conscious of the limitations likely to be imposed upon their vertical mobility by demographic, economic and political changes which they had not envisaged when they had chosen to enter the profession ten to twenty years before. Women voiced three particular concerns. Some commented on the difficulty that they had encountered, or were still attempting to overcome, in returning in any capacity to teaching after child-rearing – difficulties which are confirmed by Biklen (1985) in the USA, and Grant (1986), Acker (1987) and Evetts (1990) in the UK. Others in this position reported that they could not find full-time permanent appointments, but only jobs as 'supply' teachers or as part-time or temporary teachers. Finally, several of those holding senior management posts commented on the obstacles which women, especially those with children, faced in obtaining headships. A sub-set of these women were two Roman Catholics whose husbands had left them and who felt that they no longer had any future in the voluntary sector of education, in which, they claimed, divorced women would not be promoted. Several of those women who perceived themselves as 'having no promotion prospects in schools' had moved or were hoping to move into teacher education, notwithstanding their wish to pursue a career as teachers. As one said 'If I had any real faith that, as a woman, I would have got a deputy headship, I would certainly have stayed in schools'.

In her study of women primary and infant headteachers, that is of women who have successfully ascended the career ladder within schools, Evetts (1990) describes five strategies which she differentiates according to individuals' priorities in respect of both career and personal goals. These priorities, she argues, are influenced by attitudes to promotion, by self-image and by sources of motivation, though she also recognizes that each of these can change over time. One of these strategies (the accommodated career) is adopted by women who do not want or seek promotion; the other four are used by those who wish to seek it. When Nias examined her teachers' careers for evidence of vertical mobility, she found no examples which in her view fell into Evetts' first promotion-oriented category (the antecedent career). This term describes women who 'are career-ambitious from the beginning' and who fit 'personal goals . . . in and around career goals' (Evetts 1990: 72). It may be significant that Evetts does not illustrate this category with empirical evidence from her own research. Certainly Sarah, the subject of Aspinwall's study, had been successful in climbing the career ladder but had mixed feelings about this:

> I think one of the reasons I have been feeling problematic about my job is this thing about moving too fast. One of the parents said when I came and was deputy 'You're going too fast, you know. It won't be good for you' . . . I did take that as a serious comment and I think she could be right.

Despite her success, she did not attribute her fast move up the career ladder to ambition:

The moves that I've made and the development I've gone along with has come from my own needs. And I find it a bit shocking that it's measured in terms of whizzing up the ladder but it is because, you know – because when people say and what are you doing and when did you do it – I mean acquaintances they say 'Gosh are you a deputy head already? Crikey!' and I think that really sounds awful, it sounds like one of the people who make the right moves calculated to a year and a day and it has just not gone like that at all. It was never – I ... it sounds awful because I haven't ever even been career-minded I don't think about it in those kinds of terms, I just enjoy doing what I'm doing and don't want not to do it. It's a career and I'm succeeding in it, then all well and good, but I don't measure it myself in terms of another success marked off, and another one and another one, I don't look at it like that.

Grant found a similar rejection of the notion of 'promotion for its own sake' among the women secondary deputy heads that she interviewed (Grant 1989: 123). Evetts (1990: 80) also reports that many of her interviewees 'showed a marked reluctance to apply the term ambitious to themselves' and that they relied upon 'gatekeepers' (such as inspectors/advisers and headteachers) to push them into appropriate courses of action. Gilligan (1982) suggests that many women perceive ambition to be incompatible with their preferred qualities, such as sensitivity and compassion, and finds this attitude to career planning is consistent with their value systems.

However, although relatively few women appear to use an antecedent career strategy, by mid-career some of those whom Nias interviewed were actively seeking to ascend the career ladder. Most of them fell into Evetts' second promotion-oriented category (the two-stage career) or the third (the subsequent career). Individuals adopting a two-stage career leave teaching for parenthood after climbing the lower rungs of the ladder and attempt to build upon this experience when they are once more ready to give priority to their work goals. Those adopting the subsequent career strategy embark upon a quest for promotion after they have accomplished their family aims. Although Evetts (1990) cites one woman whose career illustrates successful use of the two-stage strategy, she also accepts that 'within primary teaching [it] does have limitations' (p. 75). Nias' teachers certainly found that if they were able to get a job at all, it was usually one that involved them starting the career ascent from a low level and undertaking it for the second time. This particularly applied to married women who had followed their husbands to another part of the country and/or who had re-entered the profession after child-rearing or a stay abroad. Most of them spoke about their experiences of re-entry with disappointment, resentment or frustration. In particular, they all considered that their previous experience was discounted by their new colleagues. A few put it mildly:

It is frustrating in a way because once you've lost your Scale 2 there's no recognition made of the fact that you were deserving your promotion. You're then back to where you started, it doesn't count for anything.

Others were more overtly angry:

This job – as a so-called 'remedial teacher' – is the only one I could get. And I had a Scale 3 for language in my last job. So here I am doing things I don't approve of and watching someone else do the language job here that I know I could do better. But no-one ever asks you what you did before.

Another reported:

I came here first as a supply teacher so no-one knows I was a deputy before I had my children ... They never ask, and if you're a Scale 1 teacher you can't tell them.

Similarly, those of Nias' interviewees who had adopted Evetts' 'subsequent career' often expressed frustration about the difficulties which gender, especially their perceived responsibility for child care, placed in their way. These problems are well documented in Acker (1987).

However, although these women seemed to be voicing anxieties and resentments about the obstacles they encountered in their search for vertical mobility, Nias came to realize that her interviewees were attaching other meanings, too, to the lack of promotion opportunities which they perceived to lie ahead of them. In particular, they were less concerned about a relatively low income than about the probable effects of non-advancement upon their self-esteem and the associated constraints upon the development of their potential – as Connell (1985), Sikes (1986) and Poppleton and Riseborough (1990) also remarked of Australian and English secondary teachers in mid-career. Permanent, full-time teachers spoke with anxiety of 'good people getting stuck', of those who 'haven't got promotion being bitter and frustrated and worse teachers because of it', of 'good teachers losing heart because they have nowhere to go'. They wanted to take on additional responsibilities, to extend their spheres of influence, and were afraid that if their efforts continually met with lack of reward or recognition, they would begin to put less into the job. For such teachers diminished promotion prospects appeared to relate closely to an expressed dread of professional stagnation.

The same was true of those with temporary or part-time jobs who found it hard to teach as they wanted to, to think of themselves as 'real teachers', to participate fully in the wider life of the school. Their most common complaints were being unable to reach the level of performance, for themselves or their pupils, to which they were accustomed, and the frustration engendered by the resulting need to accept lower professional standards. As one recalled:

> During the five years of part-time work, I kept on thinking, 'One day it'll be real again. One day I'll be doing the real thing'. I suppose seeing so many people who don't do it very well, you just keep thinking, 'One day I'll be able to get back in my own classroom and do my own thing and make a good job of it'.

Being unable to 'make a good job of it' was partly due to the constraints of time and space which their curtailed role imposed upon them. These constraints were, however, felt to be compounded by the attitude of some heads and class teachers who, Nias' interviewees bitterly commented, simply wanted them for what they called 'child-minding'. For example: 'At some schools, they say, "Just go along and find something to do!" That's dreadful. I kept thinking, "This is ridiculous. I'm being paid to do odd jobs"'.

Nor did they feel they were seen as full members of their school staffs. Instead, they perceived themselves as 'on the periphery', 'just a spare part', 'filling in'. In consequence, they felt undervalued or excluded, either by default or because they were actually prevented from making a contribution to staff discussions. For example:

> It's frustrating in some ways . . . At staff meetings I know that when we are discussing the curriculum it doesn't really affect me as much as everybody else. But I think it shouldn't be like that, because although I'm on temporary contract now, I'm still making a contribution and some of the things that they're planning in the curriculum depend on my being there. I don't think that people mean to exclude you but you're not taken into account the same as an ordinary member of staff and that's quite difficult . . . Without meaning to, the staff are excluding you from the group.

The cumulative effect of employment under these conditions was a damaging loss of professional and personal self-esteem. Typical comments were:

> My training and skills weren't being used, I didn't feel they were appreciated in supply teaching . . . My self-confidence began to go.

> When I was a full-time, I was important to kids, but [as a part-timer] I'm just somebody who comes in on Thursdays and they don't care about me.

> I can remember that confidence I felt because I'd been [at that school] a long time and I knew all the staff, I knew the children and I knew the parents . . . I would like that feeling back again, not so much that you're important but that you are as important as everybody else.

To self-doubt was added a sense of injustice, for, as these women were quick to tell me, 'I wouldn't be doing much more work if I had a full-time job than I am in a part-time one'. As one reflected, 'No-one seems to realize how much thought and effort goes into being a good supply teacher ... In a lot of ways, it's harder than having a class of your own'. Done well, they said, temporary and part-time teaching involved flexibility, sensitivity, vigilance and a great deal of preparation. Yet the circumstances in which they were required to teach tended to leave them feeling not just frustrated, deskilled, undervalued and impotent, but also lacking the affective and professional rewards of long-term involvement with children and with whole school development. No wonder they felt, as one said:

> I wouldn't consider doing part-time again, I would want to do full-time. And permanent too, if I could. I don't want any more temporary posts. It's just not worth it, if you're keen on the job and want to do it well.

There is evidence then in Nias' work and that of others, notably Evetts', that some women adopt traditional, and some would say masculine attitudes to their careers, even though they use gender-specific strategies to pursue them. Such teachers want to move upwards, to posts carrying more status and financial recompense but, above all, more responsibility, the opportunity to learn fresh skills and the likelihood of enhanced self-esteem. If they temporarily step off the ladder in order to pursue alternative goals, usually but not exclusively in parenthood, they tend to experience frustration, self-doubt and lack of esteem when they attempt to climb back onto it.

'Horizontal' careers: stories of self-extension

But not all Nias' interviewees saw their careers in such negative terms. Some women, usually with children, but also one single woman with no dependents, had made a virtue out of necessity. Disadvantaged, in terms of the single line vertical structure of teaching, by the multiple roles they carried, by the prejudice which existed against their promotion to senior posts in schools, and by the mobility sometimes enforced upon them by their husbands' jobs, they had redefined the concept of career to mean progressive opportunities for personal learning and extension.

They pursued these 'horizontal' careers in two ways. First, the fact that some of them returned to teaching in roles which were peripheral to conventional classroom teaching gave them a good deal of freedom. This they relished, as Ball and Goodson (1985) also noted was the case for some female secondary teachers. They appreciated the flexibility afforded by part-time or temporary work and the potential for personal and professional development offered by moves into, for example, theatre workshops, teaching English as a second language or work with children with special educational needs. Lyons and McCleary (1980) and Acker (1987) have noted the same trend, while Smith *et al.* (1986: 110) claimed of elementary teachers in the USA: 'Beyond the self-contained classroom . . . there exists a huge array of other options for teachers. Our [women] teachers found and created a number of those'.

In the UK, the 1980s were marked by the growth of school-based in-service education and by an increase in the number and responsibilities of support and advisory teams for primary schools. These developments increased the options available within what has become a network of short-term opportunities. Within this network, information often appears to pass in the first instance by word of mouth (see also Evetts 1987, 1988). In other words, an alternative career structure exists, its potential recognized and exploited by many women. One put it this way:

> Mine is hardly the accepted way of pursuing a career, but in terms of personal development and learning, I regard it as very satisfactory. I'm not concerned with status, which is fortunate, because both as a supply teacher and as a part-timer, I am always the lowest status person in the school. But during the past few years I've had a wonderfully wide range of experience, all of which has fed me. I'm very enthusiastic about the life I've chosen.

A second group of women, all married, had returned after child-rearing to permanent, full-time posts in school. Reconciling themselves to the fact that they might not find the promotion that they felt they deserved, they had however turned their energy, talent and enthusiasm to improving not just their own professional competence, but also that of their less experienced colleagues (see Biklen 1985, 1986, for similar American evidence). One in eight of Nias' mid-career interviewees named as 'a woman in her 40s' the person, other than headteachers, who had most influenced their professional development. These influential teachers were all either late entrants to teaching or 'returners'. A similar late-entrant who worked in one of the Primary Schools Staff Relationships project schools exerted a tremendous amount of school-wide influence. Reflecting on her failure to obtain a headship, she said that she had eventually realized that she did not need to pursue a vertical career in order to fulfil her professional aims, that there was little that she wanted to achieve educationally that she could not bring about through her influence on others as a deputy (Nias 1987). Evidently, some older women teachers are able to create a satisfying role for themselves in primary schools without becoming headteachers. They find they can exercise a profound influence on their colleagues while still remaining in the classroom. It is possible that Poppleton's (1988) finding that women secondary teachers tend to experience more job satisfaction than men also reflects a similar trend.

'Parallel careers': Switching and juggling

However, the individual's subjective career is sometimes more than a vertical or horizontal progression through a series of posts which involve promotion or opportunities for personal extension. Several studies have suggested that individuals may also pursue 'parallel careers', that is, they may hold personal and professional goals to be of equal importance and seek to achieve both simultaneously or in alternative sequence. There appear to be several reasons why they do this. Some feel they have exhausted the possibilities, in terms of personal satisfaction and extension, which teaching can offer them, but are tied to their jobs by domestic commitments. The 'stories' of secondary teachers in English schools (e.g. Benet 1983; Woods 1984; Sikes *et al.* 1985) note a tendency for individuals to offset boredom or frustration in mid-career with the development of interests such as pottery, antiques-dealing, car repairs, market gardening or social community work (paid or unpaid). Huberman *et al.* (1987) hint at the existence of such expedients among older teachers in Swiss secondary schools. Nias followed Goldthorpe *et al.* (1968) in calling such teachers 'privatized workers', because the important part of their lives appeared to go on outside school.

The second form of parallel career is similar to the first in that personal and professional goals complement and compensate for each other. One 'self' is temporarily held in suspense while another comes to the fore. Evetts (1990) sees such teachers as adopting her fourth promotion-oriented strategy: the compensatory career. Nias identified a small group of women who switched between their family and work goals at different times in their lives, in response to the dictates of felt need. However, she does not see this type of parallel career as necessarily being related to a desire for promotion. Rather, since work has to take its place alongside other life-age commitments, it is likely to be used by many teachers at different times in response to the fluctuating demands and satisfactions of their varied roles. For example, she interviewed some teachers who, reacting to the pressures in their personal lives, had transferred their attention temporarily away from classroom and school, while others were seeking – or had sought – refuge in school from domestic circumstances. As one woman said, recalling the period after her marriage broke down, 'I felt rejected . . . I turned to something I knew I could succeed in and that was my job. Through that, my confidence improved'. Another explained: 'I needed to find something I was good at again'.

A third reason why women pursue parallel careers appears to lie in their developed capacity for creative improvisation 'in ways especially sensitive to context, interaction and response' (Bateson 1990: 2). Unlike 'privatized workers', who are motivated by the felt need to seek personal significance, self-esteem and self-extension in their non-work roles because of frustrations or failures at work, such teachers attach equal importance to personal and professional goals at the same time. Since both sets of aims are perceived as worthwhile and experienced as demanding, the lives of the women 'improvisers' who opt for parallel careers are characterized not just by creativity, but also by compromise and negotiation.

Evetts (1990) argues that the resulting pressures are part of the price that women pay for adopting a two-stage career strategy. Sarah (Aspinwall 1985) does not fit unambiguously into any of Evetts' categories, but she was very aware of the tension between her role as deputy head and that of parent to her two daughters. She saw both careers as important and demanding:

> It [teaching] is such a demanding profession because there is always something more you can do . . . I always feel therefore under a greater pressure, because if I could just manage to do this I might be able to help and influence more, so there's almost no end limit.

And

> It's because it [mothering] will always be open to doubt that I find it so worrying. Because if it could be measured and if one knew how much one had to put there to be sure what could be described as fair – or even more than that, I would want it to be more than that – you wouldn't have to worry about it.

Indeed, the tension between these two parts of her life was sometimes experienced as conflict:

> There have been times when – I haven't neglected the children – but there have been times when I've felt at the end of the day I have hardly spoken to my children.

This caused her considerable concern: 'because you only have the experience of those children once and its got to be as good as you can possibly make it'.

The sensitivity to context and interaction which characterizes improvisation is not, it appears, an easy option for women to undertake. It may be that the level of satisfaction which they derive from parallel careers depends upon their capacity to 'juggle' their competing interests (Sikes *et al.* 1985; Spencer 1986) or to build 'bridging' devices between them (Woods 1990).

To sum up the argument so far, the stories which women tell of their careers suggest to outsiders that they attach different meanings to the term. Many use it in its conventional, vertical sense, perceiving their careers to have been 'broken' or 'interrupted' by, for instance, service abroad or a period of child-rearing. For such teachers, 'career' is often experienced in negative terms, damaging to their sense of personal potential and self-worth. This feeling is also reflected in the comments of those practitioners who came into the profession during a period of relative expansion and who now work in a much more constraining economic and political climate. However, others (predominantly married women with children), construe 'career' in horizontal terms. Some of them choose, with a sense of fulfilment and self-determination, to move around a network of short-term posts, often peripheral to or outside mainstream classroom teaching. Others create satisfying roles for themselves within schools, which enable them to grow professionally and to exercise considerable influence over their colleagues. Lastly, a minority of teachers treat their jobs as one of several careers which they pursue in parallel, offsetting the frustrations of one life with the rewards (among them status and recognition) offered by another.

Telling the story: 'life as a work in progress'

Researchers seek to identify the themes that exist within lives that others have composed, even if in doing this they rely heavily upon the artists' own interpretations of the patterns they have created. Yet no matter how sincere and painstaking their attempts are, they always remain the work of outsiders. In this sense, many commentators on women teachers' careers – and in this context, Nias (1989a) in particular – can be accused of perpetuating the authority-dependence which writers such as Lortie (1975) suggest is characteristic of primary school teachers. However, in the next part of this chapter, Aspinwall argues that it is not only the researcher who imposes meaning in these circumstances. She offers evidence of how the subject of her study, Sarah, used their conversations to engage in an active but largely unarticulated process of creative improvisation. She seeks to present an 'insider's' view of the challenge which women face as they compose their lives, and of the ways in which being legitimized to talk about her biography assisted Sarah to see her 'life as a work in progress' (Bateson 1990: 1), in which she could trace continuities and over the future shape of which she had some control.

The design of the study of Sarah's professional biography was strongly influenced by an awareness of the impact on individuals of the process of re-viewing and recounting their life experiences. For example, after spending just one day on an INSET course reflecting on their professional biography, teachers made the following discoveries.

Life has just continued. This day has given me *time* to consider myself and relationships. Generally I'm too rushed and stretched by various forces to fully consider myself and what I want, where I want to go. So I need to make more space and time in my life.

Not to be afraid/guilty about examining my past, but to see it positively. That things which seem crucial, happy/painful today may not be significant in the long term.

That me 'the teacher' cannot be separated from me 'the person'.

This demonstration of the direct impact on present understanding of reflection on one's life experience and the recounting, explaining and making meaning of this life to others was the consequence of one day's workshop. It seemed highly probable that the more intensive and longer-term process of recounting an individual professional history to an interested researcher would have greater impact.

When she was asked about the effect of talking about herself during five biographical conversations, Sarah's response was unequivocal:

As a process it has helped me enormously . . . It's helped me to come to terms, to face what I'm doing in a calmer, more rational way because I realize why I'm here and what I'm doing . . . It seems to me the benefits have been greater, I mean so much better than anything that I can think of for a very long time . . . I would much rather have done this than anything else.

It is clear that the need to make sense of her own experiences and to present a sensible account were both important to Sarah. She felt a particularly strong need to understand her present situation because of the problems she was experiencing as a relatively new deputy head in what was widely acknowledged (by, for example, LEA advisers and HMI) to be a difficult school. At intervals throughout the conversations, Sarah made such comments as: 'It's giving me the opportunity to clear my thoughts', 'It's helping me to clear a lot of things', 'You just don't see it as a whole' and 'Unless somebody makes you, or asks you or invites you, to stand outside and gives some time and support you don't do it'. She several times stressed the significance of being asked to tell her story:

And you need – someone needs to make you sit down, not with a threat, but you know it's coming and you've actually got to do it. Because you can sit and think about it – but until you actually come to try to tell someone else about it.

. . . some of it is just talking to you about it.

In speaking of understanding herself much better she said:

I think that's what people desperately need ... They need the time to come to terms with what they're doing, particularly if they are feeling fairly uncertain.

She described in some detail during the final discussion of the effects on her of what had happened, how she had felt about the process at the beginning:

I was very nervous of doing it at first. I felt that it was going to be – not just difficult for me but that I might be in danger of appearing simple to you and I was bothered about that. 'Kath'll think I'm an idiot'. That mustn't be surprising to you after going through what we've been through in terms of putting yourself in the situation and not knowing how it's going to go and I was terribly, terribly nervous. And because of that I think it was just as well we started where you suggested we start, which was in a chronological, secure position for me to be in terms of a straight remembering and picking up of events that had happened. After the first one I thought, 'Well that was easy and that wasn't too bad at all. Next time it's going to be hard'. But in fact it never ever turned out like that. Although we've done most of them at the end of a school day when I've been thinking 'I'm drained, I need at least a couple of hours' ... after doing one of them I've never felt 'Oh, that's taken a lot out of me'. And because of that I'm a bit worried that I haven't put enough into it to help you to do what you've done ... It hasn't turned into what I feared it might which is a really difficult mind-bending exercise, a psychological search in a sense. Or if it has in parts, it's because it was a natural thing for it to do. It wasn't an imposition. So I never did feel under any kind of threat or difficulty.

Sarah wanted both to understand herself and her situation better and to present a coherent account. It is possible to trace through the conversations four different elements that illuminate the process of clarification and making sense. Two reflect the way in which Sarah's story-making helped her to discover continuities in her life and some of the consequences of these; two indicate how telling her story led her to reconsider some of her perceptions of herself and her life.

Elements of the process

Recurring themes

One element of conversations was the recognition of both Sarah and the listener of themes that recurred throughout her story. Some of these were well established. For example, what Sarah referred to as her 'love of learning':

> I've always loved learning and wanted and searched after knowledge and wanted to know more and never felt I knew enough. [first conversation].

And, with reference to in-service:

> That's why I keep going, because I need to find out if I'm keeping up, if there's more recent research. [first conversation]

> I need a theoretical framework behind me. If I didn't know about the early stages and what can be expected and looked for I don't think I'd be so confident. [second conversation]

To her years at university:

> It was a wonderful decision honestly. It was in that department that I really did take off in terms of intellectual development. It was incredible to be be part of taking the boundaries of knowledge further. [second conversation]

And their continuing impact:

> The need to – to develop my mind further and to go on and come to different conclusions and to try different things and work things out is always there . . . so I am still doing that, although it's at a different level of course but no, I think I do it all the time. I still always am thinking and changing and reviewing. [second conversation]

And with reference to having her own children:

> Not being sure I was doing the right things and wanting to learn more about children, wanting to do a lot more and know a lot more'. [third conversation]

It is clear that for Sarah this 'need to know more' was a familiar explanation of much of her behaviour in many different circumstances. This perception was confirmed rather than changed by the conversations. However, other perceptions were influenced by the reflective and reflexive process.

Familiar themes and present problems

Another recurring theme was the idealistic way in which Sarah viewed the task of teaching. This was both a familiar and important influence on the way she approached her work and a matter of some pride. None of this was challenged by the process of telling her story, but for the first time she came to see how this way of seeing things was magnifying problems she was experiencing with her colleagues. She traced this idealism back to her decision to become a teacher. She had originally entered teacher training college on leaving school but left the course disappointed by its low quality and went to university instead. She only went back into training after having her children. Therefore, unlike many of the teachers in Nias' study, rather than 'interrupting' her career, Sarah's children provided the impetus for it:

> What made me do it was almost certainly being involved with my own children. I think that was the biggest influence and secondly seeing what I considered as a raw untrained mother to be awful things that were going on – really bad practice. I didn't want anybody's children to have to go through that as an introduction to those early years when it should be so good.

This experience also influenced her attitude to teaching and the commitment to ensuring a high-quality experience of schooling for children that pervaded her story. For example, in speaking of her concern about the colleagues with whom she worked, she said:

> I cannot for the life of me understand how people teach without some idea of where the kids are and where they're going and they put something in and don't evaluate it . . . They go on in such a haphazard way . . . And I can't work like that – be like that.

Sarah had always recognized and valued her idealistic commitment to teaching. However, in telling and retelling aspects of her story, she began to reach a new understanding. She realized that her difficulty in recognizing that others might approach the job quite differently was getting in the way of her task, as deputy head, of influencing the behaviour of her less committed colleagues:

> One of the things I feel I can't get across to people is the importance of teaching. For some people it's just a time they spend away from home . . . But it's so vital to me – I can't just feel it isn't important and you forget that all people don't feel like that about it.

She realized that her feelings about the importance of teaching were getting in the way of developing strategies to change the situation:

> I realize that it would have been very much better . . . to have a shot at one thing at a time . . . to look at the problem and highlight the ones that can be dealt with and I've never worked like that. I've worked like that at children's development, doing term plans and half term's and weeks and even days . . . but I've never worked like that with adults. I tend to expect more of them than I'm ever going to get.

Coming to terms with this, and recognizing the need to live with the possible, enabled her to move from a sense of despair about her current situation to beginning to see some possible steps forward. Schön (1982: 310) describes this process as 'frame analysis'. As Sarah became able to see the 'frame' through which she was viewing her work with adults and compare it with the way she worked with children, she became able to 'reframe' the problem and see alternative courses of action.

Changing perception

Sometimes the process led to a change rather than a reframing of perception. Another recurring theme was Sarah's belief that she lacked self-confidence. This again appeared in several different contexts. To give but two examples, in speaking about her time at university she said: 'I was very surprised, I mean I think it took two years to get over how surprised I was that I could match up to the other people who were around'. She had only began to feel confidence in herself as a teacher after an affirming visit from an HMI. She described herself as 'always under-confident' and 'sensitive to criticism', saying: 'I have always been like that right from a very young child. It's always been like that with me but I don't know where it comes from'.

After reading the transcripts of our first four meetings, Sarah returned to this theme to wonder whether her childhood experience being 'special' to her father had led her to need similar strong affirmation from all those around her and to lack confidence when this was not available. However, there was also considerable evidence in the conversations that contradicted this perception. For example, when she was half considering applying for a job at the polytechnic, her head had said, 'You realize you can't do that, you can't go into lecturing until you have been a head'. Sarah's response had been to apply. 'It wasn't a serious intention to lecture. It was just that I wasn't prepared to be told that you can't'. She was also well able to reject what she saw as inappropriate interventions during the conversations. For example:

> I tend not to think about it like that to be honest . . . I mean thinking about what you said earlier I don't think my life would have been very different if I'd been a man . . . perhaps I'm just not prepared to accept that because I'm a woman doors have been closed and I haven't been able to do things that I want to do. Because I made quite a few of the decisions and the choices about saying 'Yes' and 'No'.

As Sarah speaks slowly and softly and is a generally a gentle person, her lack of confidence was easy to accept in a face-to-face conversation. However, the process of data reduction that is inevitable in transcribing had interesting consequences in this context. Once such factors as facial expression, tone of voice and body language were eliminated, the actual words often appeared much stronger. Insight emerging from the original conversations was reinforced by reading the transcripts. This led Sarah to begin to reconsider this aspect of herself and to the point of acknowledging that despite her habitual belief that she lacked self-confidence, 'underneath I probably am fairly secure and sure'.

Recognizing change

The process of telling the story to someone else can also reveal changes that have taken place so gradually that they have passed unnoticed. In such cases, 'some incident is needed to bring home the extent of the shift' (Strauss 1959: 93). For Sarah, retelling her past was such an incident. For example, during her first long, sequential account of her history, she mentioned having been awarded a Commonwealth scholarship to read for a PhD in politics at UCLA but that she had not taken it up. At the beginning of the second meeting, she said that on thinking about this afterwards, she had been very surprised:

> I hadn't realized how unimportant the research post had become to me ... I realized I had got it out of my system ... that it had almost gone away ... I suppose it ought to by now ... but it was some-thing I really wanted to do when I was in middle of applying for it and going for interviews and winning the scholarship and feeling better at getting it and then, suddenly, it was different. And it took me a long time to adjust to it and the fact that I was pregnant and life was completely different. And I did find it strange that I mentioned it as an afterthought.

These factors, the affirmation of familiar themes, the testing of these themes in telling the story to another (reinforced by reading it again in a transcript), and the revelation of unrecognized changes, all contributed to the development of new insight and understanding. This was not a con-clusive shutting down of alternatives. Sarah said, 'It certainly hasn't frozen me where I'm at ... it's not cleared completely where I'm going', but the sense of clarification was helpful and important to her. Being the subject of this study appears to have made a significant contribution to the process of composing this life.

This study is unusual in that the subject was asked to do more than tell her story. Sarah knew from the beginning that at the end she would be asked to describe what the process had contributed to her understanding of her self and her career. In addition, she was able to read through, and reflect on, transcripts of the account. This clear articulation of purpose has something in common with the work of those such as Abbs (1974), Pinar (1975) and Grumet (1981), who have involved student and practising teachers in written autobiographical writing during their initial training or as part of their study of curriculum theory. In his work with teachers, Butt (1984) claims that the consciousness of past, present and future that are inevitable in biography work have the 'significant potential of recording the *development* of teacher thinking as it happens' (p. 99). Conscious of her own thinking processes, Sarah spoke of almost feeling her mind working when she read through some parts of the transcripts. In the context of this study, she felt not only her original expressed need to understand her present situation and its implication for her future career, but also a responsibility to share with the researcher the sense-making process.

Conclusion

The women in these two studies were all recounting and, to a greater or lesser degree, reflecting upon aspects of their professional lives. From their accounts, it is possible to identify themes that recur across the stories and the themes within a particular individual's life. There is evidence to suggest that, in addition to the sense that can be imposed from outside by researchers, the tellers are making their own meaning of their lives. The act of telling their story to another also actively influences this sense-making process. The created meaning is a manifestation of present understanding, a consequence of reflection on past experience and an indication of once hoped-for, or still anticipated, futures. There is a sense of both clarification and impermanence, the chance that if the conversations had taken place at a different time, at least, some of the conclusions might also have been different. Bateson (1990: 13) reminds us that 'fluidity and discontinuity are central to the reality in which we live. She refers to 'an improvisatory art' and to a process similar to that of playing jazz which is 'both repetitive and innovative' (p. 3) to describe the bringing of some coherence to the story of our lives.

This sense of flux can be difficult for researchers, anxious to establish the validity of their account and to move from data to theory. Yet the subjects of the research have their own needs to be coherent, to present their lives, to clarify their purposes, to feel more than the victims of circumstance. They need to live up to their image and aspirations of themselves as individuals and as teachers and their perceptions of the expectations of those around them. The teachers in Nias' study were aware of the conventional view of career and held their experiences against it. Sarah did not want to appear 'an idiot'. Plummer (1983: 68) speaks of the 'quest for generalisability [which] imposes order and rationality upon experiences and worlds that are more ambiguous, more problematic and more chaotic in reality'. It may be helpful to acknowledge that there is more than one way of knowing. For example, Polanyi (1969: 132) notes two:

> Research is an intensely dynamic enquiry while knowledge is a more quiet research. Both are ever on the move, according to similar principles towards a deeper understanding of what is already known.

In the context of the stories told so generously to us, the art of interpretation seems to necessitate combining and holding in tension the general and the particular, the outside and inside perspectives, the inner and outer meanings, the present and past understandings, and the sense of both clarity and flux. These are the ingredients that researchers and researched use, both in attempting to reach generalizable conclusions and in the act of composing a life.

Notes

1 For the sake of clarity, we have used 'she' to refer to ourselves and each other. However, we both would have preferred to write as 'I', since our writing is, in its turn, part of the personal meaning-making which this chapter explores.

References

Abbs, P. (1974) *Autobiography in Education*. London: Heinemann Educational.

Acker, S. (1987) Primary school teaching as an occupation, in Delamont, S. (Ed.), *The Primary School Teacher*. Lewes: Falmer Press.

Aspinwall, K.A. (1985) 'A biographical approach to the professional development of teachers'. Unpublished MEd dissertation, University of Sheffield.

Aspinwall, K.A. (1986) 'Teacher biography: The in-service potential'. *Cambridge Journal of Education* 16(3), 210–15.

Ball, S. and Goodson, I. (1985) Understanding teachers: Concepts and cultures, in Ball, S. and Goodson, I. (Eds), *Teachers' Lives and Careers*. Lewes: Falmer Press.

Bateson, C. (1990) *Composing a Life*. New York: Plume (Penguin) Books.

Benet, C. (1983) Paints, pots or promotion: Art teachers' attitudes towards their careers, in Ball, S. and Goodson, I. (Eds), *Teachers' Lives and Careers*. Lewes: Falmer Press.

Biklen, S.K. (1985) 'Can elementary schoolteaching be a career? A search for new ways of understanding women's work'. *Issues in Education* 3(3), 215–31.

Biklen, S.K. (1986) 'I have always worked: Elementary schoolteaching as a career'. *Phi Delta Kappa*, March, pp. 504–8.

Butt, R. (1984) Arguments for using biography in understanding teacher thinking, in Halkes, R. and Olson, J. (Eds), *Teacher Thinking: A New Perspective on Persisting Problems in Education*, pp. 95–102. Lisse: Swets and Zeitlinger.

Connell, R. (1985) *Teachers' Work*. London: Allen and Unwin.

Evetts, J. (1987) 'Becoming career ambitious: The career strategies of married women who became primary headteachers in the 1960s and 1970s'. *Educational Review* 39, 15–29.

Evetts, J. (1988) 'Returning to teaching: The career breaks and returns of married women primary headteachers'. *British Journal of Sociology of Education* 9, 81–96.

Evetts, J. (1990) *Women in Primary Teaching: Career Contexts and Strategies*. London: Unwin Hyman.

Gilligan, C. (1982) *In a Different Voice*. Cambridge, MA: Harvard University Press.

Goldthorpe, J., Lockwood, D., Bechofer, F. and Platt, J. (1968) *The Affluent Worker: Industrial Attitudes and Behaviour*, Vol. 1. Cambridge: Cambridge University Press.

Grant, R. (1986) 'A career in teaching: A survey of middle school teachers' perception with particular reference to the careers of women teachers'. Paper presented to the *British Educational Research Association Conference*, Bristol, September.

Grant, R. (1989) 'Heading for the top – the career experience of a group of secondary deputies in one LEA'. *Gender and Education* 1(2), 113–25.

Grumet, M. (1981) Restitution and reconstruction of educational experience: An autobiographical method for curriculum theory, in Lawm, M. and Barton, L. (Eds), *Rethinking Curriculum Studies*, pp. 125–48. London: Croom Helm.

Huberman, M. (1988) 'Teacher careers and school improvement'. *Journal of Curriculum Studies* 20, 119–32.

Huberman, M., Grounauer, M., Marti, M. and Retord, A. (1987) *Le Cycle de Vie Professionelle des Enseignants Secondaires*. Geneve: Universite de Geneve.

Lortie, D. (1975) *Schoolteacher: A Sociological Analysis*. Chicago, IL: University of Chicago Press.

Lyons, G. and McCleary, L. (1980) Careers in teaching, in Hoyle, E. and Megarry, J. (Eds), *World Yearbook of Education: Professional Development of Teachers*. London: Routledge and Kegan Paul.

Nias, J. (1987) One finger, one thumb: A case study of the deputy head's part in the leadership of a nursery/infant school, in Southworth, G. (Ed.), *Readings in Primary Management*. Lewes: Falmer Press.

Nias, J. (1989a) *Primary Teachers Talking: A Study of Teaching at Work*. London: Routledge.

Nias, J (1989b) 'Subjectively speaking: English primary teachers' careers'. *International Journal of Educational Research* 13(4), 391–401.

Pinar, W. (1975) Currere: Towards reconceptualising, in Pinar, W. (Ed.), *Curriculum Theorising*. Berkeley, CA: McCutchan Publishing.

Plummer, K. (1983) *Documents of Life*. London: Allen and Unwin.

Polanyi, M. (1969) *Knowing and Being*. London: Routledge and Kegan Paul.

Poppleton, P. (1988) 'Teacher professional satisfaction'. *Cambridge Journal of Education.* 18(1), 5–16.

Poppleton, P. and Riseborough, G. (1990) 'A profession in transition: educational policy and secondary school teaching in England in 1980's'. *Comparative Education,* 26(2/3), 211–26.

Schön, D. (1982) *The Reflective Practitioner: How Professionals Think in Action.* London: Temple Smith.

Sikes, P. (1986) 'The mid-career teacher: Adaptation and motivation in a contracting secondary school system'. Unpublished PhD thesis, University of Leeds.

Sikes, P., Measor, L. and Woods, P. (1985) *Teachers' Careers: Crises and Continuities.* Lewes: Falmer Press.

Smith, L., Kleine, P., Prunty, J. and Dwyer, D. (1986) *Educational Innovators: Then and Now.* Lewes: Falmer Press.

Spencer, D.A. (1986) *Contemporary Women Teachers: Balancing Home and School.* New York: Longman.

Strauss, A.L. (1959) *Mirrors and Masks: the search for identity.* Glencoe, IL: Free Press.

Woods, P. (1984) Teachers, self and curriculum, in Ball, S. (Ed.), *Defining the Curriculum: Histories and Ethnographies of School Subjects.* Lewes: Falmer Press.

Woods, P. (1990) *Teacher Strategies.* Lewes: Falmer Press.

Index

TEACHER EDUCATION AS TRANSFORMATION

C.T. Patrick Diamond

This book argues that the major challenge for all who are involved in the professional development of teachers – whether in initial or in-service training – lies in providing means by which teachers may become more critically aware of their own values, thinking and practices and thus empowering them to find new and more effective ways of teaching. Pat Diamond views teachers as essentially self-directing and self-determining but, citing examples from Australia, England and North America, he sees them as being under threat from forces of production and accountability which have seized the political and moral initiative with calls for a more perscriptive education curriculum, more 'value for money' and quality control. He makes many practical suggestions for teacher educators and teachers themselves which can be enable them to be released 'from the paralysis of being hurried and harried'.

Contents
Teaching: a besieged perspective – Conceptualizations of teacher education – Preservice teacher education: expansion of perspective – In-service teacher education: countering contraction of perspective – A meeting of perspectives – Ways of eliciting teachers' self-narratives – Ways of reflecting upon narrative perspectives – Conclusion – References – Index.

160pp   0 335 09254 3 (Paperback)   0 335 09255 1 (Hardback)

MAKING SENSE OF TEACHING
Sally Brown and Donald McIntyre

This book helps us to understand better the nature of teaching in schools and, in particular, to understand teaching from the perspective of the people doing it: the teachers. The authors seek to gain access to teachers' professional craft knowledge and to facilitate teachers' own articulation of the ordinary, everyday teaching which they do routinely and spontaneously in classrooms. Their emphasis throughout is on investigating 'good teaching', on what goes well in the classroom. They are also concerned to identify how an understanding of the professional craft knowledge of teachers is particularly important for, and applicable to, the pre-service and in-service training of teachers, effective curriculum innovation, and teacher appraisal. They help us to make sense of what goes on in good teaching, and draw out the significant implications for policy and practice.

Contents
Making sense of teaching: a priority for theory, policy and practice – Identifying 'good teaching' – How do teachers talk about their good teaching? – Generalizations across teachers: goals and actions – The conditions of teaching and a theoretical framework – The routines teachers use to achieve their goals – Making sense of teaching: conclusions and implications – References – Index.

144pp   0 335 15795 5 (Paperback)   0 335 15796 3 (Hardback)

TEACHERS TALK ABOUT TEACHING
COPING WITH CHANGE IN TURBULENT TIMES

Judith Bell (ed.)

This book considers the impact of some of the far-reaching educational reforms introduced in the UK during the last decade, from the point of view of those people who have been required to implement them. All the contributors are, or were, teachers and all are committed to providing the best possible education for school students. Their views on the impact of some of the reforms provide an insight into what it is like to work in schools today and the effect the many demands placed on them have had on their lives. They consider the impact of the National Curriculum (and the associated methods of assessment), career prospects, appraisal, the changed role of governors, the influence of local management of schools and the low morale of many teachers. Throughout the book, the unifying threads are how teachers are coping with change and ways in which their interpretation of autonomy and professionalism differ from those of some ministers and administrators. These messages from the 'coalface' are worthy of serious consideration by all who have a concern for quality education and for the well-being of learners and teachers alike.

Contents

Contributors

Judith Bell, Ken Bryan, Rosemary Chapman, Karen Cowley, Ann Hanson, Jill Horder, Gill Richardson, John Ross, Andrew Spencer, Peter Swientozielskyj, Lorna Unwin, Stephen Waters.

144pp   0 335 19174 6 (Paperback)

LIVERPOOL
UNIVERSITY
LIBRARY